The Mating Game

The Mating Game

HOW GENDER STILL SHAPES
HOW WE DATE

Ellen Lamont

UNIVERSITY OF CALIFORNIA PRESS

University of California Press
Oakland, California

© 2020 by Ellen Lamont

Library of Congress Cataloging-in-Publication Data

Names: Lamont, Ellen, 1979– author.
Title: The mating game : how gender still shapes how we date / Ellen
    Lamont.
Description: Oakland, California : University of California Press, [2020] |
    Includes bibliographical references and index.
Identifiers: LCCN 2019040602 (print) | LCCN 2019040603 (ebook) |
    ISBN 9780520298682 (cloth) | ISBN 9780520298699 (paperback) |
    ISBN 9780520970724 (ebook)
Subjects: LCSH: Dating (Social customs)—California—San Francisco—
    Case studies. | Equality. | Sex. | Youth—California—San Francisco—
    Case studies. | Sexual minorities—California—San Francisco—Case
    studies.
Classification: LCC HQ801 .L2775 2020 (print) | LCC HQ801 (ebook) |
    DDC 306.7309794/61—dc23
LC record available at https://lccn.loc.gov/2019040602
LC ebook record available at https://lccn.loc.gov/2019040603

Manufactured in the United States of America

28   27   26   25   24   23   22   21   20
10 9   8   7   6   5   4   3   2   1

For Andrew, who told me, "Now that you're
a real author, I'll let you edit my work,"
and for Mama, who taught me how to write

Contents

Acknowledgments

There is one person without whom I wouldn't have finished this book, so I'll start there. stef shuster provided both academic support and friendship at a level I never thought possible. Before they arrived at App State, I felt lost as to how to manage a heavy teaching load while also making time for scholarship. stef taught me how to fiercely guard my time, but more than that, stef was someone to actually talk *ideas* with, helping move my work forward and giving me a space in which to think deeply about sociology. They have read and commented on every aspect of this manuscript with insight and generosity. Thank you stef for giving me an intellectual home.

When I see people write about the horrors of their graduate school experience, I can't relate, most certainly thanks to the endless support of Kathleen Gerson. Kathleen was a warm and caring mentor, but one no less rigorous for it. I got many marked-up manuscripts back—with a ratio of red to black no one wants to see!—and my work is infinitely stronger as a result. Like any great mentor she has been a wonderful advocate of my work and career. Most of all, I appreciate that Kathleen gave me the space to develop my ideas independently of her, allowing me to chart my own course, while supporting *my* vision for my work. That is the true definition of mentorship.

Two pieces of scholarship came out at just the right time, inspiring my work and providing me a way forward when I felt stuck. The first was Cecilia Ridgeway's *Framed by Gender*, truly one of my all-time favorite books. The second was Paula England's *The Gender Revolution: Uneven and Stalled*. Just my luck, right after that Paula moved to NYU. And while I had already moved back to the Bay Area to collect data, she responded to my e-mail expressing genuine interest in the project and agreeing to be on my dissertation committee. Since then Paula has provided consistently insightful feedback on my work with a quantitative eye that forces me to think methodically about the claims I can actually make. And she has the fastest turnaround time on feedback I've ever experienced!

Thank you to Cameron Lippard for having faith in my scholarship. His support is what brightens my workday and his constant advocacy for the people in our department is what makes him an excellent and worthy chair. Martha McCaughey's book, *The Caveman Mystique*, was the first sociology book I bought in grad school. Imagine my delight at getting the chance to work alongside her many years later! Martha, too, has proved a wonderful advocate and mentor, giving me advice and feedback whenever I need it. Plus, who better to discuss current controversies in academia with or marvel with at the hypocrisies of carceral feminism?

I am grateful to all of those who have provided feedback on my work in one form or another. I have had the privilege of being part of a number of awesome writing groups. Thank you to Jessi Streib, Abi Ocobock, Jaclyn Wong, Clare Forstie, Monica Liu, Sushmita Chatterjee, and Teresa Roach. Each brought a different lens to the manuscript, helping me strengthen the many moving pieces. In addition, thank you to Teresa for her friendship and the support she shows in so many ways. Thank you to Sarah Damaske for being always willing to provide advice or guidance; I often use her work as a road map. Thank you to Steven Lukes, Lynne Haney, and Larry Wu for their help on my dissertation committee. Larry gave me confidence in both my teaching and my interviewing skills. Steven was the first to support this project and I'm somewhat sorry all the power theory fell out of the manuscript along the way. But his power theory seminar is where all my thinking on this project started.

Thank you to Naomi Schneider, Benjy Malings, Kate Hoffman, Jeff Wyneken, and Summer Farah at UC Press for their hard—and very fast and efficient—work on this book. They made it a breeze (if that word ever belongs in a sentence about writing a book!). Thank you to Dawn Raffel, who helped me take this book to the next level. Thank you to Jennifer Randles, Amy Wilkins, Kathleen Bogle, and one anonymous reviewer for their supportive and constructive reviews. They all provided important guidance while not undermining my vision for the work, and I am grateful. I also have to include a thank-you to the nine anonymous reviewers who supported the work in article form. They too pushed my thinking in a supportive manner.

Appalachian State University generously funded this research through a University Research Council grant, a College of Arts and Sciences summer research grant, a Student and Faculty Excellence grant, and a Department of Sociology grant.

Now to thank some people who probably never expected to see their names here, but only because they don't realize what a pivotal role they played. Thank you to Sarah Wiliarty, who was the first to make me think that maybe I could do this. She was one of my advisors on my undergraduate honors thesis and generously provided me with the space to learn how to think through my own research. I feel like I badgered her weekly at Cafe Milano. She was always patient and supportive, even though I constantly asked her when she would be done with her dissertation, something I now understand as a deadly sin. Still, she inspired me to do one of my own. Thank you also to Lisa Lancaster and David Sundelson. Supportive to the utmost in so many ways, they too inspired me to return to school to get a PhD, and voiced support for my intellectual abilities. I also have to thank David for ripping apart my writing sample for my grad school applications. His intolerance for jargon made my writing so much stronger.

I am lucky to have an extremely supportive family. I want to start by thanking my grandparents, Mama and Papa. They thought so highly of me that I don't think I can ever live up to their vision, but their love and support and cheerleading meant the world to me. They pushed me academically and edited so many of my papers. They also taught me that aggressive intellectual debate is fun! While this has not necessarily served me well, it's something I carry with me. I wish they had lived to see the end result of this project. I'm pretty sure no one would have been more excited or proud.

My mom is wonderful. She is always there to take a phone call, even though she's heard it all before. She watched Andrew when I needed to do interviews, made space in her home, and steadfastly supported me in everything I tried. My dad, too, championed my work, even though he still thinks I should have been a lawyer. He paid for transcription costs, took Andrew to the Bay Area Discovery Museum while I worked, and sent me to conferences. They both made this book possible. My dog, Nola, was my "study buddy" throughout the last year of writing, insistent that I move her bed next to my desk for all my writing sessions. My sister Julia was always there for Facebook chats when I needed a break from writing. Sometimes that meant that my breaks ended up much too long, but it was time well spent. Andrew is my most precious guy, providing me with much needed respites from work whether in the form of games or hikes or funny conversations. He was born just as I started this project, and while he may have slowed it down, *a lot,* I wouldn't change a thing.

I don't think many people could have gotten through the last five years with me, but Jacob did a bang-up job of being a rock through it all. He kept me supplied with the gummy bears necessary to fuel the writing process and never guilted me when I was supposed to be working but was actually watching *Buffy* or *NCIS.* And besides more tangible forms of support, he also reminded me to focus on what really mattered. That bugged me, but he was right. As he'll say when he reads this, "According to Lamont (2020), I was right."

Finally, thank you to my respondents. Without their generosity, this book wouldn't exist. They gave me rich accounts of their lives solely to help out a budding academic. It's hard to live in a period of social change; what are the new rules? It's unclear, but to me it felt like they were trying their best. I wish them the best of luck in all their endeavors.

Previous versions of this work appeared as 2014, "Negotiating Courtship: Reconciling Egalitarian Ideals with Traditional Gender Norms," *Gender & Society* 28(2): 189–211, https://doi.org/10.1177/0891243213503899; 2015, "The Limited Construction of an Egalitarian Masculinity: College-Educated Men's Dating and Relationship Narratives," *Men & Masculinities* 18(3): 271–92, https://doi.org/10.1177/1097184X14557495; 2017, "'We Can Write the Scripts Ourselves': Queer Challenges to Heteronormative Dating and Courtship Practices," *Gender & Society* 31(5): 624–46, https://doi.org/10.1177/0891243217723883.

1 The Puzzling Persistence of Gendered Dating

Karley Sciortino writes a recurring opinion column for *Vogue* on sex, love, and relationships. Recently she asked, "Can I Be a Self-Sufficient, #Empowered Woman and Still Enjoy It When a Guy Picks Up the Check?" Sciortino's conclusion? Yes, as she finds herself feeling "like a whore—in a good way," and "confused" as to why "wanting to blow someone for my dinner is seen as 'regressive.'" As she explains,

> Look, I'm a feminist or whatever, but I still like it when a guy picks up the check on a date. . . . In terms of gender equality, we've come a long way in recent years. At 32, I often earn a similar income to the men I date, and I like being in relationships that feel equal. And yet, there's also this old-school part of me that likes it when a guy takes the reins, in ways that extend beyond just his wallet—like, offering me his jacket when it's cold, or helping me down the stairs when I'm wearing nonsensical shoes, or spanking me when I get too drunk. You know, lovingly misogynistic Don Draper shit.[1]

Sciortino's take on dating is not an outlier. But how do we make sense of her perspective?

A gender revolution is underway. Talk to middle-class young adults in the United States today, and you'll see how firmly many embrace the new cultural messages of gender equality. Young women are, more than ever, investing in their educations and careers, while putting their love lives on the back burner. When they do partner, they expect to do so with someone supportive of their ambitious professional goals and they plan to continue to support themselves financially. Heterosexual men are encouraged to desire and respect these independent, go-getter women and adjust their relationship goals accordingly. But while many progressive young adults claim a feminist identity, they define it by opportunities in the public sphere and meanwhile fail to examine the inequalities stemming from their most intimate desires. As a result, in spite of significant progress, the gender revolution remains "uneven and stalled."[2]

While young adults now have a clear set of professional goals and a vocabulary with which to understand them, the social scripts for dating and courtship have not undergone a similar transformation. Despite enormous changes in how people construct relationships in 21st-century America, contemporary understandings of heterosexual romance, desire, and intimacy remain firmly rooted in assumptions of gender difference.[3] Dating norms and scripts continue to presume that men initiate sexual and romantic overtures, and women react. Men are still expected to ask for, plan, and pay for dates, initiate sex, confirm the exclusivity of a relationship, and propose marriage.[4] These conventions feel both safe and right, and heterosexual men and women actively desire them.

But these seemingly benign rituals may lay a lasting foundation for inequality. Once a couple marries, the gender division becomes more entrenched, with women taking on more of the housework and childcare than men.[5] This doesn't only influence the home. Women's caregiving responsibilities limit their availability for paid labor, leading to lower wages and greater challenges moving up in their careers in the long run.[6] Women are also more likely to make career sacrifices for their families, such as stepping out of the workplace for extended periods of time or relocating in support of a partner's career.[7] Men, on the other hand, are less likely to take time out of the workplace when they become parents, even when they have the option to do so.[8] Even women who out-earn their partners often end up doing more household labor to compensate for their success in the workplace so as not to threaten their partner's status in the family.[9]

Lesbian, gay, bisexual, and queer (LGBQ) people are not immune to this contradiction between an egalitarian ideal and established expectations as they navigate the tension between assimilation and innovation.[10] True, they often seek to form relationships that take critical aim at heteronormativity, and express greater support for egalitarian practices than do heterosexuals.[11] Yet having recently won a hard-fought battle for inclusion in one of the most conservative social institutions—the married couple relationship—some find themselves affirming more than challenging prevailing understandings of how relationships should work.[12] As a result, many gay and lesbian individuals still enact domestic inequalities in their relationships.[13] For everyone then, conventional norms compete with the stated desire for progressive relationship practices.

The Mating Game looks at how people with diverse gender identities and sexualities date, form relationships, and make decisions about commitments as they negotiate an uncertain romantic landscape. As college-educated residents of the San Francisco Bay Area, the young adults (ages 25–40) in this book have the economic resources and progressive social environment that should enable them to construct their lives in opposition to conventional practices. Yet surprisingly, for most of them, their intimate relationships are firmly shaped by entrenched inequalities. In the following chapters, I uncover how gender upheaval has only partly done its work; in fact, old gender tropes are firmly in place, shaping our personal lives, but raising little concern. Indeed, a tepid feminism has taken hold in which many people fail to interrogate how the personal is political. Yet others see the danger, sounding the alarm that reveling in gender difference is a recipe for gender inequality, and they advocate unconventional ways of building relationships. A showdown between traditionalism and egalitarianism is underway.

THE DEATH OF DATING?

Popular media narratives might have us believe that we are in an era of apocalyptic "anything goes" romance. In 2013 the *New York Times* ran an article proclaiming "the end of courtship." According to journalist Alex Williams, traditional dating rituals are obsolete, replaced with a casual and individualized approach in which young adults put limited effort, and money, into their dating lives.[14] Dating websites jumped on the bandwagon, declaring new rules in the "'post-dating' landscape" and encouraging women to look for romance in nontraditional ways and contexts.[15] And supposedly, it's no longer only men running the show; economically empowered women now set the terms of intimacy. They purportedly aren't playing by "The Rules" as outlined by the 1995 bestselling self-help book that encouraged women to play hard to get in order to secure commitment from men.[16] Reluctant to even use the word "date," young adults now "talk" or "hook up."[17] As *Rolling Stone* argues, millennials and Gen Xers are taking the sexual revolution a step further than their baby boomer parents, avoiding early commitments altogether in favor of casual sex, eschewing monogamy to leave space for flexible relationship structures, and refusing limits on their sexual orientation.[18] In what is portrayed as a welcome and freeing change from an overly rigid past,[19] young adults are no longer confined to just one relationship pathway, but instead feel free to pick and choose what works for them. As *Slate* states, "good riddance" to courtship and the sexism and heteronormativity embedded in its rituals.[20] Yet this assessment certainly doesn't reflect the experiences of the majority of the people with whom I spoke.

In spite of the supposed and much-trumpeted rise of hooking up, the majority of young college-educated adults remain committed to gendered dating and courtship practices. Once college ends, even those who avoided dating in favor of hooking up tend to follow conventional dating patterns as they begin the search for a committed, long-term partner.[21] Those without college educations may be upending traditional courtship, but it's the result of financial constraint, not empowerment. Struggling to attain the economic resources and stability that Americans understand to be the foundation of a good marriage, young adults who are low income or working class often feel shut out of the dating and marriage markets altogether.[22] Even so, many of the steps they *can* enact are often taken in a rather traditional manner.[23] Thus, alongside these narratives of gender role reversal and relationship anarchy, outlets such as *New York Magazine*, *The Atlantic*, and *Women's Health* puzzle over why young adults, especially young heterosexual women who are vocal in their commitment to gender equality, remain so attached to old-fashioned rituals. As one article asks, "You're a Feminist . . . So Why Don't You Date Like One?"[24]

These competing messages about how intimacy should look leave young adults with a murky sense of what constitutes an ideal romantic relationship. Very few of the people with whom I spoke either expressed a desire for a fully traditional, male breadwinner, female homemaker type of relationship *or* articulated a radical, gender-neutral worldview. Instead, I heard story after story of how, while the division of paid and unpaid labor in partnerships should be equitable and not determined by gender, gender-traditional romantic behaviors should be preserved. This was especially the case among heterosexual women and men. Indeed, three-fourths of heterosexual women and men wanted or expected some semblance of a traditional courtship, and almost everyone wanted at least certain aspects of one. In contrast, 80 percent of LGBQ young adults wanted relationships that explicitly reject traditional dating conventions in favor of gender-neutral and egalitarian practices. This raises interesting questions about how, why, and among whom gender norms persist in romantic relationships.

DATING AS AN AMERICAN INSTITUTION

Current courtship conventions may put men in the proverbial driver's seat, but historically women and their families had substantially more control over the process. Prior to the 1920s and the advent of the modern dating system, wooing often took place within the confines of women's family homes.[25] Under the "calling" system, interested male suitors would visit women in their homes, where they would sit in the parlor and have a conversation. When a woman first came of "appropriate" age, dependent on her social status, her mother or guardian would invite eligible men to call on her. As she matured, a woman was able to invite her own suitors to the house. Those deemed unsuitable or undesirable were turned away at the door. Widely embraced, "calling" was created to emulate the wealthy counterparts of a newly formed and rising white middle class.[26]

After the 1920s, the United States saw the ascendance of "the date." Courting was no longer relegated to the private sphere, but instead took place in public. Originally a lower-class response to a lack of private space in which to receive suitors, dating was rapidly embraced by the middle class who saw it as exciting and freeing and who established it as an "American institution."[27] And as middle-class white women increased their presence in the public sphere, entering college and professions, they also demanded broader access to public spaces. Yet ironically, as these women took their place in public life, they lost control over courtship. The date took women and men away from the prying eyes of family but also required transportation and money, as couples went out to dinner or a movie theater. In the process, control over courtship shifted to men, as they were the ones expected to ask for the date, plan the date, pick up the woman and drive, pay for the date, and then take her home again. As the relationship progressed, the man was supposed to ask her to go steady and, if things went well, to propose marriage. The woman could pick and choose among suitors, but she was never to initiate.[28]

Based on an assumption of a breadwinning, dominant male and a dependent, passive female, these courtship norms dictated distinct behaviors for men and women. They were premised on the belief that men and women are innately different and that these differences are reflected in their skills, activities, desires, and the separate spheres they inhabit. Cultural narratives about gender associated men with power, agency, ambition, and the public sphere, where their breadwinning activities were used to support their wife and children in the home. Women, on the other hand, were represented as nurturing, reactive, and expressive, ideal for homemaking in the private sphere.[29] Courtship conventions reflected these beliefs, situating men as the initiators. These norms were prevalent enough to shape people's experiences and perceptions of courtship to the present day, establishing these behaviors as the most ideal and appropriate way to progress through relationships.[30]

Of course, the narratives and resources that undergird conventional courtship practices were not available or applied to everyone, but rather centered and reflected the experiences of the white middle class. Public dating required money, and concepts of what constitutes romance were constructed around affluence and consumption.[31] The family ideal of separate spheres was the result of a growing white middle class that had the resources to rely on one income.[32] By contrast, dominant narratives of women as weak and in need of men's protection, one driver of the separate spheres ideology, have never been extended to women of color. Many men of color, on the other hand, were prevented from fulfilling the male bread-winner and protector role. Racial discrimination and oppression made it difficult if not impossible for people of color to fulfill these supposed ideals.[33] In the decades leading up to the start of the gender revolution, women's self-reliance was seen not as a sign of empowerment or equality, but rather as a result of men's failure to enact their role as heads of household and a dysfunctional breakdown in appropriate gender roles.[34]

In spite of these exclusions, dating remains a widely understood and accepted means of developing committed, long-term romantic relationships, particularly among white college-educated Americans. Powerful cultural messages perpetuate particular beliefs around how and what types of relationships we should form. Even those who are excluded from dominant relationship pathways frequently don't question the pathway or the end goal itself, but rather their own ability to enact it, delaying committed relationships until they have the resources to do so.[35] However, while traditional dating and courtship practices dominate the public imagination of how relationships should play out, the assumptions about gender difference on which these practices are based have been significantly destabilized.

GENDER AND INTIMACY IN UPHEAVAL

Since the 1960s, the United States has experienced a massive transformation in the gender system. So far-reaching are these changes that they have been referred to as a gender revolution, emphasizing the radical changes in women's educational and career attainment.[36] The narrative of revolution resonates most strongly with a particular demographic, the white middle class, who reaped the rewards of the increased opportunities for self-development among women. But the expectations for professional success are widely embraced as both ideal and necessary.[37] Middle-class parents raise their daughters with professional ambitions,[38] and now that women's college graduation rates exceed men's, these women are far more likely to expect career trajectories that mirror those of men.[39]

The decline of formal sex discrimination has increased women's access to a wider range of jobs, which are also better paying.[40] Well-educated women are delaying marriage until their late twenties and early thirties in favor of establishing careers;[41] this significantly increases their earning potential throughout their lives and their ability to support themselves independently of men.[42] The increase in the availability and reliability of birth control has given women greater control over their reproduction, allowing them to invest more heavily in their careers. They no longer have to worry as much about an unexpected pregnancy and can delay marriage in favor of starting a career without having to forgo sex, thereby making space for women to enter into a succession of dating and sexual relationships.[43] Indeed, it has become increasingly acceptable for women to be sexually active outside of relationships, signaling a decline in, though not an end to, the sexual double standard.[44]

Women have also seen a decline in the status of the homemaker, making it a less desirable pathway, even among couples who can most afford to support a family on one income.[45] Couples are having fewer children, who are born later in a woman's life. Women, especially those with a college degree, can expect to spend fewer years of their lives with young children in the house.[46] These changes make permanent homemaking less appealing in light of the opportunity costs of staying at home. At present, the majority of women continue to work after having children;[47] well-educated, well-compensated professional women are most likely to quickly return to full-time work.[48]

At the same time, men can no longer count on being the sole breadwinner. Currently, only 19 percent of heterosexual married couples rely on the male breadwinner and female homemaker model,[49] while the woman brings in an equal or larger share of the income in 31 percent of heterosexual marriages or cohabiting relationships.[50] Women's wages have become increasingly important to attaining or maintaining a financially secure status,[51] and romantic relationships based on women's financial dependence are for the most part no longer viewed as either desirable or sustainable.[52] The gap between men's and women's mate selection preferences is narrowing, as men's preferences are increasingly coming to mirror those of women. More focused on women's career and income prospects, men are less concerned with women's appearance and sexual histories.[53] One consequence is that men and women are now seeking to form relationships with peers, as many middle-class young adults consolidate their class privilege by marrying those with similar levels of education and career prospects.[54] As such, the two-income family, along with women's new economic and educational opportunities, have provided men and women with an unprecedented opportunity to create egalitarian partnerships in which partners share paid labor, housework, and caregiving equitably over the life course. And young adults claim those are the types of partnerships they want.[55]

Changes are not limited to heterosexual relationships. We have also seen an increased acceptance of same-sex and queer sexual and romantic relationships, including a very visible movement to give LGBQ people the same marriage rights as heterosexual men and women. The culmination of this was the landmark 2015 Supreme Court case *Obergefell v. Hodges*, which legalized same-sex marriage in all 50 states. Although this decision has been widely lauded by LGBQ people and their supporters, the movement's focus on marriage, to the exclusion of other pressing human rights issues, was more controversial.[56] While the same-sex marriage movement in particular has emphasized long-term committed relationships, with some LGBQ people living lives that are virtually indistinguishable from their heterosexual counterparts, others continue to challenge this one-size-fits-all version of family life.[57] Alongside this movement, new cultural understandings of gender challenge the assumed connection between sex category and gender identity.[58] Young adults are increasingly coming to understand their gender outside the binary, rejecting the association of sex assigned at birth with both gender identity and presentation.[59] When they form relationships, they bring into stark relief the limitations of the assumptions people bring to romantic relationships.[60]

This means that not only heterosexual men and women but also LGBQ people face a tension as they build their intimate lives. On the one hand, LGBQ people are exposed to the same cultural messages as heterosexuals about how intimacy, romance, and love "should" look. Legibility and legitimacy are tied to emulating heterosexual couplings as closely as possible. Yet there is also an extensive history of queer challenges to normative family life. Rejection, exclusion, and discrimination by and from families of origin and other institutions have left LGBQ people creatively reimagining intimacy for decades now, and they often demonstrate a more open-minded approach to the variety of ways relationships can be constructed.[61] Indeed, queerness is frequently understood as resisting and challenging socially accepted and expected ways of living.[62]

The increasing acceptance and visibility of LGBQ relationships has created new pathways to relationships and marriage; it challenges the notion that distinct gendered behaviors in romantic relationships are based on inherent difference rather than cultural norms, undermines expectations for gender complementarity, and provides increased legitimacy for nontraditional couplings. As a result of these many social, cultural, and economic changes, the United States has experienced the dissociation of sexuality, reproduction, and kinship, as many people no longer expect sex and childbearing to go hand in hand, or either of these to go hand in hand with marriage.[63] Relationships are now expected to provide room for independence and self-fulfillment for both partners.[64] Gender norms are called into question.[65] Thus, conventional courtship rituals now compete with a commitment to self-development, individualistic understandings of intimacy, egalitarian impulses, and strong attachments to paid labor by all, meaning that young adults must negotiate contradictory expectations. While the cultural messages regarding education, career, self-reliance, and equality have taken firm hold, providing young adults with a clear path to follow and a narrative with which to make sense of it, no similar transformation in scripts has developed for dating and courtship. Young adults face a dilemma as they navigate uncharted terrain.

WHY COURTSHIP?

Looking at courtship helps us home in on one of the major questions of the gender revolution: why has it stalled in intimate relationships?[66] Is this about stagnating beliefs or unchanging structures? While people may say they want egalitarian relationships, they certainly don't have them. One school of thought argues that this is the result of structural constraints.[67] Workplaces refuse to accommodate dual-earner couples; the United States provides almost no public support for caregiving, and when push comes to shove, people have to make hard decisions about how to divide paid labor and caregiving.[68] Evidence demonstrates that partnerships are often more egalitarian when public policies support that goal.[69] But when they don't, people look to "Plan B," or what they see as their next best option, and this is often laced with assumptions about gender. Although often couched in narratives about practicality, "fallback" positions tend to reveal, or are at least justified by, very conventional beliefs about the appropriate roles of men and women.[70]

Given this, certain research may overestimate the support for egalitarianism in romantic relationships. Studies have often clustered gendered beliefs in different arenas into one measure of support for equality,[71] but recent research demonstrates that Americans often hold competing beliefs. On the one hand, there is widespread cultural support for women's educational and job opportunities. At the same time, Americans cling to their belief that men and women are fundamentally different and that women are better suited for the home.[72] They are less concerned with equality for equality's sake, especially in heterosexual romantic relationships.[73] Instead, consistent with Americans' belief in individualism and free choice, people are more likely to support women's opportunities for upward mobility, such as access to rights and opportunities in the public sphere.[74] The benefits of challenging gender inequality in the home are less clear in light of the possible social sanctions.[75] And although the most up-to-date research shows millennials moving away from this divide and expressing support for equality in the home, it is unclear whether and how these beliefs will be put into practice.[76] We have a great deal of data demonstrating that people often fail to enact their supposed egalitarian beliefs in their everyday lives, or express contradictory beliefs about interpersonal relationships.[77] Certainly this was the case in this research: young adults who stated a desire for egalitarian relationships enacted gender inequalities anyway, and found ways to justify them.

Gender functions as a primary frame that individuals use to define who they are, how they will behave, and how they expect others to behave.[78] People draw on cultural knowledge, or "shared," "common" knowledge that "everybody knows," to coordinate their behavior and facilitate social cohesion.[79] Most adults continue to believe that men and women are innately different with either complementary or conflicting needs and desires, particularly in heterosexual romantic relationships. These perceived differences are especially salient during courtship, when people tend to fall back on well-worn dating scripts to ease uncertainty and reassure themselves and others that they conform to normative gender standards.[80] Individuals are held accountable for such behaviors by others, who may sanction them for nonconformity, and by themselves, as nonconformity can be experienced as an assault on the very core of who they are. In the process of selecting a long-term romantic partner, our cultural beliefs about what it means to be a man or a woman are acted out in a ritualized manner through particular practices.

Sexism hasn't gone away; it has simply become subtler and research isn't accurately capturing the nuances. It has become less socially acceptable to express a desire for separate spheres, or women as homemakers and men as breadwinners.[81] LGBQ people, too, are attuned to the judgment leveled at unequal and gendered relationships.[82] And in response to economic need, even conservative men and women have shifted their beliefs about women's work outside the home.[83] Instead, studies on gender as "cultural rules or instructions," rather than studies on beliefs in separate spheres, may better illuminate the prevailing attitudes.[84] In addition, people tend to see courtship rituals as mere convention and preference, and therefore consistent with narratives of "free choice" feminism.[85] As a result, gender inequality in this realm tends to go unquestioned, making it less susceptible to social desirability bias and to economic need. This is thus an ideal location to explore changing (and stagnating) attitudes.[86]

Courtship lays the foundation for expectations in the relationship, so it is important to understand how dating conventions enforce gender difference and where openings for change, and greater equality, may be occurring. This book does just that, looking at how these practices influence our understanding of gender through "cultural rules or instructions"[87] in ways that perpetuate broader inequalities, all while flying under the radar.

THE STUDY

In order to make sense of how young adults are dating and forming romantic relationships, I interviewed 105 college-educated young adults in the greater San Francisco Bay Area. Sixty-five identified as heterosexual and forty as LGBQ. Given that all were between the ages of 25 and 40, they were old enough to have a relationship history but young enough to be grappling with the changing norms that came out of the feminist, sexual, and gender revolutions. The people whose thoughts and experiences fill this book spent hours with me, telling me all about their past and current romantic relationships, as well as their hopes and dreams for the future. We met at coffee shops, restaurants, wine bars, parks, and in their homes. I asked, and they answered, questions about how they find partners, who they find attractive, what they like and expect on a first date, how a relationship should progress, when sex should take place, and how a marriage proposal should unfold. I also asked questions about what they wanted their family life to look like in the long run, such as how they expected to divide household chores and childcare, how they wanted to manage finances, and how they showed love to a partner. Some of the respondents were already in long-term cohabiting or married relationships, so I was able to see how they made sense of how their preferences were playing out at home. As a result, I have information on people's past and present dating, courtship, and relationship behaviors, as well as their preferences, their attitudes about what people *should* do, and their perceptions of the social consequences of various behaviors.[88]

I interviewed participants in two waves. In 2010–11, I interviewed 81 heterosexual and gay and lesbian individuals, recruited from the alumni networking lists of two universities in the San Francisco Bay Area.[89] I returned to the Bay Area in 2015 and interviewed 24 LGBQ people in order to increase the number of nonheterosexual people in my study.[90] I recruited participants through online postings with LGBTQ organizations in the Bay Area, as well as through social media, utilizing the help of friends and colleagues. While I did not recruit through universities in this wave, I did require all participants to have a bachelor's degree. All of the trans and nonbinary people I interviewed identified as LGBQ, so they are included with that group.[91] Descriptive information for the sample is provided in appendix 1.

The young adults I interviewed were relatively privileged. First, they were more educated than the general college-educated population, as 30 percent had completed some form of graduate school or professional training.[92] The heterosexual women in the study were more highly educated than the heterosexual men, with 41 percent of the women having completed more than a bachelor's degree compared to only 28 percent of the men.[93] All but 15 of the respondents were employed full time (and most of those who were unemployed or employed part time were in graduate school). Seventy percent were employed in a managerial or a professional occupation. Many of those who were currently in graduate school will likely end up in professional fields. Heterosexual women's employment was on par with men's, but LGBQ people were slightly less lucratively employed, possibly due to discrimination but also to personal decisions to avoid corporate jobs. Still, most were well employed or in the process of finishing graduate school. As a result, the majority of the sample is firmly middle class or above, and the remainder will most likely end up there as they complete schooling and enter or build up careers.

Although this is a narrow slice of the population, my decision was strategic. Part of what makes the persistence of gendered dating scripts so puzzling is exactly *who* we're talking about. These are highly educated, professional-track young adults in the San Francisco Bay Area; they are supposed to be at the vanguard of progressive beliefs. The women, in particular, are expected to epitomize feminist liberation. We see media narratives of them happily forgoing relationships while they climb career ladders. Early committed relationships are often viewed as a threat to their career aspirations and are to be avoided.[94] As professional-track women put increased effort into their careers, remain in the workforce either longer or permanently, and make salaries similar to those of professional-track men, they bring substantial resources into their relationships, which affects their expectations and interactions.[95] And college-educated men are more likely than those without a college education to express support for gender equality and egalitarian relationships.[96] Their high status allows them more flexibility in how they enact their masculinity.[97] In fact, previous research shows that members of this group often position themselves as "exemplars of egalitarianism in their interpersonal relationships with women" as a way to distinguish themselves from lower-class men, to whom they attribute a predatory masculinity and hostile sexism.[98]

Certainly, the class and racial privileges of the majority of the respondents shaped their understanding of the relationship pathways and opportunities available to them. Two-thirds came from middle- to upper-middle-class backgrounds. College was all but guaranteed. The four-year university is a privileged path to adulthood that structures people's beliefs about appropriate courtship. Well-educated Americans face a "self-development imperative."[99] They are expected to pursue career opportunities while delaying marriage until their late twenties to early thirties, when they become financially secure enough to settle down.[100] However, throughout, they can feel reasonably secure that conventional courtship and family-building pathways will be available to them as desired.[101] They can expect to have the financial and personal freedom to "date around" and have marriageable people with good careers to choose from when they decide to settle down. And they can expect marriage to come with both personal and economic rewards. Indeed, it is this group that maintains the highest rates of marriage and marital childbearing, given the stabilizing influence of economic resources on intimate relationships.[102]

In addition to their class and educational advantages, 59 percent of the people with whom I spoke were white. Given this intersection of class and race privilege, they viewed the workplace as a guaranteed pathway to financial stability and expected to see a steady momentum of progress in their careers. The men saw only their own motivation rather than structural barriers as a potential limitation to their achievement. Second-wave narratives of feminist empowerment resonated with the women. They worried about the glass ceiling and abortion rights, and saw the home as a potential source of constraint. They were silent on workplace policies and inequalities at play in pink- and blue-collar professions, on more communal approaches to family, or on the racist sexual narratives that make certain forms of sexual empowerment available to them but not to women of color. They planned to use their own financial resources as an individualistic strategy to handle gender inequality, rather than advocate for policies and practices that would help everyone.

But while all of the people with whom I spoke had a college degree, not all of them came from privileged backgrounds. A third described their families of origin as either poor or working class. Forty-one percent were people of color.[103] Given that courtship norms center the experience of class-privileged white people, these groups have historically been excluded from conventional relationship scripts and practices.[104] The ability to enact "romance," for one, is premised on having the resources to go on dates and excursions and buy gifts.[105] The value of delayed marriage and childbearing is linked to the rewards that come from career building in white-collar professions and the security that comes with a stable marriage.[106] Even marriage as a goal in and of itself has a fraught history and feels out of reach for many still.[107] However, the process of working toward or maintaining a middle- or upper-middle-class status leaves people from different class and racial backgrounds drawing on very similar scripts for how to achieve personal and professional success. Indeed, gender projects are closely tied to social mobility projects, and those who want to end up in the professional class emphasize career building and peer marriage, goals shaped by their desired position in the class hierarchy.[108] I center my analysis on the interplay of gender, sexuality, and class mobility/stability connected to high earnings potential and significant educational investments, but also note where variations occur due to race or class background as well as how particular privileges shape participants' understandings of the pathways and life choices available to them.[109] Still, this is a limitation of the study as it doesn't engage with how those excluded from these pathways navigate relationship building differently.[110] Courtship narratives and behaviors are conceivably quite different among those who don't see themselves reflected in the cultural norms.

In addition, the San Francisco Bay Area is assumed to be a hotbed of radical beliefs, especially around gender and sexuality. And indeed, the young adults with whom I spoke overwhelmingly identified as liberal, albeit not necessarily radical. Among the heterosexual people, only three participants considered themselves to be politically conservative and the majority described themselves as center-left, explaining that they were socially liberal and economically conservative. Most participants referenced their support of feminist ideals, even if they didn't identify with the feminist label. Yet when it came to gender inequality, there was a greater focus on professional opportunities than interpersonal dynamics. The fact that the majority continued to embrace gender difference in their intimate relationships shows just how entrenched these beliefs are and how difficult they are to change, even in individuals who purport to support equality between men and women.[111]

Among the LGBQ young adults, 40 percent of the respondents identified as queer, characterized in their narratives as more politicized and progressive than gay, lesbian, or bisexual identities. This group was quite radical in its understanding of sexuality and relationships, almost certainly more so than the LGBQ population as a whole. Even those respondents who identified as LGB frequently referred to themselves and their relationships as queer in other parts of the interviews, and several of the cis women stated that they preferred to identify as gay rather than lesbian because they found "lesbian" too gendered a term. Many of the respondents reported taking gender studies courses in college and participating in explicitly queer spaces, such as groups for queer and trans people of color. This more radical understanding of queer identity among the respondents was most likely the result of the recruitment process, which relied more on social networks and LGBTQ community organizations than college alumni lists. However, this opens a window onto a group with an explicit desire to reject normative relationship expectations, revealing the challenges they face in doing so and the possibilities that arise from this approach to intimacy. As such, throughout the book I compare heterosexual men and women to LGBQ young adults to understand how a commitment to normativity, versus a rejection of it, shapes behaviors and outcomes in intimate relationships.

THE BOOK

This book makes the case that by clinging to traditional courtship scripts, young adults are unwittingly undermining the gender revolution they say they embrace. Seventy-five percent of heterosexual men and women express a desire for egalitarian relationships, with an equal division of work and household labor, equal negotiating power, and the financial independence of both partners. Yet they struggle to navigate the changing expectations of what it means to be in a relationship. They seek to reconcile independence with commitment and intimacy and try to blend equality with romance and desire. For the most part, they engage in courtship rituals that reinforce gender differences. They hold on to the persistent belief that men and women are fundamentally different, with contrasting romantic desires and needs. This belief is cemented through their dating strategies and reinforced throughout the later stages of their relationships as they become more committed. Despite the expressed desire for egalitarian relationships, they tend to form long-term relationships that mirror the patterns of gender difference established during courtship. Indeed, even the 20 percent of heterosexual men and women who didn't want a conventional gendered courtship often found themselves enacting these practices anyway due to the pressures to conform. They, too, then ended up with many of the same unequal relationship practices seen among the most ardent supporters of gender difference.

Similar to heterosexual men and women, 80 percent of LGBQ individuals desire egalitarian relationships. But in comparing the dating strategies of heterosexuals with those of people who pursue same-sex and queer relationships, the contrast becomes poignantly stark, as the majority of LGBQ individuals reject and actively resist dominant courtship scripts. They challenge gender norms by seeking relationships that emphasize balance, flexibility, communication, and frequent renegotiation. As a result, they are more likely to have egalitarian outcomes in their long-term relationships. Yet even among LGBQ people, gender norms are pervasive and hard to resist. Twenty percent of LGBQ individuals find themselves falling back on gendered practices when dating, limiting the potential challenges to unequal long-term relationship patterns.

Despite their best efforts to resist traditional scripts, the majority of respondents perpetuate conventional dating patterns. This highlights not only the persistence of inequality but the contradictions between thinking about and behaving in relationships, incongruities that stymie significant social change. Chapter 2 looks at how young adults conceptualize the types of romantic relationships they seek to build. I show how heterosexual women emphasize their self-development and how they desire to form relationships that will not interfere with their career goals. Heterosexual men, on the other hand, seek high-achieving partners in order to resist the pressures of breadwinning and ensure compatibility with their partners. Finally, LGBQ people aim for a balance of individualism and commitment in an effort to achieve mutually rewarding relationships. Across the board, young adults not only express a desire for egalitarian relationships, but seek out partners who can help them achieve this goal.

Chapters 3, 4, and 5 turn to the dating practices themselves, exploring how heterosexual women and men and LGBQ people negotiate courtship. In chapter 3, I look at heterosexual women's courtship behaviors and preferences and examine how they make sense of the tension between the resonance of feminism in their lives, the narratives of economic and personal independence they draw on, and their desire for old-fashioned romance. Chapter 4 turns to heterosexual men's navigation of changing gender norms, examining how they balance their understandings of themselves as egalitarian partners with time-warp desires and the expectations of their romantic partners. Chapter 5 looks at how LGBQ individuals navigate the culturally dominant gendered courtship practices that don't reflect their reality. I show that rather than attempt to conform to heterosexual norms, respondents actively reject them, seeking new and more egalitarian ways of building romantic relationships.

In chapter 6, I examine how the narratives employed during courtship affect relationship and care work in long-term relationships. As I show, heterosexual men and women believe that they have different interests, different skills, and different availability for their personal lives. These assumptions of difference limit their ability to question and challenge these preferences and arrangements. On the other hand, LGBQ respondents emphasize egalitarian, flexible, and nongendered care work in committed relationships; this further indicates that how people date may set the stage for the dynamics in their long-term relationships.

In chapter 7, I conclude with the implications of these findings. In spite of the rapid social, cultural, and economic changes poised to undermine gender inequality in the United States, the gender revolution remains uneven, with greater progress in the workplace than in intimate relationships. And while we have seen an overhaul in how our culture conceives of intimacy relative to self-development, when people start to form romantic relationships their intentions for egalitarianism are often undermined by their commitment to gender difference.

The stakes are high as relationship imbalances ripple out into the public sphere. As I will argue, courtship rituals are a key component of the reproduction of gender inequality in spite of changing conditions. Those young adults who directly challenge notions of gender difference are better able to craft egalitarian relationships, providing all of us with a way forward.

2 The Quest for Egalitarian Love

Keira rolls her eyes at "the kind of women who say, 'My proudest achievement is my children.'"[1] A well-paid technology researcher and recruiter, she considers herself a career woman and looks down on those who prioritize romantic relationships. But she didn't come to this perspective on her own. From a young age, Keira, 36, got the message from her parents that she needed to focus on her education above all else: "As far back as I can remember, UC Berkeley and Stanford were my options. When I was five, those were my options. A [low ranked] school was not an option." Her parents expected these prestigious credentials to translate into a lucrative profession. Keira explained, "I would say that the pressure was around finding a well-paying, respected career. My parents originally wanted me to go into medicine or engineering. Barring that, if you couldn't swing that, *maybe* law or accounting. The expectations were around academic achievement, financial achievement, but nothing around 'I hope you find a nice boy.'" This focus on personal achievement featured heavily in the lives of almost every woman I interviewed.

Yet Keira clearly sees herself as different from most heterosexual women. As she said,

I never fantasized about the wedding the way my friends did in school. I wanted to see what I could do with my life. Getting married and having kids were probably, if they were even on the list, like number 99 and 100 on the list of 100. . . . I wanted a degree of independence. I also wanted nothing to do with what I saw as the old ways, this very patriarchal, horrible power struggle. I never wanted to be tied down with children. I always saw children as anchors holding me back.

While Keira did marry, she waited until her late twenties in order to first achieve financial independence and a greater sense of self. Now divorced and remarried after her first husband proved too unambitious and resentful of her success, Keira said that what she most appreciates about her current relationship is that she and her husband feel like a team, rather than a couple that defaults "to a traditional marriage in the sense of gender roles." Although Keira brings home 70 percent of the income, she doesn't feel he resents her success, and she also enjoys the unlimited space he gives her to pursue her own hobbies and interests. As a result, she can balance her individual desires and goals with her relationship. They are currently trying to get pregnant, as she finally feels that she's ready to integrate caregiving into her life.

Like Keira, many college-educated young adults seek to build relationships that leave room for both partners to reap the rewards of professional success and caregiving. But where do these new goals come from and how do young adults make sense of the messages they received growing up?

While both heterosexual men and women expressed a desire for egalitarian relationships, women especially saw this as a priority. Raised by their parents to be successful, professional women, they were wary of romantic partners who might demand traditional homemaking. Where women feared thwarted career goals, men questioned the burdens of sole breadwinning. Although men's educations provided them with economic opportunities, they did not want the pressure of being the main economic support for their family in potentially shaky economic conditions. They also worried about missing out on the rewards of raising children and about their compatibility with, as one man said, "the kind of woman who wanted to stay at home." They sought out partners who they felt would be their equals, at least in the workplace. Both heterosexual men and women feared getting trapped in traditional roles.

LGBQ people felt the same way, if not more strongly, emphasizing the importance of equality and fairness in their relationships. LGBQ individuals were also taught the importance of independence and professional success. But their parents assumed they would be heterosexual and framed their relationship messages around that expectation. As a result, LGBQ people had to question their parents' narratives. In the process, many ended up placing even greater emphasis on personal independence and growth than did heterosexual women and men—although in ways that wouldn't undermine a partner's access to the same.

Both heterosexual and LGBQ young adults expressed progressive values that appeared to lay the groundwork for balanced relationships in which partners could focus on individual goals in the context of commitment.

FIRST COMES CAREER, THEN COMES MARRIAGE

Today's middle- and upper-middle-class, college-educated women expect to be achievers. No longer content to use college as a matchmaking service, heterosexual women resist early commitment, which they see as time-greedy and a threat to their personal development.[2] They are entering male-dominated professions in large numbers for both economic rewards and the satisfaction that accompanies career success.[3] They expect to maintain this professional commitment throughout their adult years, with limited interest in giving up paid work for childrearing.[4] These shifts mean that heterosexual women are making new calculations as they form romantic partnerships, delaying marriage until their late twenties and early thirties while they invest in education and career building.[5] In the process, they seek partners who will be supportive of their ambition.

Raising the Bar on Women's Careers

We expect boys to receive messages from their parents about the importance of professional ambition and achievement. This is consistent with what it means to be a successful man and a suitable romantic partner.[6] But these traits are increasingly valued in daughters as well.[7] Middle-class parents not only prepare their daughters for professional success but in some cases are hypervigilant, swooping in when anything threatens to derail their goals for their daughters, relationships included.[8] Most of the young women in this study internalized their parents' high expectations. A college degree would enable them to land an engaging, lucrative career, providing them with the ability to support themselves and pursue their own aspirations. Rather than getting messages about when they should marry, the type of husband they should seek out, and when the grandchildren should arrive, heterosexual women were instead taught the importance of personal achievement and the dangers of sacrificing their own desires for a man.

Of the 34 heterosexual women in the study, 29 said that there was a heavy emphasis in their families on getting a college education. Samantha, 31, described herself as very ambitious: "Growing up, all I ever knew was, 'You're getting good grades in school; you're going to college.' Because neither one of my parents completed college. And there was no question. It was just an expectation." Heather, 27, received a similar message: "[My parents] didn't get to go to a four-year college, and they always wanted my sister and I to go to a four-year college. They've always been very involved in our decision-making in all aspects of life. It wasn't even a question in my mind whether I was going to go [to a four-year college] or not. I *went*."

Like Heather and Samantha, women whose parents had not attended or completed college received the most explicit messages on the importance of higher education. But those with college-educated parents knew they were expected to go to college as well. Jane, 31, said that "education-wise it was almost implicit more than explicit. And I think also from where we were growing up, in a relatively affluent suburb, college was never a question. The only question about college was, 'What college are you going to?'"

Many of the women reported an intense pressure to attend a prestigious school with the expectation that this would lead to a lucrative career. Similar to Keira, Caroline, 31, said that "growing up there was definitely a very strong expectation that I would not only go to college, but that it would be a good college. My parents actually told me that they would be more than happy to pay for my education as long as it was a top-tier school and that, if it was not, then they would not pay for my education." Half of the women said their parents also expected them to choose majors that were high status and would translate into a well-paying career, reflecting the belief that a college education should enable a clear career path and future financial stability.[9] Nicole, 28, said,

> Well, I think at one point I had expressed interest in becoming a doctor. And [my parents] jumped all over that. And it was a very rough moment, right before getting into college, where I said, I don't think this is what I want to do. It was pretty ugly. . . . So there was that drive to be more realistic. Be more realistic. My mom less so. But she did feel like if she's going to put money toward my education, it better result in something. There was one time where they were yelling and they're like, "We're not paying for you to go to school and do arts and crafts."

Whereas in the privileged classes in the past women's jobs had been considered a supplement to men's, they are now considered an important and necessary achievement and many of the women experienced pressure from their parents to pursue masculine-typed white collar careers. In this manner, women are now being set up for careers in the same way as men, with an emphasis on a job that will pay the bills. Partially at the behest of her mother, Caroline left her job in advertising to pursue an MBA in order to increase her income, which is now over $250,000 a year:

> My mom had a lot of emphasis on making money particularly since I grew up in a comfortable household, and so I think she wanted to make sure that I could at least live well like that, and my career in advertising didn't pay very well. So I couldn't afford things that I would've liked to have been able to afford, so my mom made frequent mention of how important it was to make more money. That was probably in part what inspired me to do something else.

Very few of the women discussed pressure from family to find a husband to support them. Instead, the women were expected to establish careers so that they could gain status and economic security through their own achievements. They focused on attaining college educations, and half had attended one of the more prestigious universities in the country, reflecting the makeup of the sample. They selected majors like business, pre-med, and pre-law that would facilitate their professional goals. Parents expected romantic relationships to take a backseat to academic and career achievements, something to be pursued once the other cards fell into place. Just as marriage is now seen as a capstone experience for men, something that indicates an economically stable and established adult, so too is it for professional women.[10]

Maybe When I'm 30

While the majority of the heterosexual women discussed messages about education, careers, and achievement that started in early childhood, only a few received early messages from their parents about the importance of marriage. In fact, Ashleigh, 29, was the only woman in the study to discuss her childhood relationship goals in more detail than her career goals, which is potentially the result of her religious upbringing: "When I was 13 my mom told me to make a list of what I wanted in a husband. I think that's when I started showing a more serious interest in boys. So she said make a list and just think about that. Then when I would come home and tell her about whatever boy I liked that week, she would be like, 'Oh, does he match your list?'" Ashleigh's father would occasionally get out a video camera and interview her about her goals: "My dad used to interview me and record it. And so I had questions and I would answer them. And he would say, 'What do you want to do when you grow up?' And I would be like, 'I want to marry somebody and I want him to be like this.'" While the purpose of her parents' interventions was to remind Ashleigh to take seriously the specific traits needed in a good husband, it also served to emphasize marriage as one of the main goals on which she should focus. Incidentally, she was also the only woman in the study to leave the workplace in order to stay home with her kids.[11]

But Ashleigh was not the norm. Instead, parents encouraged women to either refrain from dating or deprioritize relationships until they finished their education and established their careers. Because of the scarcity of nearby schools in her field, Sophia, 26, was considering a move from California for graduate school. She had informed her boyfriend that she was going, regardless of his plans, and at her mother's insistence. Repeating the advice her mother gave her, she said, "Don't let anybody hold you back." Ariana, 30, said of her parents, "Both of them were like, you shouldn't really think about [marriage] until you're done with your education; don't worry about it. I mean, my mom said, later in life, after you're done with your education, like late twenties, early thirties kind of thing." Jane said, "I'd had some serious relationships and [my mom] was always like, 'Don't settle down too young. Don't be like me.' So it was more like really figure out what you want in life first before you make that commitment." Embedded in her mother's message was the assumption that what Jane really wanted in life was a career.

After Alyssa, 28, called off an unhappy engagement in her late twenties, her family even agreed to pay for fertility treatments if she needed them later. "I've already asked, if I'm not married [at a certain] age, I want to freeze my eggs. . . . And they're like—don't worry; we'll pay for your eggs to be frozen. So I'm good."

Because relationships are time consuming, parents worried that a serious relationship or an early marriage would derail a daughter's individual pursuits and career plans before she had a chance to establish herself, a valid fear considering that women's career ambitions continue to be treated by men as secondary to their own.[12] Alice, 34, recounted that her mother had been raised in a "very traditional Chinese family" where the sons were valued over the daughters. Wanting something different for her own daughter, Alice said her mother advised her to put "career over marriage." As she explained,

> And so for me, it was never like I had to be married, be the subservient housewife. In fact, I had talked about when I have kids, wanting to stay at home, and she was very adamant like that is not a good idea, you do not do that, because of the way she was raised and her expectations. So the career was definitely number one, getting married is just because it's culturally an acceptable thing, and kids. But even with kids, there's a sense that you still should work just to be independent.

While comments such as these were present throughout the interviews, they were especially common in Asian families where there was an explicitly stated worry that a relationship with a traditional Asian man would interfere with a daughter's professional success.[13]

Girls internalized these messages and they translated into adulthood. Only Ashleigh described marriage as her ultimate goal, although all but six of the women had always had marriage as one of their life goals. For the majority of women, although an eventual marriage was assumed, it was not a focus during their twenties; this was a common sentiment among college-educated women building professional careers.[14] Indeed, the assumption that marriage would be available to them when they desired it allowed for this delay.[15] But delayed marriage also reflected the fact that women saw economic and personal benefits to doing so. Working-class young adults often don't envision the same benefits to marrying later; instead, they see benefits to coupling up early, leading to divergent pathways by class.[16] Sophia noted how her new emphasis on delayed marriage distinguished her from her many male friends in blue-collar jobs. As a result, she saw her life trajectory diverging from theirs:

> I definitely thought I was going to be married right now and I thought I was going to be in my career by now, settled and working and that kind of thing. I've seen some of my friends who became police officers or firefighters so they already have a nice house. They had a nice house two years ago, not married, but a lot of them are looking to get married. Some of the guys I've dated, I just think they are looking to get married, and I've told them, I don't even have my big-girl job yet so getting married is [not a priority].

Rachel, 27, argued that people marry too young and without really knowing who they are yet as people. She assumed that if she did marry, she would be over 35 so that she could establish herself professionally first: "People change and grow, and that is why over 50 percent of marriages end in divorce. My biggest pet peeve is people who don't do anything with their lives, and I see a lot of women who get married and have no job and do absolutely nothing, and that's very sad and I would never want that for myself." As she explained, "Society has it backwards. It should be harder to marry and easier to divorce."

Young women had the same fears their parents did—that an early marriage would limit their future opportunities. Rather than worry that they would never find their "forever" partners, women assumed that this part of their life would fall into place when they were ready for it.

No Housewives Here

Heterosexual women's professional goals influenced what they were looking for in a partner, and their parents encouraged them in this respect, pushing them to marry men with similar, and traditionally valued, qualities: hard working, well-educated, ambitious, and financially successful. But these were expected to *match* women's qualities rather than complement them. A man who wanted a traditional division of labor was seen as both a liability and incompatible. Alyssa, who is Asian, said that her parents preferred that she date outside her racial group, which they considered too traditional: "So my dad and my mom have voiced an opinion that they prefer if I do date any Asian men, for instance, that they do have to be more Americanized. Because a lot of Asian males tend to still hold traditional gender roles that don't fit very well with me."

Given the strong media warnings about young men's "failure to launch,"[17] parents emphasized that men should be professionally successful, as a total gender role reversal was also not acceptable. Caroline described her mother's expectations for her future husband as such: "Probably smart and generally successful and ambitious. Someone who works hard and isn't going to be a drain on me." In fact, her mother disliked her former fiancé because even though he came from an extremely wealthy family, he was failing to establish himself as financially successful independently of his parents. Both Caroline and her mother viewed his lack of ambition as a personality flaw and Caroline ended the relationship as a result. But she held herself to the same standard, saying that she planned to stay in the workforce and support herself: "I don't want to be in a dynamic where anyone is mooching on anybody or anybody feels entitled to other people's stuff."

Rather than explicitly tell their daughters to find high-earning men, most parents used coded language to ensure the same end result, emphasizing men's level of ambition, education, and economic stability. Still, this was about more than finding a partner with high and stable earnings. As Alyssa said of her mother,

I think she puts more emphasis on education. Because she says that she doesn't think that I'd be able to communicate as well with someone that was uneducated. She thinks that someone who has at minimum a bachelor's, but more driven, has at least like a graduate degree—either a master's or a PhD—something like that would be better. Just to show more ambition, versus someone that has just remained status quo and then just doesn't really have any drive and things like that. She just thinks that we'll have a little bit more in common.

Although most parents didn't explicitly reference socioeconomic background, it was clear that they expected their daughters to find partners from a similarly class-privileged background. This would ensure higher levels of education and, as an extension, high earnings and economic stability, yet daughters also received the underlying message that lower-income men would be incompatible. Only four women stressed the importance of men as the main or sole breadwinner, and these women tended to have mediocre earning power due to their careers in pink-collar professions.[18] A more common description of an ideal mate focused instead on his willingness to support her career while at the same time being ambitious and economically successful himself. In this manner, parents encouraged the consolidation of class privilege through marriage.

Parents' emphasis on women's career success influenced how women expected to divide household labor and childcare. Three-quarters of the women described their ideal relationship as one in which household and caregiving tasks were not decided by gender. Jennifer, 27, said, "I'm never gonna assume that I shouldn't help clean the gutters. And I hope my [future] husband never assumes that he can't do the dishes. I don't think there're male chores and I don't think there're woman chores." Women applied the same expectations to childcare, although here they emphasized their need to remain in the workforce. Three did not plan to have children at all, viewing them as a barrier to professional achievement. But among the women who did want children, three-quarters reported that they had not interrupted or would not interrupt their careers to stay at home beyond a short maternity leave; however, a few of these women acknowledged that this might change when they actually had children. The general attitude was summed up best by Alison, 27, who said, "'Cause what the hell am I working, did all that work for, and then not use it; that's crazy." Caroline eventually broke up with a boyfriend after visiting his parents and seeing their traditional gender dynamic: "I think he really wanted to be with someone who would be a stay-at-home mom after we had kids, which he's perfectly entitled to how he wants his life to look, but that's not how I want my life to look. . . . I never wanted to stay at home. More power to women who can do that; I think it would make me crazy. You need something going on." Sophia concurred: "I could not be a stay-at-home mom. I would go nuts."

Many of the women expressed the same sentiment—that they would "go crazy" if they had to stay at home with children. Although they tended not to express this overtly, the subtext was that women who devoted their lives to their husband's achievements and stayed home with their children were somehow lacking. Keira said, "[My husband's] brother, who's the PhD, he and his wife are college sweethearts. They went through their PhD program together. After they got hooded, they got married and had children. They have triplets. She changed her name. *She has a PhD and she's a stay-at-home mom.*" Keira saw her sister-in-law as selling herself out, and her own goals, by prioritizing motherhood. In keeping with narratives of liberal feminism, many women I spoke with associated the private sphere with constraint and the public sphere with liberation.[19]

Not only did women enjoy their work, but they also recognized that without a job they would have less power to negotiate their needs within the relationship. In particular, there was an emphasis on supporting oneself so that money could not be used as a source of control by a partner.[20] Ariana expressed the fear experienced by many: without financial independence she would lose power in her relationship, and the ability to leave if necessary: "My mom was a stay-at-home mom and my dad had a lot of financial control over her, and she always emphasized, be independent, get a good education so you have your own financial independence and so no man can use that to control you. So that's always been embedded in my brain."[21]

Still, a few of the women already anticipated stepping out of the workplace, even if only temporarily, to care for children. One was a stay-at-home parent and one expressed a desire to be one when she had children, while six of the women indicated that they would like to stay home for a few years before going back to work. Almost a quarter of the women either readily embraced an orientation toward caregiving *or* couldn't see a way to build an egalitarian relationship after the arrival of children. Yes, they wanted careers, but they still saw themselves as the ones to do any caregiving that necessitated a break from the labor force.

Overall, women expressed strong egalitarian narratives in response to their career aspirations. Raised by their parents to put education and career before marriage, the women embraced the self-development imperative middle-class women now face. As a result, what women want from their relationships has shifted. They are not conflicted about their professional goals, and they seek a relationship with a partner who will support these goals rather than hinder them. Committed, serious relationships, whether the couple is married or just cohabiting, present a danger to these professional aspirations if they prove too time consuming or leave women financially dependent. For the most part, women express a strong desire for partners who are similarly ambitious and willing to share both the paid labor and the household loads. As such, heterosexual women initially appear to be on a pathway to the equal relationships they seek.

MARRIAGE AS TEAMWORK

Heterosexual middle- and upper-middle-class men were also seeking professional success. But given that romantic relationships have traditionally privileged men's ambitions over women's, they didn't spend their time worrying that a relationship would interfere with their career goals.[22] Instead, they reflected on the burdens of being the sole breadwinner.[23] Not content to sit on the sidelines of their children's lives, they aimed to be active participants in raising them. In order to have access to the rewards of caregiving, men expected to share both paid labor and housework. But the division of labor was not their only concern. Just as women wanted partners with similar aspirations in order to ensure compatibility, so too did men. Traditional gender roles were viewed not as a path to happiness in a relationship, but as an indication that they didn't have enough in common with their partner.

Buying In to the "Success Sequence"

Surprisingly, while 23 of the 31 heterosexual men recounted a strong pressure or expectation that they go to college, most received less direct pressure than women to pick specific majors that would earn them a great deal of money. Instead, the focus was on finding your passion, working hard at it, and doing the best you can. Rather than money, an enjoyable career was emphasized as the pathway to happiness and success. Arjun, 25, described his parents' advice as follows: "Do something you're happy about, but work hard. Simple as that, you need to work hard. Money was not it. Incidentally, we all picked business because that's where you make money. But my dad would say, 'If that's your passion, then it's your passion.'" Logan, 29, reported his parents telling him, "Don't let [money] be your primary concern because that's not going to help you be happy or succeed." Ben, 33, said his mother told him, "I have no requirements of you other than I want you to be happy with what you choose to do in life, and if that's being a teacher or a lifeguard or whatever, you can do that and I'll be fine. I just want you to be fulfilled." Yet given that cultural narratives about men's skills and passions align with the expectations of higher-paying careers,[24] men were able to follow their parents' advice, discuss their goals in nongendered terms, and still follow a gendered pathway into high-earning professions. Potentially, then, women receive more pressure to pick certain majors due to parents' knowledge that women are more likely to be pulled into less lucrative careers and pink-collar jobs.

However, while many of the men said that they were encouraged to find their own path in life, others felt subtle or explicit pressure to be attentive to financial concerns. Often this was couched as a pragmatic approach to life in the pricey Bay Area rather than as money as the be-all and end-all of happiness and success. Jeremy, 30, said, "My dad would always emphasize that it's important to make money in order to be able to do what you want to do. So like when I had political ideas about going into nonprofits, my dad would always say, 'Well, if you make money, you'll be able to support those causes more effectively.'" But in contrast to what heterosexual women were told by their parents, there wasn't a strong message to be financially independent *from a partner*.

Just as with women, men said that their parents expected them to establish themselves in a career before getting married, although unlike with women, relationships in general weren't treated with suspicion. Ryan, 28, succinctly summed up the message: "Get a career first, get financially stable, and then get married." Pressure to marry was limited and came after a career was established. Adam, 33, said, "Mom likes to drop hints. Oh, you know, now that you're at a certain part of your career, certain period of your financial security, you need to start thinking about getting married and things like that." Men, for the most part, embraced this message. Daniel, 26, said that he chose not to date much until after college: "There was an almost laser-like focus on my part to graduate and do all the right things career-wise." Alexander, 38, said that his family opposed his marriage because he was still in school: "They have their prescription, which is go to college, get your career, and then get your house, and *then* get a wife and a family."

In order to create the right conditions to attract a wife, men used their twenties as a time to invest in themselves professionally. Referred to as "the success sequence" by conservatives, this approach is portrayed as the ideal way to go about family building, emphasizing personal responsibility and delayed gratification.[25]

For the most part, though, heterosexual men reported receiving significantly less relationship advice than did women, possibly because relationships weren't seen to be as threatening to men's success as they were to women's. Two-thirds of the men recalled getting either no messages or very few messages on what they should be looking for in a partner and what type of relationship they should establish. Instead, most of the men just recalled a hope on the part of their parents that they marry. Ben said of his mother, "She communicated that finding a partner or someone to be married to was a good thing in the sense that it made your life more stable and it made life better. But in terms of whether you had to marry a certain kind of person or anything like that, nothing."

Adam said his parents had started out with specifics, but over the years had changed their tune, simply hoping that he would start dating:

> When I first graduated they wanted me to date a Taiwanese girl and then Taiwanese girl becomes Chinese girl, Chinese girl becomes Asian girl, Asian girl becomes a girl. And now we're at this stage, it goes, start dating, I don't care what you do, just start dating. And that is the focus right now.

Rather than viewing romantic relationships as a potential problem for men, their parents, in particular their mothers, saw relationships with women as beneficial and even necessary, especially once they reached a certain stage in life.

From a young age, then, men were told that there was a particular pathway they should take for success. Education, career, and marriage

should unfold in a dependable manner in order to create happiness, financial security, and stability. But in contrast to women, there was very little
emphasis on establishing and maintaining financial independence from a
partner, nor on the type of partner they should seek out, thus indicating
limited concern that a partner would potentially interfere with these
goals.

Mirror-Image Mates

Sociologist Arlie Hochschild described modern couplings as a relationship between faster-changing women and slower-changing men, as wom-
en's work and family patterns depart from their mothers' while men's continue to look remarkably similar to their fathers'.[26] As a result, professional
men are encountering a different type of woman in the dating market, one
who mirrors back their traits. While a guiding assumption is that men are
superficially focused on women's appearance over traits such as personality, compatibility, or career prospects, almost all of the men wanted and
expected their partners to be accomplished, ambitious, and independent,
just as they were.[27] Discussing what he wanted from a spouse, Ishan, 29,
said, "Probably very much an independent type, not very dependent on
others to achieve whatever she wanted to achieve." Jake, 34, broke up with
a girlfriend he felt was not ambitious enough. When I asked Jake what he
would look for in a future partner, he said, "An active brain. A curiosity
about life and about people. And then a sharpness of intellect, a learning
person, someone who's constantly learning, someone who's challenging
me. Ambition is huge. I'm looking for someone who can support themselves and is surviving on their own."

    This type of partner was encouraged by the few parents who did pro-
vide opinions and advice. Andrew, 35, said his mother weighed in on a
former girlfriend after he broke up with her. "She said, 'She just wasn't
cutting it in our book anyway.' . . . It was sort of a lack of ambition and that
played into body type and gave rise to a bunch of shortcomings." Ryan's
mother, too, had a very specific idea of her ideal daughter-in-law: "She
had to be very well educated, she had to go to, of course, preferably like [a
top-tier university]. And she had to be skinny." Interestingly, mothers in
particular emphasized a balance of normative and non-normative

femininity, in which partners were expected to be both professionally ambitious and conventionally attractive.

Heterosexual men sought partners, then, who were achievers and therefore not reliant on them for income or interests. But for their sons to attract these women, parents emphasized that *they* needed to be achievers as well. Andrew recalled another incident in which his mother gave him relationship advice. Fresh out of law school, Andrew had lined up a job in the area when his fiancée got accepted to an out-of-state MBA program. To support her career, he decided to turn down the job and follow her across the country. Andrew's mother worried that this choice would actually hurt rather than help the relationship. As he explained, "My mom was very opinionated in that she thought that my wife needed a partner who was exceptionally successful and, by sidelining my career, I would actually be doing harm to the perception that [my wife] would have of me in the future."

Coinciding with this desire for ambitious partners, a strong, intellectual, and curious personality was frequently cited as an important quality. Matthew, 29, explained why he started dating his current girlfriend: "I liked her because she had a really strong personality, like she was very outspoken, had a lot to say, and was, again, very interesting." Indeed, there was some concern that a woman who wasn't accomplished wouldn't be interesting. Dave, 34, said, "I never had a relationship with someone who wasn't on the same intellectual level as me. How would that work out?" Andrew made a similar point when he explained his decision to marry his wife. He described her as an "extremely directed individual, very passionate about life and adventuresome; enjoys travel, enjoys hobbies that are similar to mine and very well read. So there are a lot of characteristics that I could see being good in a mother *and* a companion at all times of the day. So somebody well rounded enough that wouldn't be a person I'd get bored with."

Ben agreed that intellectual curiosity was necessary in a partner:

Okay, so deal-breakers were bad at conversation or no intellectual drive, so no interest in the world around them. So for example [my wife's] brother is married to a woman who has literally no interest in anything other than fashion. She is also beautiful, but incredibly frustrating to be around because she doesn't have an opinion about anything, and so it's just, well, what do

I talk to you about even if I knew about fashion. It drives me insane that people aren't interested in the world around them or stuff like that.

Even the three men who wanted their wives to eventually stay at home emphasized the value of these traits. At issue was the sense that a long-term partnership required a certain level of compatibility and that if a partner's traits did not match theirs, the relationship would fail. Not only were men worried that their partners could become too financially dependent, but they were also worried that without a strong sense of self, their partners would become too emotionally dependent. Christopher, 34, broke up with his long-term girlfriend for this very reason and hoped for something different from his next partner:

> Someone who, you know, has a career and has hobbies. And isn't just going to become my wife. I want someone who is an individual and more of an equal partner. And not just somebody who is going to get lost in me. You know, that's how I felt with [my ex-girlfriend]. [She] just got lost in me. And she didn't ever get her career going, you know. Just someone to have their own career, you know, and want to do the family, but have their sense of self.

Only a few men expressed a preference for a more traditional partnership in which the man was the dominant partner. Dave had gone through a divorce and compared his first wife to his second, saying, "I would call [my first wife] the more dominant party. With [my second wife] I would say I'm the more dominant party. I like it. [Laughs] You know, a lot of stereotypes come up—how men aren't comfortable marrying a stronger woman necessarily. And, having been with a strong woman, I kind of understand where they are coming from."

Dave recalled his first wife's constant put-downs, in spite of the sacrifices he made for her. As he explained, when his wife got into law school across the country, he moved away from the Bay Area and the hub of his career activity to support her career goals. Yet he felt that she didn't appreciate these sacrifices, and speculated that her poor treatment of him had led to their poor sex life. Although he had said he didn't want to emulate his domineering father, he did discover that he liked being the more dominant party in his relationship.

Aaron, 40, had similar feelings, also born of a problematic, and now ended, first marriage in which an overbearing wife and mother-in-law were seen as the main obstacles. But Dave and Aaron were the exceptions and they both seemed to conflate "strong" with overbearing and mean. As a result, their second marriages were more traditional than their first.

Balanced Breadwinning

Given that the majority of the men wanted a woman whom they saw as an equal partner, they also expressed the view that men and women should both be involved in paid labor, caregiving, and housework, stressing that in particular they did not want financially dependent partners. Rather than viewing the breadwinner role as a privilege, many of the men saw it as a burden. Ryan broke up with his previous girlfriend because she supported traditional gender norms: "I didn't like having to sort of pay for everything or be alpha for everything. . . . I think I realized I was looking more for a partner as opposed to just take care of somebody and be someone's sugar daddy." Mark, 32, said of his relationship with his fiancée, "I don't want to feel that I have to hold the entire family financially together. That responsibility . . . I seem to have that in my relationships. With us, it would be nice to be relieved of that responsibility for a period of time. But . . . I make more money."

In addition, almost all of the men said that they wouldn't have an issue with a partner who made more money, and many even discussed this as a positive due to their limited earning power in a profession they enjoyed. However, they also recognized that a limited income was a liability on the dating and marriage market. Christopher said,

> I think it's harder to date if you're a guy and you make less money. I think it's definitely harder to date. Even if the person likes you a lot. You know, [my ex-girlfriend] liked me a lot, but she would talk about me doing a second career. I know [my girlfriend] likes me a lot, she's really into me. But she even says, you know, have you ever thought about doing anything besides teaching? So I think if you're a guy and you're not making a lot of money, you can try to bring it with nice poems or music, but sometimes it does really come down to money. It sucks.

Thus, most of the men still considered a certain level of income a goal even if they didn't want to be the sole breadwinners.

While almost none of the men envisioned themselves as extended stay-at-home parents, they also didn't want their wives to stay home. William, 32, said, "I would like for us both to be equal in the parenting. It's a little hard to imagine a life with a stay-home mom." Consistent with the value men placed on women's ambition, he added, "I would like someone who has an idea of what they want to accomplish in their career, not just working because they have to." Indeed, many interpreted a desire to stay at home as a lack of ambition, which indicated that a woman might end up too dependent. As Christopher said, "I don't want my wife to just get lost in me and the family. I want her to be her own person and do her 'thing' too." Mateo, 33, partially attributed the end of his marriage to his wife's dependence on him. When I asked him what he would look for in a future partner, he said,

> Someone who's very independent. They can be on their own and be happy. They can have a happy Saturday all by themselves. I want them to have a profession. Whatever they like. One of the things that I've thought about with my relationship with my wife is that maybe she wouldn't have been as attached to me if she had had a job and friends through that job. I don't really care what, it doesn't have to be this or that, just something that they enjoy.

In fact, only three of the men interviewed wanted a wife who would definitely stay at home. The remainder presented this as either a negative or as a personal choice for the woman. Only one man went so far as to express a strong desire to take time out of work for childrearing. Mark, who chafed at breadwinning expectations, also wanted the opportunity to stay at home with his child for a period of time: "So I really want the privilege of being able to stay home. But it seems more practical that she's willing to stay home. She really wants to stay home. I guess the fact that I want an equal stay-at-home time with the kids and maybe I won't get it, is kind of annoying." Mark seemed genuinely upset that although his fiancée was working toward a PhD in chemistry, she was already scaling back her career goals in anticipation of having children. Given how demanding the modern workplace is of full-time professionals, it wasn't a great leap to the realization that his breadwinning might preclude a significant role in parenting.[28]

A few others said they would be willing to stay home when I asked, but seemed to have only considered the issue in the abstract and didn't express a strong desire to do so. Unlike the eight women who planned to take time out of the workplace, they certainly weren't approaching this as an inevitability. For example, Brad, 32, said, "I'm open. If her career was supporting us more than mine was and she was more passionate and I was just working in a job, where she's pursuing a passion, I'd be a stay-at-home dad if that's what we needed and decided. Not for long, though. I believe there's a problem with that. The resentment builds. People need to maintain some sort of independence in their lives, otherwise they start to resent." Just as there was the worry that stay-at-home mothers would lose themselves in their families, so too was there the fear that this could happen to men.

Heterosexual men provided a similar narrative of equality with regard to the division of housework. Brad described his ideal of how labor should be divided: "Fairly and equitably. . . . I don't have that gender role expectation of the woman doing everything. In fact, quite frankly, I'd rather be with a woman that doesn't accept that role." For most, however, an equal division of housework was not met with the enthusiasm they had for sharing in childcare. Most of the men just vaguely described the ideal as everyone doing their part. Adam said,

> It's all about the communication. I'm willing to do this, I like to do that. There's something that I know some people just wouldn't like to do. For example, I know some ladies, they just don't like to cut the grass; I'll do it. Some ladies don't like to take out the trash; I'll do it. Some people don't like to do the dishes; I'll do it, that's fine. But as long as I'm doing something and then you're finding something else to do with me, then I'm okay. I just don't want to feel like I'm the one doing everything.

Heterosexual men were more worried about total financial responsibility and a dependent partner than about their own potential dependency. They took for granted their own career aspirations and instead discussed finding well-educated, ambitious partners. Because women shape men's behaviors by promoting traits and practices as desirable in romantic relationships, men partially construct their relationship goals in relation to what they believe women want.[29] But they also saw this relationship style as beneficial for themselves and the well-being of the relationship. They, too, appear to be setting the stage for egalitarian relationships, although with more of an emphasis on shifts in women's behavior than in their own.

QUEERING THE GOOD LIFE

Because most parents assume that their children are heterosexual and cisgender until informed otherwise, LGBQ people received similar messages growing up. Yet at some point, they were forced to reorient themselves away from at least some of these messages as they claimed an LGBQ identity. In the process, many embraced queer narratives that questioned mainstream society's definition of "the good life" and instead sought to remake traditional practices in their romantic relationships, as well as in other aspects of their lives. The majority of the 40 LGBQ people in this study wanted relationships that balanced partners' individual needs and desires with the needs of the relationship, also setting the stage for egalitarian relationships.

The Normative Nest

Like their heterosexual, cisgender counterparts, those assigned female at birth and raised as girls were taught to value educational and career attainment over romantic relationships. Just over two-thirds of this group reported explicit pressure to go to college and start a lucrative and prestigious career. Lauren, 29, a queer cis woman, felt derailed after she wasn't accepted to any four-year colleges out of high school due to an application error. From a young age, she remembers her parents telling her that it was important that she leave home for college at 18. She was frequently taken to events at her parents' alma mater: "It was like they had, all my life, literally from the time that I was like born, talked about, 'You're going to go to school.' . . . There was never any question. Like they had built that expectation that I had to and I would." Santiago, 34, a queer transmasculine person, said they experienced "typical immigrant shit—like my mom wanted me to be a doctor, a lawyer. I remember before I could even say sentences, she trained me to be like, what do you want to be? Doctor or lawyer." Santiago's mother gave birth to Santiago at 19 and didn't finish college until 22 years later. Rather than hope Santiago would marry and have children, their mother worried that early relationships would result in early pregnancy and marriage and derail Santiago's professional success.[30]

Many parents tied this expectation for education to their children's financial stability and independence. However, unlike heterosexual women, this group was more likely to resist these pressures, seeing high-paying, corporate jobs as unappealing. Adah, 34, a queer genderqueer and gender-fluid person who was unemployed but hoped to do healing and performance work in the future, said, "I think they really wanted me to have a stable, secure, nine-to-five job with good benefits." Sam, 30, a queer genderqueer person working as a bike messenger, said, "From my perspective, [my parents' pressure] was more about stability and making money. Even today—because I don't have a traditional career—my mom is like, well what about the money that you're making?" She frequently makes career recommendations to Sam, to which they reply, "I don't like that job. [And then my mom says,] but you have to do things you don't like sometimes. I'm like, no." Even Riley, 29, a lesbian trans man[31] who was attending school for a master's in social work, reported that his parents worried that a career in social work would leave him "penniless."

Unlike heterosexual women, members of this group were more concerned with maintaining freedom from the capitalist grind and finding meaningful work than in using their credentials to ensure independence from a male partner. Indeed, Ella, a 26-year-old gay cis woman who worked as a highly paid management consultant, articulated this norm, saying, "I'm selling out to the 'The Man,' right? Like, there aren't many lesbians in business. I mean, you're meeting a lesbian who is like almost sleeping with the enemy. . . . I probably have the most capitalist job out of any lesbian I know." For many, being counter-normative and queer extended to all aspects of their lives, including their professional work.[32]

But although their parents wanted them to finish their educations and establish careers prior to settling into long-term relationships, this group reported getting more explicit and conservative messages about relationships than did heterosexual women. Whether this was due to parents picking up on some form of nonconformity in childhood, or LGBQ people noting the differences in their feelings versus parental and cultural messaging, is unclear. However, a third of them originally imagined very normative romantic lives. Lauren recounted an incident that really stuck with her:

> I remember distinctly when I was eleven-ish, we were in Los Angeles visiting family. My mom and I had gotten our nails done and we were walking down the street. There was this wedding dress in a boutique, in the window. My mom was like, "That's the dress that you are going to wear when you grow up and get married." Like, we went in, looked at it, looked at the details of it. She even took a Polaroid of it, I think. Like, it was serious. *I was eleven years old.*

Tina, a 27-year-old bisexual cis woman, said of her parents, "In terms of relationships, heterosexual matrimony has definitely always been the angle in their mind. . . . They always talk about when you get married, or someday your husband will be X, Y, and Z." It wasn't until they came to identify as LGBQ that many in this group started questioning their parents' expectations for their romantic relationships as well.

In contrast, parents of boys, only one of whom no longer identified with their gender assigned at birth at the time of the interview, provided their children with the same narratives as those given to heterosexual men. While parents expected their sons to go to college, there was significantly less pressure to select a certain career path. When asked if his parents voiced expectations for his college major and career, Brian, 30, a queer cis man, said, "Not really. I think at 16 I decided I was going to be a fiction writer and so, like, they were sort of behind that. Or a high school teacher was something I thought about a lot and so, yeah, they were on board with it." As with heterosexual men, the focus was on doing something that inspired them, although still with the expectation that whatever inspired them would pay the bills. Sean, 26, a gay cis man, said, "My mom always told me that she wanted me to be happy no matter what and not pick a career just to be stable and financially secure. So I never had the sort of pressure that I needed to find X job to make X money sort of thing." That said, unlike those raised as girls, this group was almost exclusively employed in well-paying, masculine-typed jobs, indicating again that passion and career achievement in gender-normative professions are often conflated for men. There was also no mention of the desire to avoid a "soul sucking" corporate job. As a result, they were mainly in or entering jobs that would allow them to support both themselves and a partner. This is potentially because, unlike those raised as girls, this group was less likely to identify as queer or genderqueer, perhaps indicating a more normative orientation to life.

Like heterosexual men, those raised as boys received limited advice on their romantic relationships. As Ken, 33, a gay cis man, said, "Just no kids at 15! That was the one rule." Coming from a low-income background, the advice Ken received reflected worries in low-income communities of color about the risks of early childbearing.[33] But for the most part, given the class background of most of the respondents, parents didn't express a concrete worry over early or even nonmarital childbearing.[34] Again, they were simply expected to follow the "success sequence"—go to college, start a career, find a wife, have children. This expectation resonated, and 80 percent provided some variation of an American Dream and white-picket-fence narrative when asked how they had expected their lives to turn out when they were younger. Nicholas, 36, a gay cis man, said, "When I was younger it was the American Dream, kind of like, wife, two kids, dogs, a house with a white picket fence. That's what I always envisioned that I was supposed to have, who I was supposed to be." Jocelyn, 36, a bisexual trans woman, said, "I assumed when I was young that I would have a wife and be married and have kids and that whole white-picket-fence dream was definitely stuck in my head." This trajectory and end goal represented the culmination of successful upper-middle-class masculinity.[35]

Even those who identified as gay or queer from an early age simply switched their narrative to replace a wife with a husband. Evan, a 27-year-old gay cis man, said,

> Before I came out, I wanted to be with a girl. I thought that was what I was supposed to do—have a family, have kids, all that jazz. I had these sexual urges. My body's telling me one thing. I am not attracted to girls, I'm attracted to guys. I didn't know how to deal with it. I came out at 16 and things sort of stayed the same. I still wanted a committed relationship. I still wanted the same things as everyone around me, just "with a guy."

A few of the gay cis men said their mothers took a similar perspective on the men's relationships, simply substituting a man for a woman in order to maintain some semblance of normativity. Ken said, "My mom is the worst! It's her main goal in life to get me married off, partnered with a boy. . . . She tells me that she can get on the internet and find the right boy on Match. com, 'cause that's so successful at hooking people up." Fathers struggled more. Not only were they less likely to give advice on relationships, ceding this responsibility to their sons' mothers, but they were less accepting of their sons' sexual identities and were more likely to partially disconnect from them. Many simply settled into a "don't ask, don't tell" relationship.

"An Empty Void"

In spite of the so-called deinstitutionalization of relationship pathways and the expectation that people pick and choose the type of life that works best for them, one relationship ideal remains culturally dominant, especially among the college educated.[36] Many LGBQ people simply reconfigured this expectation for a married, monogamous coupling to mean a same-sex partner, finding pleasure and comfort in following at least some conventional markers of the "good life." Others either played along to fit in or simply couldn't see a future for themselves. While only 20 percent of those raised as boys provided this narrative, 70 percent of those raised as girls did, potentially indicating how much more prevalent traditional relationship narratives are in the lives of those assigned female, and how much more oppressive those narratives feel.

While some attempted to go along with the expectations of heterosexual relationships, their hearts simply weren't in it, yet they lacked the concepts to understand why. Jamie, 30, a queer cis woman, recalled how she cheated on all of her male partners while growing up, as she attempted to play along with the expectation that teenage girls are supposed to want boyfriends: "I didn't have a long-term vision of having a life with a partner until I was in a queer relationship. And that was the first time that I did not cheat on my partner and that I really saw myself having children with them."

Others couldn't see alternative options for themselves given that the ones provided to them did not resonate. Andie, 27, a gay genderqueer person, said,

It was sort of like an empty void . . . I never pictured getting married and having kids with a guy. But I also couldn't bring myself to imagine a woman in that place. So I sort of couldn't picture it and couldn't imagine what I could possibly do. It was bleak. I'd say that was pretty traumatizing for me to not be able to picture what a future happy life would look like.

Alek, a 38-year-old gay cis man, also couldn't see a future for himself, saying, "I was quite a rebellious kid and I was the sort that I could hardly imagine life after 30. I thought I would live until like 20-something and then I would like brightly die somewhere. I didn't care about the future and marriage or something like that."

As a result, many focused on sexual relationships or opted out of romantic relationships altogether. This was perhaps a defense mechanism in response to the exclusion they faced at the time from the institution of marriage. In addition, they lacked models for queer relationships and potentially feared hostile reactions if they did form them. Tina said,

I never thought too seriously about marriage. It was hard for me to ever picture myself choosing one person. So even though I was constantly getting those messages from my mom and my dad and people around me, I just wasn't interested. So I definitely thought about sex a lot, but not really dating or marriage per se. For a long time I really didn't want to be in a long-term relationship and thought they were so boring and everything. So my long-term expectations were like hopefully I can just sleep around forever and no one will ever call me on that and that'll be great.

While heterosexual women, too, often delay commitment in favor of hooking up in college,[37] they still understood marriage as a goal down the road, which is distinctly different from the sentiment expressed by this group. When I asked Jen, a 31-year-old queer cis woman, if she saw herself getting married when she was younger, she replied, "Not really, no. I saw myself getting laid." Melanie, 29, a queer cis woman, said, "I was always the odd person out. I think not having expectations was sort of like a coping mechanism or like a self-preservation mechanism. . . . But I think in high school my expectation was like, oh I'm not a datable person. I'm not an attractive person so I'm not really gonna think about myself in terms of dating or relationships. I'm just gonna be whatever." Beck, a 33-year-old queer trans man, said, "For a long time, I didn't see that part of my life playing out. I just didn't have an interest in relationships."

Others focused instead on envisioning career success. Jessie, a 28-year-old queer genderqueer person, explained, "I felt like I grew up sort of awkward, so I don't know. Like when someone says, 'Oh you want to go out? I find you attractive,' I'm like, really? This is exciting. No, I always thought I would be kind of like married to my career or something like that." Yang, a 36-year-old gay cis man, also focused more on educational and professional goals rather than worrying about how his romantic life would turn out: "I guess I never really thought about it that much. I knew I liked men. I was concentrating on school anyway."

Although many of the LGBQ people started out without a clear sense of their hopes for the future, they all eventually discovered queer communities that opened their eyes to the variety of possibilities in relationships. These were turning points in their lives as they came to see themselves as both desiring and desirable, both sexually and romantically. With the tools to imagine alternative romantic options, they were able to develop a sense of what they wanted from their relationships.

Flexible Commitment

While heterosexual men and women took marriage as a given in their future, LGBQ people did not. Many of my interviews took place as the challenges to Proposition 8, a 2008 state constitutional amendment banning same-sex marriage in California, were still making their way through the courts. The remainder took place in May and June 2015, just two years after the state resumed issuing same-sex marriage licenses, but before the Obergefell decision on June 26. In both cases, access to marriage felt tenuous. Some were eager to take advantage of this newly and hard won right, saying they would rather marry than settle for lifelong commitment without legal recognition. Ken said, "The marriage thing is an ideal; it's where you want to go." When I asked what marriage represented, he explained, "Commitment before man, God, and state. That we're gonna have kids and we have to show we're committed to each other." Sean, too, valued marriage, saying, "I would like to find somebody to be married to and adopt kids and have a family, sort of in an almost traditional way." While people talked about their desire to follow traditional relationship pathways, they also emphasized the importance of external recognition and validation of their relationships. Andie said, "I just like the idea of celebrating my relationship with friends and family. And then also just like the legal benefits and stuff."

But others were more ambivalent. Adah explained, "So much money in mainstream LGBT organizing and movement work goes to marriage equality, as opposed to all the fucking broke, starving trans people in the street. I would way rather that money be directed there. So politically, I feel in this weird place about it where I'm like marriage, as a queer person, can I even do that and be okay about myself?" While Adah was willing to consider marriage if it was important to a partner and their family, they were conflicted: "In relationships, what's been important is, are we connecting in a way that feels authentic and good and organic and are we letting things live and die as they need to? Are we not pushing to fit into some model that we think we need to be in? Are we being true to ourselves and what we actually need to be happy people?" When I asked Evan if he ever wanted to get married, he said, "Half of me fantasizes about that, just because I want to be the gay couple that can do that. But, half of me is like, 'Ugh, fuck heterosexual marriage, fuck marriage, fuck the norm. . . . I don't want to be a part of it.' I don't know. I'm torn. . . . I just want the same damn federal benefits as everybody gets, so however that comes about."

Others also emphasized the need for flexibility as opposed to rigid commitment. Sam said, "I don't see [the point of marriage]. Also, I think it's too constraining; it's just too permanent for life. Life is not permanent. But the way that I see things, people change so much and then there's an aspect of oh, now we're married; we should work on it. But what if you can't? You've just changed and you want different things? So it's just too permanent." Karina, 37, a queer cis woman, agreed: "You can only commit, I think, to being true to yourself. And that changes every second. So to say I'm yours forever, that's so untrue. I can't say that. I'm here as long as I can be. As long as we both have interest in each other." Karina felt open to getting married if it was important to a partner, adding, "But I don't think it is something that is set forever. Marriage can also be dissolved." Patricio, 25, a queer nonbinary person, had a similar perspective, saying they didn't want marriage, but rather, "commitment ceremonies. Plural. See who I'm committed to at the time and then move on, see where it goes, see what happens. Like if anything, I've definitely learned that relationships aren't forever and it's okay that they're not." But beyond the desire to avoid feeling obligated to stay in an unhappy relationship, some viewed marriage as an isolating act. Manuela, a 36-year-old queer gender-queer person, explained their resistance to marriage in these terms: "The first image that comes to mind is we're stranded on the mountain and there's an avalanche and we have to eat each other, basically. For me it just activates co-dependency."

Given these narratives, LGBQ people sought partners who valued independence and flexibility in the context of commitment, rather than a rigid adherence to norms of how romantic relationships are supposed to look. Conceptions of independence had some overlap with those of heterosexual men and women, with a focus on financial independence and personal ambition. Lauren said, "I feel like financial independence is critical. I've had lessons from my parents' mistakes, mainly my mom's, in giving up her financial freedom. I'm not going to do that." While Lauren focused on the importance of her own financial independence, common among cis women, Yang, like other cis men, focused on his partner's. Yang said, "I explained to [my boyfriend] why I didn't want more commitment. Financially, he's just not very stable. I'm talking long term. He pays his rent. It's not like he has debts. He has no health care. He's living from paycheck to paycheck." Since Yang had been willing to financially support his last boyfriend, I asked what made this one different: "Well the thing is, with [my ex], he has an education as an advancement. [My boyfriend] doesn't have a degree. . . . I just don't want to commit to somebody who's just a little bit unstable for the long term."

It wasn't only financial independence that was important, but the traits and values that this reflected. Leslie, 25, a lesbian cis woman, described what she was looking for in a long-term partner:

> Someone who is ambitious. I really like someone who is ambitious and intelligent. . . . I really like to see right off the bat where people are in their lives and where they want to be. So it's like the girl I was talking to, she was like, yeah, I'm going to go to therapy school to be like a therapist. And I was like, oh cool. And then as I got to know her more, I was like, you're not going

to therapy school at all. You're like sitting at home being lazy. So I like to see where people want to be in their lives. Because I'm thinking more long term.

Again, not only did this indicate compatible values; it also indicated that partners would have more in common with each other in other desirable ways. For example, Evan wanted someone with a career, income, and education comparable to his own: "I find that university-educated guys just come with a whole different experience set than guys who aren't. They just have more culture, or life experience." These attitudes reflect the cultural trend among the college educated that individualism and self-development should be key features of long-term partnerships. They also made clear that only partners with certain class backgrounds were acceptable.[38] These narratives are consistent with those provided by the heterosexual men and women.

But rather than view relationships as something one creates *after* building sufficient independence, many saw independence as something that should take place within the context of intimate relationships and be balanced with commitment.[39] Marco, 30, a queer cis man, said of his ideal relationship, "We accept and support each other, we both work our asses off for the future, we're very independent and we aren't overly wrapped up in each other's lives." Jen envisioned "someone who understands that relationships take work. They're something you build together. Someone who can respect my independence and autonomy, but is supportive." Rather than expect commitment or independence to supersede the other, they wanted independence to take place within the context of commitment, where both needed to be negotiated to achieve the desired balance for both partners. This is not entirely distinct from the approach taken by heterosexual women and men, but it does emphasize relationship building as an ongoing process rather than as a culminating experience. LGBQ people placed significantly more emphasis on flexibility, indicating that relationship practices should be crafted around the needs of each partner and that each partner should be open to change. Adah used the question of monogamy to discuss this perspective, saying, "It's exciting to have the kind of partner where your partner is your priority and then you kind of figure out the rest of the relationship. . . . So it's not like I'm so married to the idea of monogamy or nonmonogamy or whatever. It's more like, are you going to be my primary person? Okay, cool—let's figure out the rest to support that."

Given the importance placed on intentional rather than default decision-making in relationships, many questioned whether they would have children at all. A third said they didn't want children, while another third said they were still unsure. When I asked Evan if he wanted kids, he said, "Maybe. When I'm ready to die—when I'm like forty or forty-five. To me, I see the gay culture and I see partying until you aren't attractive anymore. And, at that point, when I would be forty, is when I would want to settle down. I'm young and I'm fit, I want to do all these activities and things, and I don't want to get held back by kids."

Like heterosexual men and women, only a few LGBQ people wanted a more traditional division of labor where one partner stayed home with children while the other focused on breadwinning. More frequently, they said they wouldn't want to stay home, nor would they be attracted to someone who wanted to do so. Jack, a 25-year-old gay cis man, said, "I just don't think I'm attracted to someone who'd want to stay home." He added, "I don't want to be the provider. No, I worry that I'll be taken for a ride." Jen said,

> My career is the most important thing to me right now because it's not just connected to finance. Finance is actually not it. It's connected to my spiritual health because it's like what I am here to do. And it's super important that my career makes me happy. So it's connected to my happiness. And then lastly it's connected to my finances. But I can always do shit for money. It's like nothing is more important to me than my career right now and myself, my spiritual health.

Given this perspective, Jen was unwilling to give up a career to take care of a child, but she didn't expect her partner to do so either. Melanie hoped for an equitable split, one she saw modeled by her parents:

> So like you know the way my parents did it, it's like my mom stayed home with my sister when my sister was a baby and then my dad stayed home with me when I was a baby. And like because they had joint custody, it ended up being that like the way they invested in us was much more equal than maybe it would have been. So that's like very, very important to me that both parents are like equally parenting the children.

Only Caitlin, a 30-year-old gay cis woman who described herself as a "den mother," envisioned staying home at least part-time with kids.

If childcare and parenting goals were murky, housework was less so and was expected to be either divided relatively evenly or outsourced. Samuel, a 37-year-old gay cis man, said, "Half and half. I'm definitely not going to be someone's bitch, nor do I expect someone else to be that. But if we have a problem with that half-and-half splitting, then just hire a housekeeper." Jack said, "We'd hire a lady" for both cleaning and childcare. Elizabeth, a 27-year-old bisexual cis woman, said, "I'm not someone's mommy. And if you still need your mommy to clean up after you then you need to grow up." Only Alek described himself as a "romantic type" who was above such petty concerns:

> I'm not stuck that much to the material things, to the money. I don't mind paying the bills. I do not care that much about how we split the chores equally or not equally. Who cares? Like if things are going a good way and we are in a good partnership, I'm more, like I discovered the value of the spiritual life. As long as we do not stay in a certain place and we are moving and we are educating ourselves.

The messages LGBQ people received from their parents were similar to those received by heterosexual people; parents emphasized the importance of education, career building, and economic stability. But members of this group discussed more pressure from parents to get married, perhaps because they remembered the messaging more acutely due to the dissonance it created, or perhaps because parents sensed their nonconformity and stressed conformity in response. But while heterosexual people internalized these messages, LGBQ people drew on queer narratives to resist some of the expectations. Certainly they still placed value on an education, but there was variation in the importance placed on professional success and financial gain. They were also more likely to question marriage and children as crucial goals in life and constructed more fluid understandings of commitment. Still, they too wanted egalitarian relationships and sought to make space for both personal growth and the personal growth of their partners in the context of commitment.

PRIVILEGED PATHWAYS TO EQUALITY

This chapter demonstrates the power of class-based narratives in shaping young adults' visions of what constitutes a successful life and how to achieve it. Especially for heterosexual men and women, the expectation was to invest in self-development through academic credentials and career building, establish self-reliance and independence, couple and marry, and then have children. Privileged narratives about whom to marry—couched in coded terms such as "ambitious"—ensured that young adults would be seeking out partners with similar resources. These narratives for social mobility/stability and personal success transcended race and gender, as almost all the young adults in this study drew on them. The relationship pathways and preferences help the well educated consolidate their class privilege, but also shape their understandings of gender in their personal relationships. Most reached the conclusion that an egalitarian relationship was the ideal. The vast majority wanted to divide paid labor, caregiving, and housework as evenly as possible, and they had the backgrounds to make this happen. Most partners were meeting each other as true equals in terms of their educational backgrounds and earning power. As such, these young adults, even across demographic divisions, seemed ideally situated to establish egalitarian relationships. In the next chapters, I explore how and why young adults construct gender difference in their dating relationships, in direct contrast to what they say they want from their long-term romantic relationships; I also examine the strategies of those who successfully resist those constructs.

New Goals, Old Scripts

HETEROSEXUAL WOMEN CAUGHT
BETWEEN TRADITION AND EQUALITY

"It's a deal breaker if a man doesn't pay for a date," Aashi, 29, told me over dinner. "I would just never call them back." As she made clear throughout our conversation, although she ultimately wanted an egalitarian relationship, she had firm dating rules that she expected men to follow. They needed to ask her out, plan the date, and pick her up. She had rules for herself as well. On a first date, she said, "I'll probably initially be a little more demure. . . . I'd probably play up my more girly, feminine side." And she liked playing hard to get: "I just feel like I don't want to come off as more into them. *The Rules* is a really good read; very applicable," she said, explaining that women are more attractive to men when they appear unattainable. And yet, when I asked Aashi if she considered herself a feminist, she answered with a resounding yes. "I know it feels counterintuitive. . . . I'm a feminist, but I like to have a guy be chivalrous. I feel like men and women should be treated equally as far as their career and their political lives. It's not like a woman can't open the door, it's not like she can't pay for herself, but when a man does it, it's a nice gesture and it's just a nice thing."

Given that heterosexual women overwhelmingly express desire for equality, why do they still want traditional courtship practices? And how do they make sense of this in light of their feminist identities? As I showed in the preceding chapter, the vast majority of the 34 college-educated heterosexual women I interviewed want to share paid labor, housework, and childcare in a relatively balanced manner with their partners. To them, this type of relationship seems fair and they believe it will allow for more productive careers and more satisfying marriages. It also reflects their understandings of themselves as empowered, independent women. After all, they are achievers who put a lot of time and energy into developing their own skills.

Yet when it comes to dating, over three-quarters expressed a desire for many of the traditional courtship practices. For the most part, women expect men to ask and pay for the first date, confirm the exclusivity of the relationship, and propose marriage. They also monitor their own sexual behavior in accordance with notions of "proper" female sexuality and plan to change their last names on marrying. To support these courtship practices, they offer popular narratives about the differences between men and women that seemingly contradict their narratives about the importance of equality at work and in marriage. Although these beliefs are in tension with each other, heterosexual women hold them simultaneously, compartmentalizing the realms in which they support gender equality and those in which they support gender difference. In the process, they reconcile their desire for gendered dating practices with their sense of themselves as independent, egalitarian women. This chapter looks at how heterosexual women attempt to make sense of these competing narratives.

A HOW-TO GUIDE TO DATING

There is an embarrassment of books designed to help women secure a long-term commitment, preferably marriage, from a man. *The Rules* is the classic and the one most women reference; this 1995 *New York Times* bestseller advises women to feign disinterest and set firm boundaries with men. Don't pursue him. Don't accept a date for a Saturday after Wednesday. Don't have sex too quickly. Let him pursue you to always keep him wanting more. Follow these rules to drive him crazy with desire and you'll secure a marriage proposal in no time.[1] This is assumed to be the holy grail of any romantic relationship for women. *The Rules* "feeds into a nostalgia on romance,"[2] which can be appealing to both men and women, especially as they become more similar in their work lives.

Twenty years later, the authors, Sherrie Schneider and Ellen Fein, updated their dating manual for young women, now dating in an era of social media. But while the medium may have changed ("Don't follow him on Twitter first" is substituted for "Don't call him first"), the underlying concept remains the same: play hard to get to increase your allure. In spite of the uptick in mainstream feminist discourse in recent years, these traditional dating messages permeate the cultural imagination of what dating should look like. As Schneider and Fein argue, "Feminism is about equal pay for equal work, owning a condo, or running a marathon. But, it's not about asking men out, paying for dates, or being a man. Women cannot be men, romantically."[3] These narratives resonate with the heterosexual women in the study, and the majority voiced little interest in deviating from this cultural script. While many of the women specifically referenced self-help books about dating, many did not, yet they still drew on similar messages as they made sense of how they wanted their courtships to unfold.

Asking a man for a date remains a particularly taboo practice. Of the 34 heterosexual women, only six said they were willing to do so. The remainder of the women said that asking for a first date was the man's role, or indicated that they were too shy to ask a man out for fear of rejection. Sienna, 30, echoed the sentiments of most of the respondents, saying that she wouldn't ask a man out because she saw that as his role: "I guess I see it as they should be doing that." This practice is so embedded in our cultural imagination that like Sienna, many simply accept it with little reflection as a matter of fact.

Women voiced popular beliefs about men's need to be the assertive, dominant partner. Over a third indicated that they did not ask men on dates because it is in men's nature to like "the thrill of the chase." In this narrative, repeated throughout pop culture outlets, men are positioned as animalistic predators compelled to pursue.[4] As Aashi said, "I feel like it's just the way men are. I feel like if they really want something, they go after what they want." Jenna, 26, said, "It's just partly biological. In animals, the guy always flashes. The male bird always flashes his colors—his feathers or something—to go after what he wants."

By locating behavioral differences in biological difference, women framed these behaviors as natural, inevitable, and legitimate and so did not challenge them. And because they assumed that men *need* to be the dominant partner, they argued that women who undermine men in this respect would be considered unappealing partners. Caroline, 31, said, "I feel like men need to feel like they are in control and, if you ask them out, you end up looking desperate and it's a turn-off to them." Nicole, 28, explained her strategy in the same terms: "Yeah, sort of that playing hard to get, because the other girls would go at it hardcore, like I like you, let's hang out type of thing. And guys are always scared of that . . . I'm like, I'm too busy for you, or nah, I'm not really interested. It sort of reels them in." Implicit in Caroline's and Nicole's statements is the assumption that all women are desperately looking to secure a relationship, a charge that doesn't haunt men when they ask for a date. Men's assumed need for control was repeated throughout the interviews. Anna, 40, agreed with Caroline, saying, "I know that with a man they like to take charge." Although Anna admitted that she, too, really liked to be in control, saying that she liked to ask men out, she attributed this to her personality rather than to her nature.

Only two women made these same types of essentialist arguments about *women's* needs. Instead, like Anna, just under a third of the women discussed their own preferences in terms of their personalities, giving this as the rationale for why they were unwilling to ask men for dates. In this narrative, "personality" is conceived of as individualistic attributes specific to oneself and not tied to gender, while "nature" refers to broad patterns of behavior assumedly tied to sex category. Olivia, 26, said she didn't like to approach men, "more because I'm shy than out of traditional gender roles or anything like that." Breanna, 36, said, "I would never approach a guy. . . . One is, I'm shy. Two is, I've never felt like, oh I'm gorgeous, so it would be fear of rejection." Because people are more likely to use stereotypes to explain others' behavior than they are to explain their own, their self-reports tend to be more progressive or individualistic and often ignore the influence of gender norms on their own behavior.[5] Yet while these women didn't explicitly discuss gendered expectations as a factor, they still attributed to themselves a level of acceptable passivity. This passivity was not seen as a hindrance to getting dates, a position not possible for men. None of the women acknowledged that men, too, might be shy and afraid of rejection, and none of these women admitted to shyness in their professional lives, indicating that their courtship narratives are unconsciously gendered.

Women's passivity provided them with assurance of men's interest and protected them from rejection and charges of desperation. Amelia, 33, said, "I think it's just because I'm old-fashioned that way. I want to know the guy is interested in me." Only six of the women had asked a man out, and half of them described their actions in less than empowering terms. Their experiences reinforced the cultural stereotype that if a man is interested he *will* pursue, and that women are better off waiting for the man to take the lead. Abby, 33, said, "I tended to be the one to approach guys, but those were usually the ones that didn't like me." Heather, 27, said that she had stopped contacting men on an online dating site: "When I have, they're not interested. There was this one time I saw this guy was looking at my profile two or three times. He was kind of a dick. He was like, 'Yeah. Sometimes I just click on people's profiles. It doesn't mean I want to date them.' It's funny. The times I've contacted people, I've never ended up meeting them."

Women experienced these negative reactions as sanctions for transgressing appropriate gendered behavior. Those who act "too forward" are often passed over for future dates or face destabilization in their relationship.[6] Because people know what is expected of their gender and can anticipate these sanctions,[7] many women focused on making their interest clear in ways other than suggesting a date. In particular, women used subtle cues to let men know they were receptive to being approached. When I asked Jenna how she would indicate interest to a man, she said, "Probably more looks than anything. I'll make eye contact with them a few times. That would be the first step. Actually, I'm not very aggressive, so I probably wouldn't do much more than that. And usually that works . . . Guys are easy." Sophia, 26, made a similar point: "I don't think I could ever hit on a guy. I would be too nervous. Like other than, you know, you flirt with a guy across the room, like the eyes, and like smiling. I don't think I could ever go over and say, 'Can I buy you a beer or something.' I don't think I could ever do that just 'cause I'm self-conscious."

This approach extended to the follow-up phone call after the first date. Sophia said she would encourage her date to call, rather than call herself:

"If I really like a guy, then I'll make it apparent that I really like him and I'm open to, hey, if you want to call me, I'd really like that." Amelia explained that she subconsciously followed the book *The Rules* in online dating: "I was sort of following that book, not intentionally, but I made it known if I'm interested or not. Especially if I'm interested, I think I made it known I'm interested. I think the guy should, the ball is in his court now to make the next move to show that he's interested in me as well. I typically won't e-mail or call or something unless I hear from him." Ashleigh, 29, also emphasized that she would be receptive rather than assertive: "Respond to their phone calls and respond to whatever. . . . Say they ask me to go somewhere, I would say, yeah, I want to go. Smile at them, and pay attention to them." These approaches were a way for women to encourage progression of the relationship without transgressing gender norms or risking rejection.

But while only a handful of women reported explicitly asking a man out on a first date, half reported at least one partnership in which they had pursued a man. Ariana, 30, said, "I called him and told him to come to a party and that I would make it worth his while. I told him to sit next to me and took his arm and put it around me. I said, 'Finally I have all of your attention.' He said, 'You sure do' and kissed me. Then he asked me out." Nicole said, "I saw a guy that I found attractive at a bar and was wondering why he didn't hit on me. So I went up to him and asked him what his problem was." Caroline said, "I approached him at a bar and flirted with him and then invited him [and his friends] to go to a strip club with me and my friends. While we were there I sat on his lap. But I let him call me the next day. He did and he asked me out on our first date."

In this manner, women tested rather than challenged the boundaries of appropriate gender behavior. This approach allowed women to clearly express their interest while protecting them from charges of desperation or outright rejection and preserving men's prerogative to initiate dates. The women who engaged in this dating approach were more likely to be highly paid professionals than those who played a more passive role, perhaps because the former were used to behaving assertively at work.[8] Women who did some of the pursuing, albeit indirectly, were also more likely to be conventionally attractive, allowing them to be slightly more bold given that men benefit from having a conventionally attractive mate.

At the same time, though, these women still said that they preferred to be asked out, as they were focused on determining men's level of interest. Interestingly, the above stories from Ariana, Nicole, and Caroline were provided to me as evidence that they *didn't* ask men out, but rather *waited* for these men to ask them out for "the first *real* date."[9] While they may have shown interest in the men and even encouraged the interaction, they hadn't actually requested the dates. Even as they acted quite assertively, they worked hard to play up the narrative of the man as the pursuer.

GENTLEMEN ONLY

The ubiquity of the hook-up culture on college campuses influenced women's understandings of men even after they exited college and entered adulthood. While they may have felt ambivalent about long-term commitment during college,[10] as adults in their late twenties and early thirties most of the women were looking for a partner interested in the possibility of marriage. Yet many of the women still viewed men as commitment-phobic or more interested in casual sex than a relationship, a view that was reinforced by popular narratives of men's "nature."[11] As a result, they used courtship rituals to confirm men's genuine interest in them. Thus, the formal date, with its attendant rituals, was used to distinguish men who were interested in the possibility of a relationship from men who were just looking for a casual sexual encounter.

"Chivalry" was frequently cited as a sign that the man was respectful, caring, and interested in more than sex. Olivia said, "I tend to like a formal date . . . Like, 'Would you like to go to dinner?'" Jenna emphasized how important it was to her that a man make an effort to plan a special night: "It's just part of being taken care of. Doing everything to make sure that the girl is pleased on the first date. Having a good time, and doesn't have to worry about paying. Everything is taken care of. Let's just have fun—let me show you a good time and how great I am, and maybe we'll have a relationship after that." That said, sometimes women overstated the significance of dinner plans. As Nicole explained, "He invited me over to his house to make fondue. Little did I know that he told all his roommates that he was going to fon-*do* me."

Both effort and payment for the first date loomed large in women's perceptions of the man's intentions. Ariana said,

> I mean, usually the first time they go out with me I'll offer to pay. I'm like, "Oh, let me split it with you," you know? And it's really honestly a test. I don't want them to say, "Okay." I want them to say, "No, I'll get it," you know? . . . And then if we go out like four times, by the fourth time I'll be like, okay, this is my turn now. Like I want to make sure the guy offers to pay, the guy opens my door, the guy, you know, doesn't just walk ahead of me. Things like that. And that's become more important to me, how gentlemanly they are. I've talked to guys about it before. If you like a chick and you want to impress her, you do everything you can. [If a guy doesn't pay] they just probably don't like you that much.

Over two-thirds of the women said that all their first dates were paid for by men. And just like Ariana, many of the women referenced payment for the first date as a test. If the man took them up on their offer to pay or split the check, it was a sign that he wasn't someone they wanted to date, as he wasn't "out to impress" and must not be sufficiently interested in them. When I asked Alison, 27, if it was important to her that a man pay on the first date, she said, "It's not important, but I would expect it, and then if he like expected me to pay for half, or if he like expected me to pay, then I'd be like, I'm out. So I guess chivalry isn't dead." When I said, "So it *is* important then," she replied, "Well, yeah, I guess it is, yeah. 'Cause I'd be like, man, he didn't even pay, what a douche."

Mia, 39, reflected on how women interpreted being "treated" on a date: "I think it feels like a sign of respect. It feels like a way to be treated well." Only a handful of the women, such as Aashi, indicated that men's payment was a way to confirm breadwinning ability; this was perhaps because men who couldn't take on this responsibility were screened out before the date even took place, as the majority of the women dated highly educated professional men. Indeed, as class-privileged women, they simply assumed that men had the ability to wine and dine them without any hardship. Men's payment for the first date appears to have taken on new meanings as women have gained their own breadwinning abilities. But getting treated to a date is also a privilege women have in their romantic relationships, meaning that they see little downside in the tradition and are thus loath to give it up.

These dating conventions became less relevant over the course of the relationship. Most of the women reported that once they started dating a man regularly, payment for dates frequently alternated between the two of them, or that while the man paid for most of the dates, she chipped in. Mia said that after the first few dates "he did continue paying, but I also started paying. We weren't splitting things, but probably every third time, I would pay for something." Nicole tried to pay for some dates with a man she was seeing, but was turned down. "He had sort of a macho-ness about him and he was like, no, no, no, this is *my* job." Still, a few of the women were extremely rigid with their role expectations. Aashi reported a great deal of conflict with a past boyfriend over her expectation that he pay for everything:

> I don't think he resented it, I think he was just, why do you feel like that someone has to [pay] if they care about you. . . . Why can't we sometimes go Dutch, that's what my friends do. So we did have a talk about that, that was one conflict, and I would say there were times I felt it wasn't so second nature for him to pay for me. But for me, when someone paid for me, it was very second nature. [Once], we were going to a concert and he said, oh are we paying separately, and I was like so disgusted when he asked me that and got in a big fight.

In this manner, Aashi enforced courtship norms throughout the course of the relationship, something that was unusual among the women. For most, it was during the "turning point" moments in the relationships that these norms were important, rather than on a daily basis.

"WHAT ARE WE?"

Gendered courtship conventions acquired significance again during moments that were highly scripted and where assumptions about men's commitment became salient. Men were expected to confirm the exclusivity of the relationship and propose marriage, as a signal that let women know the men were committed to the relationship; for there was a consistently stated belief that men were reluctant to commit. As a result, women initiated less than a fifth of the conversations on the exclusivity of the relationship. When women did bring up exclusivity, they tended to do so in an indirect manner, asking questions such as, "Where is this relationship going?" or "What are we?"[12] This approach allowed women to raise the topic, protecting them from a more direct rejection of their desired ends, but it gave men the power to confirm or deny an exclusive commitment.

Only a couple of women said they directly brought up a discussion of exclusivity, and even those women still reported saying, "Why don't you consider me your girlfriend?" rather than explicitly asking for commitment. Instead, the process was similar to that of getting a first date, with women initiating conversations that led to the man asking. Alice, 34, was representative of the most common approach: "I asked him, 'Where is this relationship going?' Then he asked me to be his girlfriend." Other women looked for openings to discuss commitment. Aashi said, "He mentioned something about us. I said, 'Oh, is there an us?'"

Women also used conversations about sex to discuss the status of the relationship. This might occur either before or directly after sex took place for the first time, but again, women were unwilling to ask for commitment. If the discussion occurred before sex, it was in the form of an ultimatum: "I don't have sex outside of relationships." Then the onus was on the man to decide whether or not they were in a relationship so that they could have sex. The other approach was similar: "We just had sex. What does that mean for us?" Again, this approach allowed women to discuss the level of commitment without directly stating that they wanted a commitment.

In contrast, a third of the women reported that a man had assumed commitment without a discussion. Alyssa, 28, said, "He just called me his girlfriend on our first date. Later, when I asked him about it, he said he had just assumed. I decided that I didn't care because it was just a label." Caroline reported that her boyfriend asked, "When are you going to update your Facebook status to reflect that you're in a relationship?" Whereas most of the women felt that they needed an explicit discussion to confirm the status of the relationship, they often found that men felt confident assuming a commitment. This approach implies that men feel more secure than women that the reaction will be in the affirmative. In addition, five of the women reported men insisting on commitment, something no woman reported having done. Ariana said of an ex-boyfriend, "He made me commit after a month of dating, telling me he didn't like the fact that I was seeing other people. He said, 'This is ridiculous. You have to choose.' I preferred to keep it open because I wasn't looking for a relationship, but he gave me an ultimatum." The same thing happened to her a few years later with another man: "Finally he was just like, 'Are you dating other guys?' I'm like, 'Yeah. We have an open relationship. That's what happens when you have an open relationship, you date other guys.' And he's like, 'I don't like it. I can't handle it.' So he told me I had to choose." Nicole had a casual sexual encounter, and the man she was dating was devastated: "I didn't think we were exclusive, but he did. He didn't want anything to do with me after that. I insisted we talk and he said that he wanted me to be his girlfriend and that I couldn't see other people." Nicole agreed to commit because her boyfriend's insistence on commitment "made me see how much he cared about me." But as she also explained, "Now it's clear, we're official. No more doing things with other people. Even though I didn't want to do that." Rather than view her boyfriend's demands as controlling behavior, they became evidence of his love for her. This is in direct contrast to how women's desire for commitment is usually seen: as evidence of their desperation and loneliness.

Two ideologies highlight the assumed differences between men's and women's sexuality.[13] The "sexual double standard" is the assumption that men want and pursue all sexual opportunities and try to avoid commitment, while women are expected to have sex only within committed, loving relationships. When women *do* have casual sex, they are judged more harshly than men for such behaviors. Whereas men are viewed as simply acting out their role as men, women's behaviors are seen as negative reflections on their moral character, and they are viewed as sluts and deserving of poor treatment by sexual partners. Stemming from this, the "relational imperative" is the assumption that women always want a committed relationship, with love and marriage as the goals. Because men are assumed to be less interested in maintaining a committed relationship, many of the women were left feeling that they must take advantage of every relationship opportunity. In addition, because women were assumed to always want commitment, they worried that their attempts to secure exclusivity could be construed as desperation. As a result, when men initiated conversations about exclusivity, women sometimes ended up committing to relationships before they were ready, as those men were viewed as especially devoted. In this manner, women ended up prioritizing men's relationship desires over their own, including their desires to be in open or nonexclusive relationships.

SHIFTING SEXUAL SCRIPTS

Traditional sexual scripts also position men as the initiators,[14] yet this script is in transition as more women take charge of their sexual pleasure.[15] Only 10 of the 34 heterosexual women indicated that they always let the man initiate sex the first time. Of the remaining women, six did not have sex before marriage, or were not planning to, either for religious reasons or to keep sex "special," so that first-time sex was mutually assumed for the wedding night. Two women had not had sex yet, although they weren't necessarily waiting for marriage. The remaining 16 women expressed a comfort with female-initiated sex for the first sexual encounter, although most of these women described first encounters as mutually initiated.

Yet assumptions about the desires of men and women were at work here as well. While all women are assumed to want a relationship, all men are assumed to want sex. Thus, while women may avoid directly asking for commitment due to the fear of being perceived as desperate and undesirable, women felt confident that their sexual advances would be well received. Just as a number of the women reported that men assumed a committed relationship, almost all of the women assumed a positive reaction to their sexual advances. "Of course he wanted sex! He's a dude!" As a result, they often had confused or negative reactions when a man didn't want or feel ready for sex. Alice said, "I initiated sex the first time when we were all hot and heavy one time. He said he [didn't want to] do it and I was like, 'What? You're not a guy!'"

Unlike the other areas of courtship under discussion, women's sexual initiation does not clash with common assumptions about men's desires. If men are believed to want sex more than women do, there is little reason for women to feel reluctance in pursuing their desires and initiating sex, especially if the couple has been dating for a while. While a majority of the women did not take a passive, gatekeeper approach to their initial sexual encounters, thereby challenging conventional beliefs about women's sexuality, their behaviors and narratives did not challenge conventional beliefs about men's. Still, a few of the women took a more passive approach. When I asked Jenna how she decided when to have sex with a man, she said, "I guess when the guy wants to start doing it," although she emphasized her consent. As she said, "I waited for their approach, and then I was like, 'Okay. Yeah. I want to do this, yeah.'"

That said, women *were* leery of having sex too quickly, so the majority said that they would not have sex on a first date. This was due to conventional notions about how men would perceive them. Many believed that having sex too early was a relationship killer, in that it would remain merely sexual rather than lead to commitment. They weren't wrong in this assumption. As we will see in the next chapter, men did indeed wait to have sex when they were more serious about a woman they were getting to know. Brooke, 36, said she would not have sex on a first date "because of the whole thing where guys [won't] take you seriously if you have sex with them the first night. I tell my girlfriends that. Don't do it for the first three dates." Rebecca, 40, was willing to, but only under certain circumstances: "If I don't like them, yeah. I mean, if I know I don't want to keep them." Sophia agreed:

It kind of depends what I'm looking for. If I'm looking for a long-term relationship then I kind of tend to make sure the guy is really interested, really wanting to make a commitment [before we have sex]. I didn't used to think it was so important in the past that I thought you could just, like if you have a healthy sex life, why can't you just have sex when you want to have sex and then still be dating that same person? 'Cause that has not worked in the past and I feel that I was more mature and confident and secure in that respect than some of the guys I have dated in the past.

As a result, she no longer engages in sex on the first date: "Been there, done that. I'm more cautious and I don't really see myself doing that anymore. 'Cause that leads to casual relationships."

Ariana liked that her boyfriend didn't pursue sex too quickly even though she was ready to have it: "He was very gentlemanly, and I liked that about him. Like he did not push for it at all. And when I was like, 'I'm just wondering why you aren't trying to sleep with me, because every other guy tries to sleep with me like within the first date.' And he was like, 'Well, most of my relationships that start fast, end fast, and I really like you.'" By waiting to initiate sex, men were able to position themselves as particularly desirable partners because women saw this approach as different from "most men" and reflective of something special.

Many of the women *were* willing to have sex on first meeting a man, but only if they weren't looking for a relationship. In this manner, women acknowledge the persistence of the sexual double standard—they can have casual sex only if they don't care about being "relationship material," a modern permutation of the Madonna/whore dichotomy in which a woman is either good for sex *or* good for a relationship and which, in effect, puts men in control of defining the terms of the relationship while women are left monitoring their reputations.[16] But the women in the study felt reasonably secure that as long as they waited an "appropriate" amount of time, men would consider them "datable" rather than only "fuckable."

SURPRISE-ISH PROPOSALS

As discussed in the previous chapter, heterosexual women preferred to delay marriage until they had established careers. But they certainly wanted marriage and hoped committed relationships would lead there. In spite of this desired end goal, women were unwilling to propose marriage. The dominant cultural script surrounding the marriage proposal places women in a passive role, where women receive the proposal rather than initiate it.[17] It is the man who takes action during a marriage proposal, deciding when a marriage proposal takes place and then acting it out. The woman responds with surprise and joy. The result is that women are left "waiting to be asked."[18] That said, while men are still expected to propose marriage, frequent negotiations take place between partners, demonstrating that women are far from passive players in the decision to marry.[19] Still, women concealed certain nonconforming behaviors from public view in order to present the "right" kind of proposal story.

Men proposed in each of the 22 cases analyzed in this study; in addition, all of the unmarried women expected men to do the proposing. Again, women discussed a man's initiation of the proposal as a sign that he was committed to her and to the marriage. Many of the women felt that they had been ready to commit before their partner and so wanted a clear sign that the man, too, was ready. Caroline said, "I wanted him to do it since he was really the one who had been slower to be there emotionally. I wanted him to be the one to drive it." But it symbolizes more than that. While the male-directed proposal puts him in the driver's seat, it can also be viewed as a gesture of submission, where the man goes so far as to symbolically place his body in a lower position in the hope she will return his affection and agree to marry him. Jane, a 31-year-old who was waiting for her boyfriend to propose, said, "I want to feel adored and I feel like if I was doing the proposing, it was kind of like, 'What, I'm not special enough that you're willing to put yourself out there and be vulnerable for me?'" The act of being chosen remained a powerful draw for the women in this study. To be chosen meant to be considered worthy of love and a life-long commitment.

Rather than view a female-initiated proposal as an expression of valid desires and unwillingness to remain passive, women viewed it as an embarrassing reflection of their partner's lack of love or their own desperation. When I asked Ashleigh if she would have been willing to propose to her husband, she said, "Never. In my mind, that's not my role. Like I would feel like he didn't really value me if he wasn't going to propose to me"; while Alice said, "I think I wouldn't do it because I want to make sure the other person loves me as much, if not more." In this manner, women's feelings and commitment are assumed, while men have to engage in these rituals in order to prove themselves. The traditional marriage proposal speaks to women's insecurities over their partners' interest in marriage.

Yet in spite of these narratives of women's passivity, the majority of the engagements occurred on a mutually agreed timetable. Most of the couples discussed marriage extensively before getting engaged, often going over how they envisioned their lives together, as this was considered pragmatic. After the couple decided when they wanted to get engaged, the man was expected to "surprise" the woman with a proposal. Ashleigh said, "I knew we were going to get engaged eventually. We went ring shopping. I had a picture of a ring from when I was 13 that I wanted. So I knew something was coming, but [not when]. . . . He surprised me and proposed that weekend, before I went out of town. So it was just a little surprise-ish." This approach allowed women to preserve the narrative of the male-initiated proposal, cementing their "chosen" status while protecting their inclusion in the decision-making process.

Only three women said that they "waited it out" until their partner was ready to propose. In fact, eight of the women were aggressive in influencing the timing of the engagement, often giving their boyfriends ultimatums and timelines for proposing. Just as with women who pursued men for first dates, these women were more likely to be highly paid professionals than the women who took a more "hands off" approach. Again, this indicated that their careers perhaps provided them with alternative scripts empowering them to be more assertive. When I asked Jenna what she would do if she was ready to get married and her boyfriend didn't propose, she said, "I would say, 'You need to propose.' But I would never ask him myself. That's interesting. So, I would informally ask him and tell him what I need him to do but I would never actually do it myself. That's so bizarre." Interestingly, women saw ultimatums as distinct from simply proposing themselves, as this approach still left the decision of whether or not to propose in the man's hands and allowed women to craft their desired proposal story for their friends and family.

Alice went so far as to move out of state when her boyfriend failed to propose on her timetable, and only agreed to move back after he expressed a willingness to propose within the year. "I told him, 'If I move back, there better be a ring on my finger.'" He proposed one year plus a few days later, perhaps adding those few days as a message of resistance. Caroline also expressed her frustration to her boyfriend: "I was fed up with him for not figuring out what he wanted. I felt like he didn't appreciate me and wasn't making me feel good about myself. I confronted him and told him I was sure I wanted to marry him, but if he wasn't, I was done waiting and suggested we see other people. He freaked out and brought out a ring and said he wanted to marry me." Thus, women were almost always able to negotiate desired outcomes, indicating substantial power in their relationships when they did explicitly express what they wanted, at least in terms of decision-making that didn't infringe on the privileges men were committed to protecting.[20] As I show in the next chapter, allowing women a role in the timing of the marriage proposal was an easy way for men to appear egalitarian without making a significant sacrifice.

Further evidence that women wanted a role in the timing of the marriage proposal was the unhappiness they felt at unexpected proposals. Only four of the engagements were a surprise initiated by the man without a prior discussion of when a proposal should take place. Two of these engagements ended before a marriage took place, and one relationship ended a year into the marriage. A fourth engagement lasted 12 years while the woman avoided planning the wedding until she felt ready. Caroline said of her first engagement, now ended, "When he proposed, it was an out-of-body experience, thinking, should I say yes? But I had to decide in half a second what to say and I didn't want to say no. It wasn't like I didn't want to be with him, I just wasn't really 100 percent sure that that was the next step right now. I thought if I said yes, I could buy myself some time." As Caroline explained, she thought saying no to the proposal would have been tantamount to ending the relationship altogether. While she said yes at the time, she later broke up with him. Breanna said, "I wasn't thinking forever, but I still said yes. But even though I said yes to the engagement, I still wasn't thinking marriage." These women experienced the unexpected marriage proposal as an ultimatum and felt they couldn't say no for fear of losing the relationship. In this, they had to confront the common assumption that women are always ready for marriage, when in reality this was far from the case. And in contrast to common assumptions, these engagements were more likely to be called off than those initiated through women's ultimatums.

Yet women's attempts to influence the timing of the marriage proposal were viewed very differently from men's, as it was assumed men had the right to do so while women did not. Because of the oft-repeated sentiment that proposals initiated by women, whether directly or indirectly, were coercive and indicated a lack of interest by the man, women felt conflicted about issuing ultimatums or otherwise influencing the timing of the engagement. This indicated a fear of negative reactions or the sense that the proposal (and the man's commitment to the marriage) would be suspect. Alison said,

> I definitely talk about getting married. I read this article in *Glamour* about the engagement chicken. . . . So there's this recipe for a roast chicken, and it's a super boring recipe, it's like onions and lemons, it's totally generic. But

every time someone makes this chicken and they serve it to their boyfriend, he proposes. . . . So I'm like, holy crap, I gotta make that for him. This is just this last weekend, I was like telling my girlfriend about it, and she was like, I read that article, too. I was like, yes! So I'm going to make it for [my boyfriend] and then he'll just hurry up and propose. I was like, but then I would feel like I kind of like coerced him into it.

This taboo against women's influence is so strong that even making a basic chicken dinner is framed as manipulative.

Similarly, Sophia was willing to suggest marriage but was unwilling to do the proposing: "I guess it kind of stems from how I feel so in charge all the time and the decision maker. I want to be treated like the girl. I still want to be swept off my feet. . . . I've always felt like I was so dominant and alpha that I want to feel that way." For Sophia, a traditional proposal was important precisely *because of* the sense of empowerment she felt in her life. This was a way to feel feminine and cared for in a society that often demands that women act "like men" in order to succeed. As women's and men's everyday lives become increasingly similar, these symbolic moments are a way to keep romance alive through an emphasis on difference.

But while some women were willing to play a decisive role in the timing of their marriage proposal, they preferred to keep the illusion of surprise with their peers. Caroline, who as discussed earlier issued an ultimatum one night and got the marriage proposal then and there, said, "I didn't tell any of my friends what actually happened. I told him to put the ring away so he wouldn't feel like he was backed into a corner. I said he should do it the way he wanted to and that I would say yes. He proposed three weeks later on a boat. That's the story our friends know." In this manner, women's "official" stories of their marriage proposals rarely acknowledged the behind-the-scenes work that took place. Nicole also emphasized the importance of the conventional proposal story for friends, saying she couldn't be the one to do the proposing: "I mean, people will ask you, 'Oh, how did he do it?' And if I were the one who goes, 'Well, it was me.' . . . And again it goes back to telling people. I have a coworker who recently [got engaged] and it was like, 'Oh my gosh, did he get you a ring?' And she's like, 'No.' And everyone's like, 'Awwwwww' [in sympathy]." Without the "right" story to tell friends, women worried that others would view their partner as insufficiently committed and in love for marriage. Given that men were more likely than women to discuss women's behind-the-scenes work, it's clear that a strong stigma against this remains and that it reflects more poorly on women than men.

A handful of the women also prioritized another traditional aspect of the marriage proposal: they wanted their boyfriends to ask their fathers' permission before proposing. Emily, 31, explained this preference: "Because my dad's opinion means a lot to me, and he's a very smart man, and if he approves, then I think that would make it okay for me. Even though I trust my own judgment, I just think having that is more . . . reassuring? I guess. Also, it's tradition, I guess—for the man to do that . . . to ask for the woman's hand." For the few who liked this tradition, asking a woman's father was about showing respect for her family and indicated a level of seriousness about the proposal. By going through the traditional motions, women assumed men were again demonstrating how committed they were to the relationship. For these women, the time and energy and deference to her family indicated the thought he had put into marrying her. That said, very few women expressed support for this practice. While the other courtship rituals discussed allow women a certain level of agency, this one cuts the woman out completely, perhaps creating too big a conflict between women's sense of independence and tradition.

EMBRACING "MRS."

Women were happy to reciprocate men's displays of commitment in a gendered fashion: the majority had or planned to change their last names. Emily was one of the few who didn't change her name when she got married. She was in the process of getting a divorce when she explained her choice to me:

> You know, I think intuitively, maybe somehow I knew it wasn't going to work. I respect my family a lot. My last name has a lot of say about my family, so I was a little resistant to changing my name. At the end, when we were talking about how our relationship fell apart, he blamed it on the fact that 'At the beginning, you never thought of wanting to be with me that long. That's why you never changed your last name.' I was like, 'I asked you if it would be okay not to change my name and you said it would be fine. You didn't care.'

When I asked her if she planned to change her name if she got married again, she said, "Very likely, yeah. I can see myself doing that because right now I know what it is really like to fall in love and have someone fall in love with me. And I'm more confident with myself—being comfortable with who I am. So if the next guy comes around I hope that he will prove his love to me enough that I will feel confident carrying his name."

Both Emily and her ex-husband interpreted a woman's willingness to change her name as an indicator of her commitment to the relationship. Certainly, research on women's surname choices shows that the majority of the general population see women who choose not to change their names as less relationship oriented and more individualistic.[21] Ashleigh, too, interpreted a name change as a way of showing her love for her husband and saw an unwillingness to do so as a negative:

> It was very important to my husband. It was important to me because I just figured that's what you . . . it seems like a little women-power hippie-ish to not change your last name. And I don't identify with that as much. That seemed more of like . . . not a hatred towards men, but a hatred towards like . . . old society. And I sort of identify with an older society as far as how they would do things. And so I didn't want to go be like women power, "I'm not changing my last name." My aunt did that, and I was like—that's weird. She was so angry and . . . so I relate it to anger, not changing your last name.

Implicit in Ashleigh's statement is the belief that a woman who doesn't take her husband's name is overly committed to placing herself and her individual needs above the committed relationship, and perhaps that these decisions are driven by anger at men rather than by a desire to have an independent identity.

In contrast to Ashleigh, Caroline was more critical of the assumption that it should be the woman who changes names, but justified her choice to do so by noting that while she might make this sacrifice for the family, her partner made others, which balanced things out:

> I don't like the fact that one person (the woman) is expected to alter a part of her own self-identity and the other does not. But I do very much like the idea of having one name for the family. If there were no social norms to factor in, I think the ideal scenario is that the two of us would come up with our own new last name to share together and give to our children. In my case,

my husband never brought it up, let alone pressured me to change my name. I think that fact made me more open to considering just taking his name to create a single family identity. I think he was surprised that I wanted to and I think he feels very honored by the gesture. It helps that I like his last name. I think it's another sign of my commitment to him, and I feel that he makes the commitment back in other ways.

Only a few of the women said they planned to keep their last name, and most justified this choice as due to professional recognition rather than a right to their own identity, despite their stated desire for autonomy. Keira, 36, was one of the few who got quite angry at the thought of changing her name and being treated as an extension of her husband: "I have friends who send me Christmas cards with [my husband's] last name. They address me as Keira Brown. I'm like, 'That's not my name.' My sister-in-law sends us Christmas cards that say Brian and Keira Brown. I am tempted to send back a card that says, 'Dave Fisher and Amanda Brown.' If she gets upset, 'That's not your name, right? That's not my name, either.'"

But Keira was one of only seven women in the study who either expressed reservations about gendered conventions or uniformly rejected them. These women were not any less likely to express the belief that men and women are fundamentally different, but the four who voiced the strongest objections to gendered courtship didn't prioritize marriage and children. Keira said, "I never fantasized about the wedding the way my friends did in school. . . . I think the men I was with knew. It would just be ridiculous if they were on a bended knee offering me a ring." As a result, they didn't need to rely on courtship conventions to ferret out which men were truly interested in commitment, nor did they have to worry about scaring men off by appearing too eager.

Still, even though these women disavowed courtship rituals, they often found themselves engaging in them anyway, as the men they dated fell back on these patterns and they "just didn't care enough" to challenge them. Rachel, 27, said that she let men ask her out because she "wasn't someone who always needed a boyfriend" and thus wasn't motivated enough to pursue someone. Keira always brought money to pay her share on dates, but said her partners were "old-fashioned" and insistent on paying. And while her former husband did indeed propose to her, she argued that it was because she "didn't want [marriage] enough," not because she saw it as his role: "He definitely felt more strongly about me than I did about him." This group of women described their courtship behaviors as the result of *men's* desire for convention. While they did not seek out traditional courtship, they did not actively reject it and certainly felt comfortable playing along. Still, consistent with the narratives of the women who wanted men to propose, Keira associated the initiation of the marriage proposal with the strength of her partner's love and commitment.

RECONCILING DIVERGENT IDEALS

As we have seen, the majority of heterosexual women wanted a traditional courtship. At the same time, most of them also wanted an egalitarian, long-term relationship. How did women make sense of this apparent contradiction? After all, many are claiming to be feminists and saying they want gender equality in their marriages while expecting men to ask them out and pay for their dates and take a dominant role.

Most of the women denied any relationship between traditional gender roles in courtship and traditional gender roles in the subsequent marriage. In spite of the importance they placed on gendered dating and courtship rituals, they saw these as either a personal preference or mere convention[22] and therefore inconsequential to interpersonal power relations and any goals for an egalitarian marriage. Many echoed the sentiments of Mia, who said, "In the past few years I've realized I'm appearing, or 'manifesting,' very traditional. So, I feel like I'm a feminist in the sense of equality, but I'm not very much a feminist in the sense that . . . a lot of things don't bother me. Like opening the door for me. I like it. I consider it part of manners. I don't consider it an insult or a gender issue." While Mia denies a link between ritual and gender, her insistence that men engage in certain behaviors and women in others clearly indicates that these practices are gendered. Instead, "equality" solely indicates access to rights and opportunities in the public sphere rather than cultural practices that reinforce beliefs in gender difference.

In addition, traditional courtship behaviors are believed to confer benefits to women. Because stereotypical representations of women can often portray them in a positive light, referred to as "benevolent sexism," they

NEW GOALS, OLD SCRIPTS

are able to garner the acceptance and support of women.[23] Women are seen as kind, caring, and morally superior to men and, if they conform to these representations, as deserving of a relationship in which the man protects and cares for them. Women incorporate these representations into their sense of self and endorse the corresponding behavioral norms, especially as they stand in stark contrast to the more obvious "hostile sexism." As a result, there are fewer incentives to challenging benevolent sexism in courtship than when discrimination occurs in the workplace or when sexism is more overt, even though these "benevolent" understandings of women contribute to gender inequality.[24]

Aashi's statement from the beginning of the chapter reflects women's common perception that gendered rituals and widespread gender inequality are not connected: "I feel like men and women should be treated equally as far as in their career and their political lives, things where they should be treated as equals. But when it comes to biology and manners, it's not like a woman can't open the door, it's not like she can't pay for herself, but when a man does it, it's a nice gesture and it's just—it's a nice thing." This interpretation of equality draws on liberal feminist themes, such as women's legal and economic rights, and is consistent with ideologies of American individualism.[25]

Focused on women's entry into formerly "male" spheres, women downplayed how difference narratives contribute to inequality. And because most women financially supported themselves, they did not see gestures that grant men symbolic dominance as a risk to their autonomy or power. Breanna said,

> I obviously easily could take over. I am, like I mentioned, independent and self-sufficient. So obviously if I wanted to put my foot in the ground and he didn't want to go my way, I could walk away—I'm not dependent on him. I don't need him for anything. But I *choose* not to take that position. . . . I do like a dominant man. . . . [I don't want] them to be submissive in any way. Gross. That would totally turn me off that guy. I even came to see where some women were insisting on paying on the dates to establish their independence. I think it's totally wrong. I mean, I think it's good to be strong and independent, but then to like, you know . . . kind of . . . force it out there, like I'm letting you know I'm independent. Like I don't need you—that kind of thing. I don't think that's the best. Even if he's not truly dominant, even if you're his equal, I still think you should let him feel like a man, that kind of thing.

Breanna's argument again reflects the essentialist belief that men need to be in charge in their romantic relationships in order to be happy. She frames men's symbolic dominance as a charade that allows men to "do gender" in spite of women's increased economic independence. But she also states that *she* finds this enactment of gender difference attractive, too, revealing that a submissive man would in fact be a turn-off to her. Rather, sexual attraction, desire, and romance are tied to this relationship structuring. By emphasizing this behavior as chosen, however, she denies an association between her behavior and the reproduction of gender inequality.

"Choice rhetoric" is often used by high-achieving women to disavow the constraints they continue to face. A narrative of choice is appealing because it draws on "the language of privilege, feminism, and personal agency" and is therefore consistent with how they make sense of themselves.[26] By emphasizing gendered courtship conventions as a choice rather than a requirement, and by reaffirming their autonomy, women could take comfort in gendered behaviors that felt "safe" and "right" without sacrificing their sense of an independent, empowered self. Potentially, the educational and professional attainments of privileged women transgress enough gender boundaries in the workplace and the home to allow them to downplay gender inequality as a relevant social problem in their own lives.[27]

That said, a few of the women certainly felt the contradiction. For example, throughout our conversation, Jenna appeared embarrassed whenever she expressed any desire for traditional relationship practices. When I asked her about this, she reflected on the competing messages she had received and how she struggled to reconcile them in her life:

> Especially in undergrad, I had a lot of strong female professors who were opposing traditional ways of life. Not that they were bad, just that you have these other ways and options. So I see that and I'm like, "Yeah, that's great. I can be on my own and these guys aren't everything." But then there's a strong attraction to, or a biological need within me, to have that more traditional bond. And that's also probably shaped by society; I'm sure of that too. But I think the rebel part of me is like, "Yay, feminism!" So that's why I always put the negative spin on the fact that I'm part of society, just like everyone else is.

As Jenna makes clear, she's aware that her desire for traditional court-ship practices might be at odds with the expectation that women and men be considered, and treated as, equals. Yet women aren't provided with the scripts or guidance for how to satisfactorily combine their romantic rela-tionships with their individual aspirations.[28] Well-educated, middle-class women in particular are expected to invest heavily in their career ambi-tions and are warned that men may derail these goals.[29] As a result, while some avoid committed partnerships altogether, others instead opt to invest more in their relationships than in themselves, more worried about being lonely than self-reliant.[30] Jenna is aware of which approach is deemed "feminist." But as she states, in her mind the competing social pressures are just too powerful for her to resist. So she alternates between describing gendered relationships as biologically versus socially driven, mildly mocking herself. This allows her to engage in the practices she's been socialized to want, while helping her preserve some sense of feminist identity in the form of her critical perspective. For Jenna, she *knows* these practices are imbued with gender inequality, but she wants them anyway.

COMPETING DESIRES

Heterosexual women's commitment to courtship norms competes with the goal of egalitarian partnerships, creating a cultural contradiction for women as they seek to reconcile discrepant sets of behavioral rules. They are encountering men on new terms and creating relationships that chal-lenge the assumptions underlying a gendered division of labor. They express comfort with asserting financial independence and personal autonomy. The progress they have made, however, has perhaps led them to believe that they can pick and choose, without consequences, among gendered practices. To ease the conflict between a desire for equality and conventional courtship rituals, women do not draw a connection between gendered courtship and other forms of gender inequality. They construe men's participation in unequal courtship patterns as natural and inevita-ble, and they explain their own participation as a personal choice that is rooted in their personalities and preferences. In this manner, women reaf-firm their autonomy and deny the significance of inequality in courtship.

This demonstrates how narratives of empowerment based on ideologies of individualism can be used to conceal the continuation of male privilege in ways that make individuals feel good about their conformity.

Although women argue that personal choice governs their courtship behavior, their efforts to conceal assertive behavior indicate that conventional gender norms guide their decision-making. As we saw with Ariana, who pursued a man whom she then credited with the first date, or Caroline, who demanded a marriage proposal and got it then and there, these women were often quite assertive. Yet while their behaviors often undermined stereotypes about women's natural passivity, both women anticipated social sanctions if they acted as the initiator, and both internalized the belief that proactive behavior would make them a less worthy partner. In response, they policed or concealed their behaviors in an effort to conform to the presumed needs and desires of men, revealing just how constrained women continue to be in their romantic relationships, even as they seem to take genuine pleasure in these conventions. This approach benefited men at the expense of women, as women were left waiting around and subverting their own goals or creating narratives that hid their agency. That said, the women in this study were frequently able to negotiate their stated desired ends.

Finally, although the women's behaviors frequently subverted the conventional passive script, they nonetheless did not challenge gender stereotypes. Viewed from the outside, these relationships appeared to proceed in gender-typical ways. The only women who fully and openly questioned courtship scripts were those who were not seeking to marry and have children. These women provide potential alternative models for courtship, but they also suggest that equality is attainable only for those who do not wish to form families. They also send the message that *marriage* is not available to those who subvert gender norms, as self-reliance undermines cultural narratives of what it means to be a good wife and a good woman.[31] The next chapter looks at how men respond to these same cultural narratives very differently, indicating a lower level of commitment to traditional courtship but a keen desire to retain certain male privileges in their relationships.

4 A Few Good (Heterosexual) Men

INEQUALITY DISGUISED AS ROMANCE

Gavin, 31, always envisioned ending up with a strong, educated, and career-oriented woman, explaining, "I think of myself as a feminist, and the women I date are very independent." While he had taken the lead in most of his relationships, he wished that women were more assertive in pursuing him: "I know there are guys that like the thrill of the hunt, but I'm not like that. I have the flip view. If you're into me, that's a huge plus." Throughout his interview, Gavin stressed his passion for relationships, describing himself as a serial monogamist and turning the stereotype of the commitment-phobic man on its head. Unfortunately, Gavin's desire for strong personalities led to conflicts. A dominant personality himself, he admitted to problems in his past relationships with "strong-willed" women and described his current girlfriend as "accommodating" and therefore more compatible. He also expected to be taller than his partners, saying, "That's just an ingrained stereotype. It's embarrassing to be shorter than the woman. But part of it is, you want the feeling of being more masculine. I want to be taller; I want to be stronger. That's just kind of natural." Not only that, it made him uncomfortable to be with women who have had more sexual partners than he has: "I'm insecure about that. I prefer being in a situation where I'm more experienced. There is a

number [of former sexual partners] at which point I go, like, whoa."
Suddenly, Gavin sounded a lot more traditional.

The tensions around changing gender norms are not limited to heterosexual women; heterosexual men too puzzle over how to approach dating
and romantic relationships. Will a woman see it as necessary or insulting
if he insists on paying for the date? Will she find it charming or predatory
if he leans in for a kiss? Heterosexual men experience a clash between
change and tradition, especially in the progressive Bay Area, and must
grapple with the changing norms of what it means to be a good man.[1]
While there has been an emerging expressed desire for gender equality in
romantic relationships,[2] men are still subject to the expectation that they
distinguish themselves from women.[3] As we saw in the last chapter, heterosexual women still want and expect men to take the lead during courtship. How can men take the role of "the man" yet avoid allegations of
chauvinism and toxic masculinity? This chapter looks at how heterosexual
men balance their understandings of themselves as good, egalitarian partners with conventional courtship practices and the expectations of their
romantic partners.

The majority of the 31 heterosexual men I interviewed seemed less
invested in traditional courtship rituals than were heterosexual women.
They went along with them because they knew what was expected of
them, but most didn't feel the same level of ideological buy-in as did
women. As a result, men's narratives revolved around what they thought
women wanted from them. In order to reconcile these traditional behaviors with progressive ideologies, men conceived of themselves in opposition to stereotypical men, whom they viewed as domineering, predatory,
and superficial. In this manner, they positioned themselves as "good" men.
They saw these courtship practices simply as nice gestures that women
appreciated rather than as gender inequality disguised as romance. In
many ways, women's commitment to these norms and men's willingness
to conform gave the initial sense that women had more power during the
courtship period of the relationship, as women's willingness to enforce
norms left men with few options. Yet men remained very much committed to certain privileges they claim in their relationships. These narratives
allowed men to claim an identity as an equal partner, without challenging
certain benefits they accrue in their romantic relationships.

NO THRILL IN THE CHASE

While women believed men needed to be the dominant partner during courtship, reveling in the hunt, heterosexual men were quick to dismiss this assumption. Only three had any interest in being the pursuer. Rather, the vast majority said that it was a major turn-on when women approached them. Not only did it make them feel desirable, but it took the pressure off, which they appreciated given that, just like women, they worried about rejection and coming on too strongly. Ryan, 28, said, "It's kind of flattering knowing that someone else finds you attractive or interesting," while Ishan, 29, said, "I actually find quite a bit of intimidation in approaching women. I actually prefer when women approach me." Gavin said,

> In the beginning, even when I've been the actor, sometimes it's been just sort of a superficial layer because I wait till I get a really strong signal that someone's interested before I'll even do anything. So I don't like the idea of being rejected. And also again, it goes hand in hand with not wanting to creep someone out. Like I don't want to be like, heyyyy—. So I like to wait till I get a signal.

Like Gavin, many of the men discussed approaching women only after they were sure that the woman was interested. They play a part in a script where both sides must show interest but in a particular, gendered manner. As we saw in the previous chapter, women take pains to make meaningful eye contact with men in whom they are interested, while others go as far as to aggressively flirt while waiting for the man to make the "first" move. Gavin acknowledged that he was more like a figurehead than an actual aggressor when asking for a date, while William, 32, told a story of a woman who asked him to ask her out, which he then did.

But while men were wary of the rejection that could come from an unwanted advance, they also discussed the issue in terms of women's comfort level. They acknowledged that women receive a lot of unwelcome attention from men who are not respectful of women's desired boundaries and who frequently act in an aggressive and intimidating manner that women often experience as threatening. Jake, 34, said,

> So I have a high respect for women being attacked all the time. Like if you go out and you're dressed up, chances are guys are hitting on you all night

and you're wading through drunk dudes hitting on you. I totally appreciate that. And having been hit on by aggressive gay dudes, I totally know there's nothing worse than unwanted male attention. And I know women. I know women have already scanned the crowd and they know who they want to talk to and not talk to, and so I'm just observant of that. Like a woman will let you know if she wants to talk to you, and I wait for that.

While these interviews took place well before the start of the #MeToo movement,[4] they certainly reflect a growing awareness that being overly assertive or aggressive in pursuit of a woman can come off as anything from unattractive to frightening, and that if you're the kind of guy who respects women, you'll be attentive to their boundaries.

For the most part, men knew that women expected them to ask for dates and so they complied, feeling that they would never get dates if they didn't. But they didn't embrace the initiator role as women thought, and almost no one mentioned the thrill of the chase except with regard to hypothetical "other men." Instead, they treated it as a hoop they had to jump through in order to meet women. A number even discussed following the advice in books or magazines about how to be more assertive and confident when interacting with women, because they knew this was expected and considered attractive. Dave, 34, discussed meeting a woman online: "We both kind of contacted each other at the same time. She messaged me, I messaged her. And so we met very casually at a bar. We went to another bar. I decided she was cute, so I kissed her. Using a technique that I got out of one of the books!" When I asked him what the technique was, he said, "It was very direct. 'I'm going to kiss you now,' or something like that. . . . A lot of guys don't know what is the proper . . . do you just go in for it? Do you say something? What is the proper approach?" As Dave explained, it was about showing that you had the confidence to make a move.

Indeed, men reported negative reactions from women who felt they hadn't made their move in a timely manner. Jake said, "I actually got yelled at by a lady when I didn't ask for her phone number after our first date. And I was like, '*You* didn't ask for my number.' 'You're the guy, you're supposed to ask!' Well, there you go." As a result, men were left with a conundrum. On one hand, they may be chastised for not being aggressive enough with a woman who is interested. On the other hand, if they take an assertive approach with a woman who isn't interested, they risk being labeled a creep, or worse. A number of men even expressed a bit of resentment toward women who took a passive approach to dating. Like Jake, a few men mentioned that women had the *privilege* of being able to just sit back and wait for men to come to them, giving them the "pick of the litter." As Ryan said, "Most girls have so many guys going after them."

Still, a few men did admit that they preferred to approach women because they felt that the women who were approaching them were not those who interested them. Jake said of women approaching, "I definitely like it. It's for sure a compliment, but I also want to be enticed enough to want to approach them as well. Even though they may have walked up to me, I would hopefully have wanted to walk up to them too." Christopher, 34, said,

> I tend to be the one to ask people out. . . . No, I wish, I wish, man, I wish girls would ask me out more. You know, like, pretty much the only two kinds of people who hit on me are old women and gay guys. Or big women and gay guys. I never get hit on by like girls that I would get with, you know? So I have no problem if somebody would ask me out.

Thus, in the same way that many women said the men they approached were never interested in them, men said the women who approached them weren't the ones they desired. This implies either that the most conventionally attractive women have the option of never pursuing, or that men subconsciously find it unattractive when women approach, leading them to create progressive narratives in which it would be acceptable if it was *other* women.

HATE THE GAME

While most of the men said they wanted a straightforward approach to dating with no games, a handful expressed some sense that dating was indeed a game that required a strategy. Christopher said he wasn't into games, but he still approached dating in a calculated manner:

> I like to leave it like, not like I don't care at all, but like, okay, I'll talk to you when I talk to you. You know? Like I did that with [my girlfriend], alright, like, let's talk again soon or something. And she seriously called me like later

that night. I was almost put off by it because she called me like later that night. But I try to, I mean, you don't want to, some people act like they totally don't care. You know, they play it super cold. And I don't play games like that. I just don't want to seem too interested even if I really am.

When I asked Christopher why it was important to him to seem less interested than he really was, he explained, "Because you don't want to scare someone away. Eagerness can be seen as weakness." Just like the women I interviewed, a number of the men felt that neither side should act too eager for a date, lest they turn the other person off. Eagerness was associated with desperation, which was considered an unattractive trait in both women *and* men. At the same time, due to the association of eagerness with weakness, men risk undermining their own masculinity by appearing too interested. Too much interest challenges their control over the situation, a requirement of an effective masculine performance.[5] Certainly this plays to the stereotypes that men must be emotionally aloof and that women want what they can't have. Christopher's game worked. His aloofness increased the woman's interest and she called him. Yet in the process, she almost risked *his* losing interest. Suddenly, she was "too" interested. As a result, both men and women are trapped between a rock and a hard place.

Of course, someone had to initiate future dates, so the belief was that it was acceptable to contact women after an "appropriate" amount of time had passed—generally agreed on as two days. This allowed men to show their interest (as it was sooner than the widespread three-day rule),[6] but not to appear that they had nothing going for them. Christopher continued,

And as far as like waiting the one-day thing, the two-day thing, the three-day thing, I think that people are getting sick of that too. That whole thing, that strategy of trying to let people cool off, I don't think you can do it too long, you know? If you go out with somebody like on a Monday night, do you call them Tuesday? Because you don't want to seem too eager, okay? So then you're going to call Wednesday? Well, they're going to be expecting you to call Wednesday. What are you going to do? Wait one more day and call Thursday? Now you waited too long. I think a day or two, not three or four days. Like you're that cool? If you really like someone, you're thinking about them, you know?

Obvious from listening to Christopher puzzle over when to call is the lack of clarity in expectations that men confronted, leaving them with anxiety over how to proceed. Men felt pressure to be the initiator while dating, without coming across as too passive, too aggressive, too eager, or too non-chalant. This left them with a difficult balancing act, as they found it hard to decipher what women wanted from them.

"JUST BECAUSE I CARRY THE PENIS DOES NOT MEAN I NEED TO BUY YOUR FOOD FOR YOU"

Beyond their making the first move, followed by a certain level of emotional aloofness, heterosexual men thought that women enforced traditional masculinity in other ways as well. Men felt women expected them to pay for first dates, and most dates beyond that. A quarter of the men were very supportive of this convention. Paul, 34, said,

> I've always kind of thought that the guy should be the pursuer and should kind of be responsible for paying. And my dad kind of taught me that way also. I guess historically men have been the breadwinners. And my parents just kind of raised me with those old-fashioned values of the guy has to work hard and support the family and so it makes sense that when you're pursuing a woman that a guy should pay and the woman should not feel guilty at all about having the guy pay.

Matthew, 29, made a similar point: "I'm not against her paying some of the time, but I would probably want to pay most of the time. I think it goes back to me wanting to show my gentlemanly chivalrous side, that I want to be the provider or at least willing to take care of you if you want." Jeremy, 33, also liked paying for dates but framed this as a feminist gesture meant to compensate for the wage gap:

> I'm making enough money to be able to pay for things. And I'm intellectually aware of the fact that there's a pay gap in this country. And like I think the *New York Times* had an article a few years ago about the difference between men's money and women's money, so I guess it was some sort of meme or something in New York in the dating scene a couple years ago. So the pay gap is conceptualized like men's money is worth more than women's

money. So basically, I feel like if I'm initiating the date, especially then I should be willing to pay for, I should be able to pay for it and I should just be considerate. If she wants to pay, I don't want her to feel uncomfortable, so of course if she wants to pay, I'm going to welcome her paying for her share. But in general, I want to live a life as a male feminist ally.

Unlike women, most of whom saw payment as a form of commitment, men viewed it as a way to demonstrate their ability to care for women financially, demonstrate financial stability, and fulfill women's expectations. None of the men brought up the issue of showing commitment in this manner, and indeed, when I mentioned it to Arjun, 25, he burst out laughing and said, "Don't women know how much men are willing to spend to get laid?!" By expecting men to pay for all dates as a matter of course, women inadvertently undermined any potential gauge of interest.

But while men liked the ability to pay for their dates and show women a good time, many resented the expectation that they pay, especially that they pay every time. To men, this signaled women's lack of commitment to *them*. Ryan said of an ex-girlfriend,

> She liked really expensive dinners, and she didn't pay for anything, of course. I asked her once and she got really pissed off. It became a fight so we fought about it. She wanted me to show that a guy was willing to take care of her for the long term. For me, I wanted to see that she was willing to commit back. . . . I don't think it's right for one person to just give, give, give and the other person takes.

When I asked Mark, 32, if his ex-girlfriend expected him to pay for dates, he said, "I think she did. . . . I started getting to the point in my life where I felt like it's important that I not pay all the time. I think it was fear of the gold-digger situation. I wanted to feel like there was a sense of mutual commitment—financial commitment—from her side of the thing." When I asked him if he stopped paying, he said, "No, I still continued to pay. . . . I just didn't *want* to be the person that would always pay as a matter of course."

In fact, the assumption that men would pay was a common complaint. A number of the men insisted that they didn't mind paying as long as women didn't expect it of them and acted appropriately appreciative. Gavin described a conversation with a friend: "I know like one of my friends, he's very particular, but he's like a doctor, makes a lot of money. But I think he went out with someone else who also was a doctor and made a lot of money and sort of expected her to do the kind of reach and she didn't, and he was actually a little annoyed by that, he didn't think that was right. She should at least offer." Arjun said it didn't bother him to pay for all the dates with his then-girlfriend "until I realized she was taking it for granted." When he confronted her about it, she said, "'Oh, I thought you cared to spend on me.' And I was like, 'No, I care to spend on you and I want to spend on you, but I don't think you understand the value of what I'm working for. . . . It's not even about a thank-you. It's about not ever offering herself to do it, or no, no, no, I'll pay.'"

Ryan, who was upset with the woman who expected him to pay for everything, was happy to pay almost all of the expenses in his current relationship: "She asked early on what I feel comfortable with. We did the splitting thing a lot. Then we took turns, but now I pretty much pay for everything because I feel that she's committed. I just make a lot more money than she does." Indeed, it seemed that it wasn't the act of paying that was important to men, but the reaction their payment elicited in women. They weren't only paying because they viewed it as their role but because they hoped women would behave a certain way toward them in response. In particular, they resented the assumption that they should always pay if women weren't willing to view this as a sacrifice, or generous gesture, on their part. While women were willing to chip in as the relationship progressed and they became more sure of men's interest in them, some men had the reverse perspective: they were more willing to pay as the relationship went on, especially if they made quite a bit more money than their partner. This of course leaves men who can't afford to pay for dates and engage in romantic consumption rituals at a disadvantage. However, because so many of the men could afford to spend money, they focused less on issues of economic strain and more on meaning.

In addition, there was some sense on the part of a number of men that they were expected to buy women's affections. William said,

> I almost always paid, if my memory serves correctly, due to some mixture of chivalry and expectation. Like the other people we were going out with were these definitely sort of male/female relationships where the male was like

the money, and the female was the peacock, the jewelry, the trophy. And that definitely wasn't our relationship. Like if anything her career was much more ahead than mine was. I mean at the time I was making literally $30,000 a year, as a consultant too, so I had to pay way more in taxes.

William was expected to show his love and commitment by spending money:

Like I was frequently buying her gifts, sending her flowers to the office. Because I knew that she liked that. She liked her coworkers to know that she was getting stuff. That she was being courted. She really liked that. I knew it would be more meaningful than me just bringing it to her at home. So, you know, it was about maximizing impact. . . . I remember buying her this like $350 Betsey Johnson dress. One day after she made me feel bad that I was text messaging with some girl. There was a lot of that. There was a lot of like you're in the doghouse; buy your way out.

As William recounts the story, he is aware that courtship is a performance for his partner's coworkers as well for her. These rituals or gestures are also about showing others how much he cares about his partner and providing his partner with status.

Still, plenty of men embraced the idea that men and women should share the costs of dating after the first date. Dave said, "We split it. We'd go back and forth. It wasn't understood that I'm the guy and so I had to pay. That's not how it worked. We went Dutch." Gavin said, "I was usually in a similar place with the people, which is neither one of us has any money, so we're gonna have to split if it's going to be sustainable." Jake took a firmer stance:

Fifty-fifty. I'm a Dutch guy. Because of the type of women I'm attracted to, they usually insist on paying every other time, like it's a point of pride to them. Like don't act like you're taking me out. I want to hang out with you too and this is my choice, so don't act like you're buying my company by taking me out. It was a very independent woman thing for sure. And I was like, thank you. That's what I like about you. . . . That goes right in line with my theory of the person I consider my equal. Just because I carry the penis does not mean that I need to buy your food for you. You're a woman, you're educated or want to be educated, you want to be independent, take your stance. . . . If every time we went out to dinner, they just sat there and let me pay for them, I would look at them like, have you no self-respect?

In this way, Jake was one of the few who connected payment of dates, or other courtship rituals, with the expressed identity of both himself and his partners. He questioned the assertion that someone could call herself a feminist while continuing to engage in traditional courtship practices. Instead, *challenging* traditional gendered behaviors was the indicator of a feminist identity. But certainly no one argued that the rituals were meaningless. From expectations to be treated on a date to insistence on sharing the cost, men understood these conventions to reflect something about the gender dynamics of the relationship.

Many men found the rigid enforcement of masculinity to be disconcerting. Mark said, "Turn-offs are . . . the expectations of what men fulfill for them in their lives. Like I want to go against the traditional men have to provide for the family, or . . . I've heard this from our friend—he's got to be six feet tall, he's got to have a six-figure income. So basically that kind of thing is a big turn-off, if I get any sense of that. I hate it." Like Mark, a number of men discussed their body size or height as a disadvantage, given that it didn't fit the ideal of what they thought women wanted. Connecting appearance norms to pop culture assumptions about human evolution, Gregory, 33, said, "Height and baldness are probably the strongest pressures. Women are programmed to go after tall men. Men are programmed to want a 0.7 waist-to-hip ratio." Christopher said, "I'm okay with my height, for the most part, but I think like I would've gotten a lot more girls if I was taller. No doubt about it."

That said, Christopher, too, enforced this norm, saying he wouldn't be willing to date a woman who was taller than he was: "I don't like that dynamic. I don't need someone who is super short that I'm towering over, but I don't want to date a girl that's taller than me. That tradition, gender thing. Power. Physical power. You know, like all those things that aren't really logical that people hang on to." Ethan, 38, said, "I've seen some responses where they're like, I'm looking for a man who could be a big teddy bear. I like a bigger man. And I say, well, okay, that's not me. And it is what it is on that front. I mean I'm in shape." Still, he felt that women found other factors to be more important than appearance as they aged: "Women who are a bit younger want . . . attractiveness, but once they get a little older they want someone who can demonstrate stability and has their stuff together and could be sort of an anchor and have some support.

At least have your own place. Stuff like that. So I try to put forth like I'm stable, but I'm in shape. So the best of both worlds." Ethan's understanding of stability for a partner wasn't gender-neutral, but implied a level of career success and emotional maturity related to breadwinning and household leadership. Thus, men felt that they had to possess and enact certain traditionally masculine traits and behaviors in order to be considered a desirable partner.

NOT LIKE OTHER GUYS

Even as heterosexual men engaged in the conventional courtship behaviors of asking and paying for dates, almost all of them (28 out of 31) still had very strong understandings of themselves as progressive partners. Conventionally, masculinity in sexual and romantic relationships is signified by men's dominance, aggression, sexual promiscuity, and emotional unavailability.[7] As a result, just as women held strong stereotypical beliefs about most men, so too did men about each other. Many positioned themselves in contrast to the misogynistic and dominating displays they associated with "other men."

This connected to their geographic location, political affiliations, and socioeconomic status. As well-educated, middle- to upper-middle-class men, they saw themselves as above overt disrespectful treatment of women. And certainly some data indicate that college-educated men are more likely than those without a college education to support women's agency and autonomy in romantic relationships.[8] They also lived in a liberal part of the country, almost exclusively voted for liberal or progressive candidates, and surrounded themselves with other political liberals. This meant that their reference points for acceptable behavior centered on liberal feminist concerns, such as women's political, labor-market, and reproductive rights. Many men expressed support for feminism as an example of their commitment to gender equality. William said, "I very much believe in the equality of the sexes. And the inequality of society to the sexes. And I actually strive for a world, like I want to see a world where men and women have equal places of power in society and influence." Matthew said, "I'm very pro-women female organizations. I haven't done anything specific for but I'm part of, I go to women—there's this women's initiative or I don't know what it's called, it's at work, and there's this women's network and they have events and I go to some of those events, so very pro-women in that way, yes." Jake said, "I love women. The more power is in a woman's hands, the better life is and I witness that all the time. . . . There's so much positiveness that emanates from a woman's perspective, that you really can't go wrong in a woman-dominated society, in my mind." While many of their narratives were superficial and underdeveloped, or essentialized women's "goodness," they were an important part of their views of themselves as progressive, egalitarian men.

While not all of the men considered feminism to be part of their identity, only two expressed direct animosity toward it. Only one of these considered feminism to be a problem for men. The other man couched his distaste for feminism in a concern for women. Both men were more religious than the other men interviewed. Paul said, "I think some [feminist] ideas have kind of hurt women, sometimes, over the years. I think a lot of women have kind of experienced a lot of heartache in relationships. And a lot of women have been abandoned and suffered a lot of abuse because of some feminist ideas." In this manner, Paul expressed a desire to protect women and saw this as a form of support for women and a way of caring about their well-being, rather than as hostility toward women's equality. Paul believed that feminism allowed men to use women for casual sex, which disadvantaged women and didn't give them the respect they deserved:

> I just wish there were more of a focus on how, you know, love is really hard, that commitment is hard, and relationships are serious and you can't just treat people as objects, you know, you can't just hook up and use people to have fun and then disregard them, because there are always long-term consequences of that. So I guess my focus is on love and commitment rather than sex for recreational fun, hooking up and all that stuff.

Cultural norms governing sexual and romantic heterosexual relationships ascribe to men an aggressive and predatory sexuality in which they are expected to want and pursue all sexual opportunities, irrespective of the context, while scrupulously avoiding commitment and emotional intimacy.[9] While many of the men engaged in or had previously engaged in casual sex, the majority now appeared to agree with Paul to some extent, emphasizing the importance of emotional connection in their sexual relationships, especially now that they were older. Again, this approach distanced them from the typical man, a "slime ball"[10] who was only out for sex and didn't appreciate women as individuals. Many prefaced their statements by saying, "I'm not like other men . . . " Gavin reported that he stopped having sex with a woman he was dating because he felt the emotional relationship wasn't developing fast enough: "We'd had sex, which I consider to be very serious. . . . [I said,] 'I can't be having sex with you and then feel like I hardly know you.'. . . Sex kinda means you're in love or it's kinda serious. The sort of thing that we were, you know, not super close, but having sex, is weird for me." Christopher said, "If I'm going to be with somebody, I'm going to invest a lot emotionally. I'm not like a casual sex person, because if I'm going to get that close to somebody, I really care about them. And it's like sharing a moment. I'm not just like getting off and then like it's Tuesday or something."

In addition, almost all the men emphasized that they found commitment more rewarding than casual sex. Henry, 28, said, "I wanted a very serious committed relationship in the sense of like, 'I'm committed to this person. I really wanna date this person. I wanna spend a lot of time with her.' I was not happy being single at all." Tommy, 27, explained why he wanted a committed relationship: "The idea that I would be in a relationship tomorrow and probably the day after and the day after and the day after. Security." Jake said, "I didn't want to get back into that casual dating sex thing. I did it. Okay, I saw that lifestyle. It's not good. I mean it's enjoyable. . . . [But a] committed relationship beats it hands down. Hands down. Quality of life is so much higher. Your contentment, your energy level, just your joy with your life is so much higher." Brad, 32, who had engaged in frequent casual sex in his twenties, made a similar point when discussing a long-term relationship that was in the process of ending: "I've never felt so loved in my life. I think that's something I needed. I never recognized that. . . . I really enjoyed that. I learned also that I'm capable of loving and being nurturing towards someone." Rather than return to casual sex, he expressed the hope of finding another long-term relationship, but with someone more compatible.

These men weren't a bunch of George Clooneys, seeing how long they could push off commitment. Indeed, as they hit their thirties, they were very interested in settling down with one person. Paul, for example, was busy getting his professional and financial ducks in a row so that should he meet the right woman, he would be ready for her. Peter, 29, said, "I would've liked to be married by this point, or at least have a serious relationship." When I asked him why he wanted to be married already, he explained, "I guess I define success as being settled down at this age. I have my degree. I have my license. A house. That was a major one. But I guess it's still an emptiness because I don't have at least some kind of relationship." Gavin even worried that his "stock" was declining as he aged. He resisted breaking up with a girlfriend, even as he described the relationship as "six good months followed by two bad years." As he said, "I didn't think I was a very good catch" and "I thought I was getting less attractive." He ended up staying in the relationship much longer than he should have, given his desire to be in a committed relationship and his fear that he wouldn't find one again.

In short, men's narratives about commitment were a far cry from the common narratives in the media that men shy away from commitment and emotional intimacy in favor of casual hookups and that women must scheme to obtain an exclusive relationship. Instead, most of the men were actively seeking committed relationships and many of them expressed frustrations similar to women's about the difficulty in securing an exclusive relationship.

"SOME EXPERIENCE AND LESS THAN A SLUT"

While many of the men gave themselves a pass on their prior sexual behavior now that they were ready for a commitment, they weren't as generous with women's sexual histories, indicating a persistent sexual double standard.[11] Certainly men expected their partners to have prior sexual experience. Ethan said, "Like did I have an expectation [she] would be a virgin? Who would really want that anyway? I want someone with more experience." But while many said that they did not care about exact numbers, many of them did. Christopher said, "I mean, I'm realistic. I'm not saying like I want every girl that I date to only have like four partners. That's ridiculous, you know what I'm saying? But if they have more than like, I don't know, like I've only been with like 13 people. So if they've been with 20, that's okay. But when we get up into like the high 20s, I don't want to mess with you." Mark made a similar point: "I think if they had way too many sexual partners, then I would have a problem with that. And I don't know what way too many is. It depends on their age, I guess. I guess if they're young and they've had like . . . a lot—20 or 30—I would be concerned." Only a couple of men were firm that a woman needed to have had fewer sexual partners than they had. Arjun said, "I guess if my [future] wife has my number [of sexual partners], that's fine. Above is not okay; below is ideal." When I asked him why this was important, he replied, "'Cause it's fewer guys. I don't like the idea. Because I don't want anybody else having touched her." When I mentioned that people had touched him as well, he shut down, saying, "I don't want to talk about it."

While Arjun was unwilling to admit his double standard about his sexual experience versus women's, a number of men were willing. Mateo, 33, said, "I expect them to have been with fewer people than me. That's the double standard I have. . . . There is a big difference between sleeping with 5 people versus 27, but if I get to know her and know the meaning behind them and see she cared about each one, then that would be okay with me. . . . If it's in a relationship, no matter how many, I think is fine." As we saw at the beginning of the chapter, Gavin also admitted that he wanted a partner who had had sex with fewer partners than he had: "It's totally arbitrary and largely unfair. I'll cop to that." Jake and I had a conversation about how many sexual partners were acceptable for a woman to have had. He said, "I would hope some experience and less than a slut." When I asked him what constituted a slut, he said, "I would say if you're a woman and you've slept with more than 20, 25 people, you've probably slept with too many. As an adult in her thirties, yeah." When I mentioned that he had had a fair number of sexual partners, he replied, "I'm right around 20. And also, you're right. There's a double standard there. For a man to sleep with 20 people, shit, that could be a busy year for a guy. For a woman, it's like Honey, what are you doing?" But Jake, like Mateo, went on to clarify that numbers weren't necessarily important if the woman was able to feel confident about her choices. Thus, men argued that casual sex and sex for "validation" were the turn-offs, perpetuating the belief that women's sexuality should be restricted to committed relationships and should mean something.[12] As Henry said, "I mean, it would be a red flag to me if she had been sleeping with several guys at the same time. If her general attitude towards sex and sexual behavior demonstrated a lack of respect for herself or if it was being used in some other way than just to show physical trust and intimacy." Still, from the consistency of the responses, men didn't want women to have had more than 20 sexual partners, indicating a persistent double standard of which men were aware but unwilling to challenge within themselves. By attributing their judgment of women who had more than 20 partners to motives other than slut-shaming or their own insecurity, they were able to maintain that double standard while justifying it with what they thought to be a respectable, rather than retrogressive, motive.

Just like women, many of the men had rules about when they would have sex with a woman, and as with women, these rules were related to how seriously they were considering a relationship. Mark was willing to have casual sex, but added, "But in terms of like a longer-term relationship, I feel that I would like to wait until I get to know the person well enough. And I think you have to have multiple conversations. And that can happen over a period of three weeks or so." Jake had created a rule that he said many of his friends now followed:

> So my rule is, if you really like this person and you're considering really dating them and you respect them, no sex for the equivalent of three weeks of hanging out. So not like you met them on the 20th and it's been three weeks and you saw them again. Twenty-one days-ish before you really have sex with them because that way you really get to know them, because there's the sex haze. . . . If every time you hang out, you get a B.J., that's kind of crossing the line. You can kiss and make out, but know them minus the sex, without coming. Basically, that's the trigger, isn't it? And so I would tell them, if you don't care and you're just having a good time and you're drinking and you want to go have sex with somebody, great. But if you're going to really want to date them, you need to know them as a person, sober almost, minus the haze of sex, and really see if you like them. And then after about three weeks of hanging out with them, you'll know whether or not you want to spend more time with them.

When Christopher started dating a woman he really liked, he had a similar plan: "I didn't want to rush into things. I don't want it to be just like, wham, bam, we just had sex, now there's no other mystery. I mean I wanted it to be more significant with her." He said that before her, he didn't really care, and wanted sex as soon as possible. By waiting, he hoped the sex would be more special and would lead to a relationship:

> 'Cause when we first started dating, we were talking about things and I was like, hey, let's keep things PG13 for a while. And she was like, okay, I'm down with that. And I was like, cool. And PG13 meant that we were never going to go like past second base. We were just going to keep it kind of, anything you can do in a movie theater that might upset your parents, but nothing too upsetting, you know? And then like first date obviously, you know, we need to establish a second date, that was a rule, third date, that was a rule. Fourth date, we went to a baseball game, we got back from the baseball game and she's like, hey, do you want to stay the night? And I was like, sure. And she seriously like threw herself at me. She was like, forget that PG13 shit. . . . Yeah, I mean, she was not going to take no for an answer. But it was, I don't know, it was a bit early.

Men's negative reactions when women initiated sex too quickly for them confirmed women's assumptions. If sex occurred too quickly, men were less likely to take the relationship seriously. Men preferred not to be pressured through sex into a commitment they didn't want, but they also assumed that a woman who had sex quickly and casually with too many partners was someone who was incapable of having the kind of serious, committed relationship for which many of them said they were looking. Matthew said he was now more cautious about having sex with women on the first date:

> I think it causes confusion and can lead to quickly being in a relationship that you don't want to be in. . . . I wouldn't necessarily not call her or not pursue her because of it, but I'd be really cautious because from what I've done, what's happened to me in the past is exactly that. You hook up, are quickly dating, and then maybe you don't want to date that person. So I just wouldn't want to set expectations. That's not necessarily going to mean that we're in a committed relationship now.

That said, men were extremely happy when women initiated sex within the context of a committed relationship. They wanted confirmation that a woman was actually into having sex with them. This made the sex more enjoyable for them due to the level of enthusiasm a woman displayed and how desirable it made them feel. When I asked Mark how he wanted a woman to initiate sex, he said, "Actually, I like aggressive. I think passive is kind of a turn-off." In fact, the majority of the men who said they were unhappy with their sexual relationships cited the woman's refusal to initiate and a lack of excitement about sex as the main source of their dissatisfaction. When I asked Mateo who initiated sex more in his last relationship, he said, "That was all me. I would say she was pretty asexual. That was something I talked to her about. I told her I wanted her to initiate more. But it didn't change. To be fair, she would say that she thought she was initiating and I would say, 'Well, turning your backside to me is not initiating.'" Logan, 29, tried to get his fiancée to initiate sex more often, saying he usually made the first move: "I mean she does sometimes, but it's not nearly as often. I'll try to wait as long as I can to make her make the first move—and just, like, wait and see if I can outlast her. Sometimes that works, and she'll initiate, but sometimes I'll just give up and I'll be like, 'Okay, let's go have sex.' She'll say yes if it's been a long time." But because of the guiding assumption that all men want sex all the time, men received very negative reactions when they turned down women's advances. Mark discussed how a girlfriend broke up with him when he declined sex with her: "She wanted to have sex. And I think I had resisted for a while. So basically she decided that we weren't moving forward together. And I wasn't really that into her was what she decided."

PROPOSAL PRESSURES

Many of the men also readily admitted that their partners' desires often established the pace of the relationship. Mark said, "We had discussed getting engaged, but then I started getting pressure. She brought it up a lot. She picked out the ring, she designed it, and then she let me know when I could purchase it. She even let me know I was expected to propose on a specific weekend." Dave, who also planned to propose, reported a similar situation: "She put a deadline on me proposing. One night she was stressed out because the deadline was approaching, and was losing it in a meltdown. So I proposed right then and there." William, whose ex-fiancée had told him to plan a dinner party and propose to her in front of her friends, said, "I planned this dinner party and got down on one knee and proposed and she acted surprised."

Just as women acknowledged the importance of the proposal story, so too did men, as they knew it was important to women. Mark said, "I think she probably wanted a story to tell about it. So rather than a conversation, a decent story. So that's probably why. And there was so much, 'Oh, we're getting engaged.' There needed to be a pinnacle." Certainly, men understood that there could be blowback if the marriage proposal didn't fit a woman's ideal image. Dave felt his marriage proposal to his ex-wife was held against him for their entire marriage:

> I bought the ring. And we were going to have lunch together. And I was late for lunch because I was getting financing in place for the ring. So she was kind of ticked at me already. And then I showed up. I didn't do the classical down on the knee . . . "Will you marry me?" I just popped open the ring and I showed it to her. And she's like, "Well, are you going to ask me?" And the thing is, it sounds cute—but later on in the relationship she held that against me. . . . I didn't do a big enough gesture. I hate her for that now. I really think, who cares? Because I cleaned my savings out for that ring.

While for Dave the act of purchasing a costly ring was the important gesture, for his ex-wife it was the proposal itself. Because the proposal didn't fit the image she had in her head of a grand gesture, she wasn't able to see love and commitment in the sacrifice he made. Unfortunately, this attitude undermined the entire marriage as the proposal took on an outsized importance in her understanding of their relationship and his love for and commitment to her.

In spite of women's concerns discussed in the last chapter, men didn't express much apprehension that women were influencing the timing of the marriage proposal. Indeed, this perspective did two things for men. First, they were able to demonstrate their comfort with commitment, again distancing themselves from the image of the typical male "commitment-phobe." Most said that they had been planning to propose eventually so it wasn't a concern when it actually happened. Second, it allowed them to show that they didn't mind a woman in the driver's seat. As such, almost all the men said that they would be fine with a woman proposing. As Brad said, "I'd be open to being proposed to. Again, that would just reaffirm the type of woman I'm attracted to—strong, independent—so yeah, I'm open to it." Of the few who expressed reluctance, most discussed the proposal as something fun that they wanted to do, but not as their right or prerogative. Matthew was one of the few who really wanted to propose. When I asked him how he would feel if a partner proposed to him, he said, "It would be odd, but if I loved them, I guess it wouldn't really matter. I'd say yes; it wouldn't turn me off. I'd be bummed out that I couldn't have done it first." When I asked why, he said, "I guess just to prove to her that I'm really serious and really committed and not just agreeing to something that she proposes." When I suggested that the same could happen in reverse, he said, "I mean, I don't know. Maybe I'm just more trusting of her."

Many men assumed that most women were very eager to get married. This made them feel confident in proposing. One man even jumped the gun, proposing to his girlfriend on the assumption that she was hinting for a marriage proposal. Logan said of his fiancée, "She read an article in *Details* magazine that said it was in vogue right now for women to ask men to marry them. . . . So she was bringing up this article with me. And before that, she was talking about what kind of ring she would want, and all this stuff . . . so I thought she was totally into it." As a result, he caught her off guard with his proposal and although she did accept, he referred to her as "Miss 'Already?' But we're so young." Popular narratives around women's interest in marriage led Logan to read into his girlfriend's behaviors in ways she didn't intend. It also meant men were sure a yes would be forthcoming, even more confident in their partner's commitment to them than in their own feelings.

LOOKING GOOD

Finally, a number of men even emphasized their acceptance of supposed undesirable physical traits in women as evidence that they were not superficial but instead focused on what was important in a partner. Again, this was a way to distance themselves from what they saw as the focus of the stereotypical man.[13] While describing an ex-girlfriend, Gavin said, "She was cute, and I came to appreciate her more. But she was probably the least attractive [woman I dated]. She didn't have the most attractive face or anything really distinguishing about her. And didn't dress really well. . . . Sort of ordinary looking. . . . It wasn't a selling point." Instead, he emphasized that he was drawn to her because "she was book smart. She was probably the sort of book-smartest girl I ever dated." And Dave said of a partner, "She's not the most beautiful woman I could have got. But that doesn't matter." Rather, he was attracted to her because she was "funny," "gregarious," "good with people," and "forgiving." Mateo said he felt his ex-wife had all the physical specifications that he desired, but that he wasn't as physically attracted to her as he could have been due to how she presented herself: "She was super skinny, which was a plus. Physically she was pretty, she just didn't try. . . . She wore really baggy jeans and baggy shirts. She hardly ever put on make-up. I think it's important that we try to look our best. . . . I didn't need her to do a 10, but the difference between a 0 and a 2 would be nice." Still, he felt other stuff (such as her personality) outweighed her appearance. Yet while the argument made was that appearance was not important, the implication was that appearance was indeed important, only they were enlightened enough to know that other traits were more important and thus were willing to "settle" in the looks department.

A few men explicitly insisted on conventional ideals of female beauty in their partners. Ben, 33, said, "I tend to prefer short blondes with larger boobs. Actually, I think I would also prefer tall blondes with larger boobs too." Ryan asked out his current girlfriend because they had similar interests in computers, gaming, and comics, which he thought was rare in women. Still, he enforced a particular appearance with her. He described his girlfriend as "normal sized," but trying to lose weight because he wanted her to be skinny: "I do like a thin woman, so she has to stay thin. . . . I try to be nice about it, but I don't believe it's right to hold back. She's really nice about it. She's trying." Ryan framed his request for his girlfriend to lose weight as an example of the value he placed on honesty and communication in his relationships. In addition, men who wanted a particular body type simply reframed their desire in terms of health and physical fitness to distance themselves from men's perceived superficiality and the hostile sexism that underlies objectification of women's appearance.[14] Ethan said, "I'm not that superficial, but I take care, like I try to stay in shape, so I kind of want someone equal. And I always put a body type on Match. Just like 'athletic' and 'in shape,' something like that." Yet he later went on to say, "I think women should have all the same rights. They could still shave their legs though." This allowed men to enforce traditional norms without acknowledging their behavior as such.

On the flip side, a third of the men also discussed allowing women to dress them or change their style. If men were asking women to look a certain way, so too were women asking this of men. Logan discussed battling with his fiancée over his wardrobe:

> These pants are very tight for me . . . they're so uncomfortable. But she wanted me to wear all this stuff. . . . At some time in our relationship, we went shopping at the mall and I got some of these pants that are so fricking tight. . . . And my shoes . . . she's switched me to these stylish shoes. I mean she bought half the stuff for me. We'd go out and I'm like, "You're the one who wants this, not me."

William recounted a similar experience:

> Almost immediately I became her little, like her fashion doll. So since she's in the fashion business. . . . So she would take me to these designer shoe stores and get me these gay-ass freaking shoes. . . . One night she had me dressed up in these like pointy cowboy boots, linen pants, and like some sort of denim embroidered shirt. . . . And I remember feeling like a geisha. You know? Like I felt my feet were bound and I couldn't walk right.

But William was one of the only men who found this to be disempowering, possibly because his fiancée's control of him extended to all aspects of their relationship. The other men said that they went along with their partners' fashion advice to make them happy or appreciated the help in an area which they considered to be women's expertise. As Gavin explained of an ex-girlfriend, "She was definitely one of those people who really pushed me towards like, oh, you should dress like this. Have you tried this kind of thing. . . . I was wearing this old pair of jeans that had tapered legs, and that was like ten years out of date. So she was, oh, you need to get boot cut—which probably now is out of style again." When I asked him why he went along with these requests, he said, "I mean, she had a good sense of style and I wanted to be attractive for her and it wasn't like I had some fierce sense of my own style anyway. It was like, yeah, whatever, I mean, sure. Again to limits. There are points where I would see myself, no, the polo shirt with the linen pants thing is just not me."

Certainly if a man dictated what his partner should wear, it would be perceived negatively as patriarchal dominance and the enforcement of problematic beauty standards. In fact, the women didn't discuss men making requests or demands of their appearance. One woman even told me that would be an immediate red flag to get out of the relationship. On the other hand, women's fashion requests of men were framed as the result of their greater fashion expertise and interest. These men accommodated their partners' style requests as ways to position themselves as supportive of their partners.

CALL ME OLD-FASHIONED

Even though the majority of heterosexual men provided what they viewed as feminist narratives and distanced themselves from the image of the stereotypical man, gender inequalities did emerge as they engaged in traditional courtship rituals and supported certain gendered practices. Since this contradicted their views of themselves as progressive men, they, like heterosexual women, had to find ways to reconcile their behaviors with their identities. Men took two approaches. First, they emphasized their desire to care for women. This approach relied on understandings of gender difference but in a manner that allowed men to continue to view themselves as "good guys." Second, when men did acknowledge an inequality, they emphasized all the ways in which they *were* egalitarian to make the issue seem less relevant and to blow off concerns. Thus, the progressive identity that they had constructed allowed them to perpetuate inequality in certain ways without feeling badly about it.

Men were able to engage in what they saw as chivalry while retaining their understanding of themselves as nice, caring, and respectful, even feminist guys, again in contrast to men who use and abuse and throw away. Like many of the heterosexual women, men distinguished between support for women's rights and gendered courtship practices. As Henry explained,

I consider myself a feminist in the sense that I fully believe that women should be equal in all areas of society. You know, jobs they can hold, pay they should earn, things they can accomplish, roles and responsibilities they can have. Absolutely, completely equal. On the other hand, I do feel that men have a certain responsibility to be chivalrous, to be caring, to provide in a lot of ways. And not in a way that's condescending, but in just a very traditional old-fashioned way. So again, opening doors for women, pulling out chairs, paying for dinner, wanting to be the chief breadwinner in the home, things like that. There's all this talk about what it means to be a man, to be manly. And I think those things are really what makes a man.

Unfortunately, this approach to gender norms, called benevolent sexism, uses positive attitudes toward women to justify restricted roles for them and often masks hostility for women who don't conform to gendered expectations.[15] For example, Gavin said, "I always offered, and I always probably did pay [in the early stages of dating]." But remember that when confronted with the hypothetical of dating a woman with more sexual experience, he said, "I prefer being in a situation where I'm more experienced. There is a number [of former sexual partners] at which point I go, like, whoa." And Henry, like many men, didn't want a partner who had sex for the "wrong" reasons. Men who support benevolent sexism are also more likely to express hostile sexism, making these beliefs two sides of the same coin.[16]

Finally, men stressed the many ways in which they *were* progressive in order to justify what they thought of as important gendered conventions. Christopher, for example, was adamant that his wife should take his last name: "Why are we married then? You're not going to take my name? You know, you'll take my ring, you'll have my kids, but you won't take my name?" When I pushed him on why this was important to him, he said,

> Well, because it's a gender role. And it's a traditional gender role that I'm against being broken, personally speaking. Again, I don't want to put down other people, but me personally there's some gender roles that I don't—I wouldn't mind being a stay-at-home dad, but I want her to have my last name. You know what I'm saying? Like I don't care if she makes more money than me, but [if you are just going to keep your name] why are we married then? Like a marriage is like you're bringing things together. . . . It's property. It's saying this belongs to me. It's why do you wear the ring, and you take the last name, it's that this is off limits, it's now mine.

Mateo, whose wife was pursuing a PhD and opted not to take his name, said, "I think it would have been a nice gesture to do it, even if she didn't want to, for all that I had done for her, but I understand why because I wouldn't have wanted to change mine either." It was important to him, however, that their daughter be given his last name: "I feel like we had already broken tradition a little bit with her keeping her last name. At one point we did discuss giving our daughter her last name, but I just felt like that's weird. Okay, fine, you don't have my last name, but at least give it to my daughter." Thus, while men acknowledged the inequality of family names, they were unable to shed the discomfort that goes with bucking tradition. There was a sense that men could only be expected to change so much. At the same time, gender norms became more important as the relationship turned familial. Suddenly, roles and obligations took on greater significance to men as they became less willing to let go of the traditions that established men as at least the symbolic heads of households.[17]

While the man was expected to prove commitment during courtship, changing her last name was seen as a way a woman could return these symbolic shows of commitment with her own. When I asked Tommy if he would want his wife to change her last name, he said, "Last name? Not particularly attached to any tradition of changing names. I think it might be nice if she changed her name. Like as a gesture on her part. But I wouldn't expect it." When I asked him what the gesture would represent to him, he said, "Let's see, like her part, like a commitment on her end." Just as women found the traditional proposal to be romantic, Gavin understood a name change by the woman in the same manner: "I've always sort of wanted the person to change her last name. It was a traditional way to do things, I thought it was romantic; it was nice to have the same last name. So anyway, it's one of those things where we decided this is okay for us because we liked it and it's romantic. But we don't think someone *has* to do that."

As we saw in the previous chapter, narratives of choice serve as a form of ideological work to justify unequal outcomes while preserving egalitarian identities. When "cornered," men made light of the situation in a manner that allowed them to dismiss concerns and end the conversation. Christopher said, "I'm the man. See? And in my double standard, sexist world, that's how it works. It's not rational, but I understand it. I mean I'm admitting to it at least. I'm not going to try to dance around it. It is sexist. It's a double standard and I'm okay with it."

SHIFTING MASCULINITIES

This chapter has looked at how heterosexual men construct their masculinity in the context of courtship. Professional men, in particular, have been increasingly exposed to egalitarian ideals;[18] 28 of the 31 heterosexual men provided at least partial narratives of a progressive masculinity in courtship. While most of them also conformed to conventional courtship, it was framed as the result of women's desire for traditional masculinity in men rather than the result of men's own beliefs and preferences. The men also contrasted their own behaviors and beliefs with the stereotypical image of the domineering, emotionally unavailable, and promiscuous man.[19] Not only were they sensitive to women's feelings and respectful of their boundaries, but they sought out commitment and emotional intimacy, rejected superficial evaluations of women, and were more than happy to allow women to take the lead in relationships. These changes are not insignificant and indicate an increasingly egalitarian approach to courtship among middle-class men.

However, these progressive narratives also allow persistent gender inequalities to function within their relationships as most men fail to view themselves as only partially changed. Unequal practices within their relationships get dismissed, given men's so-called progressive views, or are recast in a positive light, again confirming their sense of themselves as respectful of women. A sexual double standard persists as many of the men contrast women's "promiscuity" with their own interest in serious, committed relationships, allowing them to critique women's sexual behavior in a manner that is framed as rational. Men want women's gratitude when they pay for dates but don't want the obligation to do so. In this way, progressive narratives serve as a form of identity work that allows these men to think of themselves as better than the average man without having to fully challenge gender inequality.

Once marriage was on the horizon, heterosexual men were very invested in the traditional symbolic gender norms. Indeed, they were more than willing to resist certain gendered practices during courtship because it was of very little benefit to them. Women found an adherence to courtship norms to be important, as they helped them navigate a terrain in which women face great scrutiny for nonconforming behavior, and in which they feel disempowered to openly seek their desired relationship goals. Men didn't feel the same need to confirm women's commitment to a relationship since commitment was assumed given cultural narratives that all women want a relationship at all times.[20] Thus, men went through the motions without the same intense emotional investment.

Heterosexual men do, however, benefit from their position as head of household, especially when they have the economic resources to claim this status. This makes challenging norms a greater sacrifice as they form families. Indeed, they were less likely to do so as they moved toward greater commitment, arguing for the right for their last name to become the family name. Consistent with previous research, privileged men continue to "talk the talk" but fail to completely "walk the walk," as progressive definitions of manhood remain compatible with male privilege.[21] In particular, egalitarian narratives may actually serve to perpetuate gender inequality, demonstrating that progressive masculinities can allow gender inequality to function in hard-to-recognize, yet still pernicious ways.[22] As we shall see in chapter 6, men's reluctance to change, combined with men's and women's insistence on gender difference, results in unequal outcomes in committed relationships in spite of stated desires. In contrast, as demonstrated in the next chapter, LGBQ individuals are more likely to directly challenge gendered courtship practices, leading to more equal partnerships.

5 Queering Courtship

LGBQ PEOPLE REIMAGINE RELATIONSHIPS

We had been talking for over an hour when I asked Alek, a 38-year-old gay cis man, his perspective on heterosexual dating practices. His response was swift and harsh:

> Jesus Christ. When I think about straight dating norms, I feel nauseous. This is so boring. What I see in the films or in the streets, how can you guys live like this? Because you do not have any space for imagination. All your family life is scheduled from the very beginning, especially when you are a woman. You know that you are going to have a date and gosh you're so obsessed about the wedding and what comes after the wedding. After that you should have kids and then kindergarten and the company of the other young moms and the kids go to college and then you need to separate from them somehow and in this way until death.

As Alek explained, he saw no room for deviation from the set pathway provided to heterosexual men and women, and no room to change course once on that pathway. He referred to queer relationship practices as both more "interesting" and "inspiring" than "that tomb of the traditional family." Interestingly, Alek's perspective is in conflict with popular liberal narratives that position LGBQ people as victims of chance rather than agents of choice. Trying to counter right-wing claims that LGBQ people are sick and can be cured, liberal tolerance narratives attribute sexuality to biological reality and often imply that those who are LGBQ deserve sympathy rather than scorn. After all, why would anyone *choose* to be LGBQ when being heterosexual is supposedly so much easier (and in many people's minds, better)?[1] At the same time, one of the iconic slogans of the same-sex marriage movement—love is love—seeks to normalize same-sex relationships as the same as straight ones in order to make them palatable to the mainstream, heterosexual public.

But many of the LGBQ people I interviewed saw their intimate partnerships as distinct from the mainstream, and thankfully so. Rather than seek to emulate straight relationships or wish they were straight, they indicated the opposite, stating that being heterosexual and following heterosexual norms would be an unappealing way to live life. Indeed, of the 40 LGBQ respondents,[2] two-thirds explicitly described heterosexual dating and relationship norms as constraining and boring. They emphasized how heterosexual lives are predetermined by scripts, with no room for change or individuality. For them, the appeal of queer life is the opposite— "the promise of life outside the predictable constraints of heterosexuality."[3] Throughout, their interviews reflected the view that heterosexual culture, and in particular relationship practices, were something to be pitied and avoided rather than desired or emulated. LGBQ young adults viewed heterosexual men and women as too interested in playing it safe within the constraints of normative culture to reimagine the possibilities for life outside the dominant narrative.

As I show in this chapter, LGBQ young adults sought to remake dating practices to better suit their understanding of how relationships should look. In particular, most found highly gendered and scripted conventional dating practices to be the antithesis of the kinds of relationships they hoped to create. In response, they aimed for both equality *and* flexibility when they dated. In addition, they were more highly attuned than heterosexual men and women to potential inequalities that could arise, and factored this into their relationship practices. In the process, they "queered courtship," remaking relationship formation outside of dominant understandings. Still, relationship scripts and normative expectations are hard to avoid and many still found them appealing. Thus, while the majority worked to distance themselves from these practices, others embraced them, meaning that some LGBQ relationships still drew on elements of conventional dating expectations.

MAKING THEIR OWN RULES

Heterosexual dating practices are highly scripted and, as we have seen, widely followed by heterosexual men and women who take them for granted as how dating is done. After all, they reflect the mainstream messages perpetuated everywhere from movies to self-help to lay opinions from trusted friends. But many LGBQ people look elsewhere for their worldview. For many, queerness is about making "life choices distinct from those considered more socially expected, celebrated, and sanctioned";[4] it is about resisting normalization and radically transforming society in the process.[5] Consequently, queer people are "dually socialized": they are exposed to queer politics that subvert normative constructions of intimate life, while at the same time they are embedded in a culture that promotes a particular vision of romance, love, and family life.[6] In spite of having to navigate these widespread cultural norms about how men and women "should" be in relationships, LGBQ people frequently and explicitly seek to undermine conventional relationship practices.[7]

As I discussed in the first chapter, many of the people I interviewed identified as queer rather than gay, lesbian, or bisexual. They viewed this as an identity that was more politicized, progressive, and inclusive, and they were most likely more radical than the LGBQ population as a whole. Brian, a 30-year-old queer cis man, explained, "I mean I do queer studies and I think there's a real history behind 'gay' that's like, especially in this day and age, it sort of has assimilationist tinges, and I find that I'm more aligned politically, socially, with people across the spectrum as opposed to like really identifying super strongly with gay culture." While for some, queer identity indicated an attraction to people with a range of gender identities, for others it was about positioning themselves outside of or in opposition to what they viewed as the status quo, or both. Jen, a 31-year-old queer cis woman, said, "When I say I'm queer, that means I recognize several things. I recognize that there's more than just man/woman. There's more than just a binary. When I say I'm queer, I recognize that I might date someone with a female body who might identify as a man. Or I might date someone with a biological male body who identifies as feminine or a woman. You know, queer is more progressive in a way."

Many LGBQ people emphasized how freeing it was to be queer and not feel the need to worry about normative heterosexual expectations. Instead, they concentrated on figuring out what would make them happy as individuals. Adah, a 34-year-old queer genderqueer and gender fluid person, said, "I feel privileged that I live in a place and a time that I get to more or less live how I want. Yeah, happy that I get to chase happiness in that way, and I wish more people felt free to make up their own rules a little bit more of the time." Sam, a 30-year-old queer genderqueer person, agreed, explaining, "I'm not normal. I feel like I'm living a life how I want to live it; I'm not being constrained by rules and how you're supposed to be. That's who I am; that makes me happy." Indeed, most LGBQ people said an important benefit of queerness was the freedom to make your life according to your own vision, not one that is predetermined. According to Emma, a 27-year-old gay cis woman,

> We have explicitly said we're not normal or traditional, so we can write the script ourselves. We don't have to buy into this belief that the guy is gonna be kinda dopey but well-meaning and enjoy sports and the woman is gonna withhold sex and demand to have things paid for. And that feels really, really good to say we don't have to buy into this bullshit; let's craft our own relationship.

This individualism is a key element of queer culture in which people position themselves as free from societal constraints and instead draw on a "'be true to yourself' philosophy."[8] Only one person expressed any resentment over not having a script to follow, although even he acknowledged the constraints that came with heterosexual scripts. Charlie, a 32-year-old queer trans man, said, "I would definitely like to have some role models. Sometimes I feel it's so unfair I have to figure all this shit out for myself. I feel like I'm this total freak or something. Not that I want to be heterosexual necessarily, just having some benefits of it. But I could see also the harm, I think, of getting locked into that as well."

Similar to Charlie, Riley, 29, a lesbian trans man,[9] discussed how there were benefits to normativity. Riley was engaged to a queer cis woman and they had just bought a house together, no small financial feat in Oakland, California. They were in a monogamous relationship and talking about having two children. Both were in professional fields. Discussing his life, Riley said, "Like how fucking radical is that?" Riley stated that his life no longer felt outside the norm and he felt some loss over that, but also said, "Sometimes it's really comforting, you know, that I'm like, this is just life now. Like it's not a fight. It's not a struggle as much." Thus, while the majority of LGBQ people discussed strongly rejecting heterosexual relationship norms, Charlie and Riley were able to see some value in a life where they didn't feel as though they were constantly swimming against the tide. Interestingly, both Charlie and Riley reported facing greater challenges as LGBTQ-identified individuals than the rest of the sample. Charlie grew up trans in the rural South and Riley was rejected by his family of origin. Thus, a wholehearted dismissal of normativity could potentially be linked to greater family and community support, making people feel freer to break the mold in their personal relationships.

SEXIST SCRIPTS

Like Alek, who opened this chapter, when other LGBQ people discussed the constraints of heterosexual dating scripts, they almost exclusively referenced the limits placed on heterosexual *women*. They viewed the scripts as not only too rigid but also as sexist in that they were more disadvantageous to and obligatory for women than men. Jamie, a 30-year-old queer cis woman, reflected on a conversation with a heterosexual woman:

> I remember talking to a friend who's also 30 and single. . . . She was interested in a guy and she'd be waiting for this person to ask her out. And I'm like, "Why don't you just ask him out for lunch or something?" She's like, "I could never do that, like that's completely inappropriate." People who are straight are really stuck in societal expectations where they're so rigid they can't move out of it.

Because relationship and courtship norms are built on gender inequality, broader discussions about rejecting norms often included critiques of gender norms. While heterosexual men and women faced strong pressures to engage in heterosexual dating scripts, LGBQ individuals often expressed the opposite, indicating that there was an explicit pressure to *avoid* gendered dating scripts. Rather, those who subscribed to normative gendered behaviors might be openly taken to task. Ella, a 26-year-old gay cis woman, said,

> Even the butch-femme thing is antiquated. When I date women my own age, it's very much like I don't ascribe to butch or femme. I was at this music festival where there was this big fight because someone called someone else a floppy-eared butch. Basically implying she wasn't butch enough. And there were genderqueer people there and trans people and they were so upset at this one old butch woman who called this girl a floppy-eared butch because they were like, "We don't buy into that anymore, you know?"

Those who were read as heterosexual when out with their partners felt uncomfortable being viewed and treated as heteronormative, even by strangers. Lauren, a 29-year-old queer cis woman, dated a trans man and didn't feel that they took on gender roles in their relationship. However, others treated them as though they did. She said of her former partner,

> He was uncomfortable with gender roles. When we were in public, we were read as a hetero couple. He didn't like that. That was really uncomfortable for him to have that privilege all of a sudden. Before he transitioned, he was sort of a freak. That's how he felt and that's how people responded to him. As soon as he transitioned, he all of a sudden had white male privilege. He was like, "Oh my God, this is insane!" Like when we would go out to eat, waiters would talk to him and not look at me because he was the man at the table. He didn't like that. That made him feel really uncomfortable. He felt like he lost himself. I was so femme and he passed so well. No one ever questioned.

Emma discussed her comfort level with different terminology and how it reflected her queer identity:

> I was never really comfortable calling [a former partner] my boyfriend. I used to call him my partner a lot partly because I really identified with being a bi woman and I didn't like that it looked like I was just in this heterosexual relationship and like anybody looking at me would assume I was just a straight person and had no idea that I also really like women. . . . But then I

really, really like calling my girlfriend now my girlfriend and she calls me her "partner" 'cause she think that conveys the seriousness of it. And I like "girl-friend" because it's clear to people right away that I'm dating a girl.

The relatively young ages of the respondents and widespread repudia-tion of gender norms indicates a generational shift in what is expected in LGBQ relationships. As Ella discussed, in contrast to her relationships with older women, when she dated women her own age there was an expectation that the relationship be free of gender norms. But these expec-tations also reflected microregional community expectations. A number of people expressed their sense that San Francisco held the more conserv-ative gays and lesbians, while Oakland was home to more radical queers. Jen explained, "When we go to Frisco, that community tends to just be more butch-femme. Although you have your people of course who fall out-side of that. But there's more butch-femme versus Oakland, which actu-ally tends to be a little bit more queer." As a result, she sometimes felt her identity was misunderstood when she went out in San Francisco, given the rigidity she saw in lesbian communities organized around butch-femme dynamics: "I am a feminine-identified woman, but I identify as a butch queen. Which means that I sometimes look butch, I dress butch, but I'm actually femme. So it's like butch on the outside and femme on the inside." Yet she felt that in San Francisco you had to "either be butch or be femme." Jen said, in San Francisco "I see a lot of phobias. I see bi phobia, I see trans phobia. It's like if you're gonna be a lesbian, be a lesbian, but you can't date women and date men. I know from lesbians, they're just like that's nasty, you're bringing disease into the community. You can't be a switch hitter. It's looked at as slutty." On the other hand, she explained that the queer community in Oakland looked down on the butch-femme dynamics of the lesbian community in San Francisco: "Oh, you're butch-femme. Well, you're just enforcing the heteronormative patriarchal oppressive thing."

Queer spaces often give rise to a "queernormativity" premised on an "alternative respectability" that dictates how to be the "right" kind of queer.[10] Thus, despite the assertion by LGBQ people that they could write their own scripts, community-level pressures provided guidelines for how relationships should look. These expectations were highly localized, as respondents discussed the different expectations that came from different groups of people. Because the LGBQ people I interviewed were more heavily skewed toward those who identified as queer, they were also more likely to express a resistance to gendered behaviors. Not only did this align with their understandings of themselves, but they were also aware of the condemnation that comes with being too mainstream. This meant that many LGBQ people worked hard to resist conventional dating practices and remake dates as more egalitarian.

REMAKING THE DATE

Part of rejecting heterosexual dating scripts was an emphasis on egalitarian, nongendered dating practices. There were no rules over who should ask for dates, who should contact the other person first after a date, or who should pay for a date. Indeed, when I asked this question, it was frequently met with confusion and questions such as, "What do you mean by rules?" For example, when I asked Adah if they tended to initiate contact after a first date or preferred to let the other person contact them, they asked, "Do I like the person?" After I replied in the affirmative, they said, "If I like the person, I probably will let them know right away." This is in direct contrast to the narrative of the heterosexual "game" in which a woman must play hard to get to generate a man's interest, a man lives for the thrill of the chase, and an easy "catch" is a turn-off.[11]

Instead, LGBQ people said that engaging in "direct communication" was a crucial relationship practice. Assertiveness by either interested party was a positive trait, and the idea that one partner should make all the effort was a turn-off. As Jack, a 25-year-old gay cis man, said, "If they're not going to give me signs that they're a communicator, that kind of is a turn-off to me. I don't like it when people wait for me to constantly initiate any kind of text message or phone call. . . . It's like tying your shoes. You have to have good house training." Still, many people struggled with making the first move. Sam, for example, explained that they preferred to be approached. However, in their most recent partnership, they had decided to go outside their comfort zone in order to break the habit of ending up with people in whom they weren't particularly interested. The results were positive. As Sam said,

One of the things that I like about this thing [with my current partner] is that I was the one who approached her; I started it. So it's kind of like I liked you, I went for you, and I got you, and that feels kind of cool. In a way, since I am on a streak of getting involved with people that I want to be involved with, I feel like I should take that step to be more outgoing and reaching out to people. It's hard for me, it's not in my nature, I prefer to be approached. Why? I don't know, it's easier and it just feels kind of nice. Then I can choose yes or no.

Emma also shifted her attitude beyond the pursued/pursuer binary when she stopped dating men and started dating women. She explained,

Historically in my life I was always the one to be approached. I liked the idea of having the guy chase me and being the more disengaged one. And then I realized that if I like a girl, I want to tell her and say, "This is what I'm feeling, do you feel the same way?" I realized that it's kind of screwed up to want to be the prize woman. And it's not healthy to have this sort of expectation that you'll fall all over yourself trying to impress me and like win me over and making grand gestures.

Thus, it wasn't that LGBQ people didn't get shy or nervous asking for dates, or find pleasure in being pursued, but rather that they were more likely to acknowledge the relationship patterns created by certain practices. In Sam's case, this was ending up with partners without a mutual level of interest and attraction. For Jack, it was about good and equal communication. And Emma didn't like the gendered connotations of wanting to be chased. By acknowledging how the behaviors in which they were engaging related to particular undesirable outcomes, they were more willing to self-reflect and then challenge their default expectations and actions.

In addition, almost everyone stated that dates were paid for either by splitting the check or taking turns. Nicholas, a 36-year-old gay cis man, said about paying for dates, "Always Dutch the first time. Always Dutch probably the first few times. Sometimes the guy wants to pay, if I'm with somebody who makes more money, and I'm like no. . . . You know, it's like, I don't know you well enough so why would I want to do that?" Patricio, a 25-year-old queer nonbinary person, said, "We always split," but was also attempting to move away from dates that involve money at all, explaining, "Lately I've just been like, let's not pay. Let's just do something that doesn't involve having to pay. It's really dope and it works out really well." This way, they focused on doing a fun activity, such as a hike or a free concert, investing time and energy rather than money as an indicator of interest. This made space to interact with and find a broader range of attractive people, as the ability to pay wasn't being used to weed out potential partners. Almost no one indicated that this led to an awkward conversation or a decline in interest on either party's part. Tina, a 27-year-old bisexual cis woman said, "It's not even an issue because that's mostly a heterosexual thing."

Only a couple of LGBQ people said that their default was to expect to pay on the first date. Amit, a 27-year-old queer cis man, said, "For the most part I pay . . . I don't feel like it's expected of me. It's something I *like* to do." Interestingly, all the respondents who said this were cis men. Just like Amit, while they were often very critical of gender norms in other aspects of their lives, this norm went unquestioned and was portrayed as a nongendered practice. Amit, for example, explained that his interest in paying was connected to his desire to choose the location of the dates so that he could pick a restaurant "with good politics and good sourcing," thereby turning payment into a progressive political act.

But for the most part, there was discomfort with heterosexual payment scripts and a sense that these practices were disempowering to the recipient of the largesse and potentially exploitative of the one paying. Jamie said,

> Often the other person would pay. It was fun at first when they would pay, but then it felt like I didn't have any power, like there was a power dynamic where they insisted, and I didn't have a voice in being able to pay. After a while it would feel frustrating. And I don't want them to assume that I owe them something whether sexually or otherwise if they keep paying for dinner. It made me feel vulnerable and like I had very little power.

Kylie, 29, a queer cis woman, agreed: "I'm not gonna pay for somebody's meal. I think it's like creepy and presumptuous and like somebody owing you. And whenever I hear about people buying, I just kind of think of it that way, it just icks me out a bit." Lauren found that the people she dated appreciated going Dutch rather than seeing it as a negative. As she said, "I would just take my card out and be like, 'Let's just split it.' I've had

people actually tell me they're happy about that. . . . I'm like, 'I'm not asking anyone to pay for my shit.'" Unlike heterosexual women who see
benevolent sexism as a practice with benefits for them or who emphasize
their engagement with it as an individual preference,[12] LGBQ respondents connected these practices to broader power dynamics in relationships. The one who paid was also, in effect, buying a certain level of control in the relationship. This attitude was similar to that expressed around
initiation of dates. Rather than view these practices as disconnected from
social inequalities, LGBQ people were more willing and able to apply a
critical lens to how they might reflect and promote inequalities between
partners.

As people became more socially aware, they shifted away from the conventional practices they had previously embraced. Emma, who initially
liked to be pursued, had changed her attitude on payment of dates as well,
as she rethought her expectations for romantic relationships. Of an early
relationship with a man she said, "He paid. I manipulated him into asking
me out by being like, 'Nobody takes me on a date. Why do boys blah blah
blah?' Which is just real, real shady. So it started with manipulation and
kind of joking, but then during it was clear that it was a real date and like
he paid for the cab to the restaurant and stuff." Later she moved away from
this practice as she stopped identifying with heterosexual dating scripts,
started dating women, and wanted more balanced expectations for each
partner.

When one person did cover the cost of the entire date, the gesture was
still presented and interpreted through an egalitarian lens. For example,
Caitlin, a 30-year-old gay cis woman, said of a partner who insisted on
paying for their date,

> My preference is always to split unless there's a big occasion or something
> like that. But I think I justified it as I was living in San Francisco and I had
> just come down. She goes to Stanford and I had come down to Palo Alto to
> see her and so the justification was that she was gonna pay 'cause I came
> down. Next time I could pay when she came up. That kind of thing.

Tina explained how a woman she was dating turned swapping payment
into a romantic sentiment rather than something negative: "She really
liked to have just one person pay rather than split, so we would switch off

that way and she said it was just because it meant we would see each other again because the debt was never quite settled. I liked that a lot."

Yet at the same time, for a few there was an emphasis on splitting the costs of dates symbolically rather than equally, in a manner very similar to heterosexuals. This was much more common when there was a large difference in income between the partners. Melanie, a 29-year-old queer cis woman, explained how paying for dates changed over the course of her relationship: "Early dates I was like pretty adamant about wanting to split everything. . . . Later on, it definitely shifted and like he like clearly was making a lot more money than I was. And so we would more like symbolically split things. Like he would pay for like something more expensive and then if I took us to dinner it would be like tacos." For Melanie, this was a way to maintain a semblance of equality in her dating practices, even though she couldn't afford to pay for the more expensive activities. This differed from heterosexual women, who viewed this practice more as a way to chip in while still maintaining and enforcing the expectation that men will pay for dates. Yet Melanie also challenged the payment norms. Rather than expect her partner, a heterosexual man, to pay early on to test his commitment, she insisted on splitting payment from the start to make clear her expectations for an equal relationship. Only after that pattern was established was she willing to allow him to cover more of the dating expenses. In sum, the emphasis among LGBQ people was on creating egalitarian relationship expectations from the start of a dating relationship.

PICKING PARTNERS

LGBQ people were also attuned to other ways that social inequalities might affect their romantic relationships (as well as the world more broadly), which was reflected in how they discussed whom they wanted as partners. This is partially the result of a diverse sample of LGBQ respondents, which included more brown and black people and people from working-class backgrounds than the sample of heterosexual respondents. White people, both heterosexual and LGBQ, almost never mentioned race except to allude to being more attracted to other white people. And very few upper-middle-class people throughout the whole sample discussed social class; rather, they focused on individual traits, such as ambition and having a work ethic, that they related to economic success. Among LGBQ people, there was also more discussion on how normative gendered expectations should be challenged as well. Still, some of the respondents perpetuated inequalities through their mate selection practices.

The role of race in intimate relationships loomed large in the narratives of LGBQ people of color. Among heterosexual women of color, only a few mentioned race and then only to distance themselves from the men in their racial group, whom they deemed overly conservative and who they worried would prevent their own self-development projects.[13] And a few heterosexual Asian men discussed being deemed "unattractive" when compared to masculine appearance norms. However, LGBQ people, in particular queer and trans people of color, spoke openly about the importance of race to their partnerships. In particular, they felt that dating other people of color gave them important support and reference points that were missing from their relationships with white people. Jamie, who identified as Chicana, spoke of why she was so attracted to a former partner: "She's Latina and she mostly only spoke Spanish. I thought that was really attractive. I just felt like we could possibly share something culturally that I hadn't been able to share with other partners."

Speaking of what drew her to her fiancée, Jamie said, "So I remember on our second date, she invited me to a café to read poetry with her. Which I thought was so romantic. But to read these poetry books of queer Chicana poets like Gloria Anzaldua and Cherrie Moraga. And I had never been able to share that with anybody and that felt really significant to me." Explaining why the relationship became more serious, she said, "There were so many things that I felt like I had to compromise in other relationships, like whether it was my politics, being with somebody that didn't politically align with my own beliefs. Or culturally being with somebody that didn't have the same cultural upbringing as me. . . . I just felt like I didn't really want to waste time with other people."

Amit also searched out partners of color, specifically relocating for this purpose: "When I moved to the Bay, I moved here to meet radical South Asians, like radical queer South Asians and to do work with them. When I met [a former partner], we had this moment like, 'You're brown. I'm brown. Let's be friends.'" As Melanie, who was biracial black and Asian, explained, being with a person of color meant someone with shared experiences. Melanie distinguished between her relationships with people of color versus those with white people, discussing the difference between two of her former partners:

> So Reyna is also half black and half Asian. Katey is white. A really, really hard part of our relationship was our conversations and arguments around race and class. She also grew up very wealthy. And Reyna is half black and half Asian. And grew up with kind of a crazy parent situation. Parents who didn't really parent her and grew up without a ton of money. And so I really loved that those things became nonissues in our relationship. Like we didn't talk about race and we didn't talk about class, because we didn't have to. Like those were things we understood about each other. Which was incredible.

But loving a person of color could also be understood as a potentially radical act, given how beauty norms are constructed. As Patricia Hill Collins argues, loving a black woman undermines the dominant narratives that position them as unattractive and unappealing partners.[14] Jen, who identified as biracial black and white, took a similar perspective when she discussed loving a former partner whose identity she felt had been devalued: "She was just this lesbian brown girl who loved basketball, down to earth, and I wanted to love her for who she was. I wanted to validate who she was naturally because to me it was a beautiful thing." But Jen also tied her admiration to her partner's gender presentation, saying, "You know, to be a masculine woman is a beautiful thing and her family didn't really support that." There was an awareness among many that standards of attraction privilege certain racial and ethnic groups and gender presentations over others and many tried to recognize and resist when they saw these preferences in themselves. Santiago, a 34-year-old queer trans person, struggled with being more attracted to white people, while acknowledging the challenges that came from dating white people:

> You know, it's funny, like 97 percent of my friends are people of color. I became fairly politicized in QTPOC[15] spaces and yet I still keep dating white trans guys. There's a lot of reasons—I think there's the internal stuff in me, like oh am I not attracted to people of color? Am I not attracted to Asians? There's all this internalized racism around standards of beauty. All of [my partners] are generally white, skinnier, trans masculine, men. So what's wrong with me, I'm just attracted to the white men?

While Santiago reflected on whom they were attracted to in a critical manner, they also realized that dating white people meant an inability on the part of their partners to always understand their perspective on race and discrimination, including "the complications around the daily ways I experience invisibility and things like that."

Like Santiago, other LGBQ people also openly discussed excluding partners by race and favoring white people. This is not to say that heterosexual men and women didn't do this, but rather to emphasize how much more explicit LGBQ people were about discussing their preferences. For example, while heterosexual men and women spoke in more veiled terms about racial preferences, saying things such as, "I prefer blonde hair and blue eyes," LGBQ people specifically noted which racial groups they were attracted to or not. Jocelyn, a 36-year-old bisexual trans woman, said, "I'm not so into Asian guys or Indian guys. I'm not so into Hispanic guys either. They tend to be short. I like my men to be as tall as me or taller. I definitely like black guys. That's a plus." Gay cis men, especially, were open in these discussions.[16] But others were more critical of this attitude. Brian said, "I feel like I get suspicious when people say that there are certain races they're attracted to in the sense that I feel like there are so many different characteristics between people of the same race. It's like, there are some black guys I'm attracted to and some I'm not. Same with Asian guys, you know?" This sexual racism was especially apparent to people of color who had to contend with these preferences and often felt left out of the dating market as a result. Ken, a 33-year-old gay cis man, discussed the challenge of finding gay men who were willing to be with a black man. When I asked how he screened potential partners on the basis of their online dating profiles, he explained,

> There's a lot of guys whose profiles say white or Latino only, or white and Asian only, white only. So I have to go through and weed all that shit out so that's pretty much unfortunately probably the number one thing that I look for—are they open to different types of guys? I'm athletic, I do good fun things, but a lot of times people really don't see past color, so being able to assess whether they are going to be willing to date or go out with a black guy is huge. It's caused a lot of ire in my life.

While there was a great deal of awareness around the significance of race in romantic relationships, in most cases anything more than a surface-

level acknowledgment and an actual willingness to challenge racial inequalities was limited to people of color.

Still, for many, an engagement with social issues was a necessity in their
partners, once again in line with seeing themselves as constructing lives
outside of the complacent norm. Andie, a 27-year-old gay genderqueer
person, said she wanted someone who was "thoughtful about the world."
Sam wanted someone who was "socially aware" and found that dating an
activist opened a door of awareness for them, enabling them to see "things
outside the matrix." Adah discussed how similar politics made them more
attracted to a partner:

> I think the political stuff is important because there was a lot of explaining
> we didn't have to do with each other. . . . If some man was like fucked up to
> me in the world and I went home and talked to my partner about it, he
> understood what I was talking about. I didn't have to justify or explain. Or
> if something clearly racist happened, or if we were like both devastated at
> whatever atrocity is happening in the world today, we were on the same
> page. There was something really comforting there.

Similar to an understanding and awareness of racial inequality, finding a
partner who was socially aware gave LGBQ people an important source of
support and commonality in a discriminatory world and helped them find
partners who were similarly averse to living a normative life.

A QUEER AESTHETIC

LGBQ people also discussed cultivating a queer aesthetic that would be
desirable to the people they were trying to attract and clearly mark them
as queer. Ella said,

> So like normally in the old days I would definitely get femmed up and like
> look really, you know, maybe even put on some makeup, at least do my hair
> and wear cute clothes. But lately I've been trying to look more natural and
> normal. And just like how you might see me in the every day 'cause I don't
> wear makeup usually. I've been growing out my armpit hair. I think it's
> queer and fun and like feminist. So I want them to be able to see that. I used
> to really care if an outfit was flattering and now I'm like, I want them to see
> me as I am.

In fact, the politics of hair came up quite a bit in the interviews, as people sought ways of distinguishing themselves from heterosexual cis women. Adah explained, "I feel the most 'me' when I'm pretty bald. So these days I usually shave my head like once a week and that's important. I feel comfortable. . . . I feel like it reflects something core about my gender that even though it's always changing, there's something that's really like non-normative about having a shaved head. I'm like not a normative person—like you may as well know that right away, world." Jamie also changed her appearance to be read as queer: "I think that this coincides with me being embraced more in a queer community, and so I started dressing what I interpret as being more visibly queer, because I'm feminine presenting I always feel like I'm read as being straight. And so having like an asymmetrical haircut was something that I did."

While many discussed embracing a queer aesthetic to mark themselves as queer, some also brought up how they subtly shifted their appearance in response to their partners. Santiago discussed how they changed their appearance to fit the preferences of a partner:

His history is with more feminine women, like he was into boys for sure. His current partner is like tomboy femme, but she's definitely like a more femme woman who wears dresses and skirts and is comfortable with that, but she's also like ragged and stuff. Before that was also like the similar tomboy femme stuff. So I was definitely more in the transmasculine spectrum [than his previous partners] so I think he did like it when I shaved or wore something more feminine and I had boobs back then, so it was a different experience. He was really into my tits and things like that.

As Santiago explained, "I've always played with gender; my gender is definitely gender variant. So no, I didn't do anything against my desires or whatever, but I played with things. But it wasn't necessarily what I needed for myself." While Santiago said they never felt forced to remake their appearance to please a partner, they did find themselves emulating the gender presentation they felt would be most attractive to a partner. Evan, a 27-year-old gay cis man, said of getting ready for a date, "I'm trying not to trim my body hair as much. I'm finding smooth guys like hairy guys so I like smooth, because I'm hairy. And they like me." These beliefs relied heavily on the notion that people wanted at least some form of gender complementarity in their relationships. Adah made a similar point:

I make assumptions based on what I know about people and their preferences in the past. So I mean it's oversimplifying it, especially because so
many people I date are like gender-fucker weirdos. But I think if I see someone who presents in a pretty masculine way and I know that the last couple
of people they dated have presented in pretty feminine ways, that that might
influence me to want to look a little bit more femme for them. Then sometimes I have a defiant day where I'm like oh, you really like me the way I am?
Well I feel really masculine today and this is how I'm going to look and so
what do you think? Can you hang?

While the expectation was that queer people could challenge and
remake normative expectations, they still faced pressures to present a certain way within their communities and frequently struggled with having
their appearance fetishized. Sean, a 26-year-old gay cis man, discussed
both the challenges and opportunities that come with being a bit heavier:
"Sometimes bigger is more of a hindrance. But then again there's the bear
culture.[17] So when I got to a certain point [in my weight], it's like I got
more attention. That made me more self-conscious because it's like I'm
obviously big enough to be a bear now." Kylie, too, felt boxed in by appearance norms, although more by heterosexual cis men than by LGBQ people.
Explaining how she crafted her OkCupid profile, she said, "I recently reno-
vated. Somewhat more successfully. I had to put 'gender nonconforming,'
which is not something I necessarily—it's hard. The descriptor fits, but is
not something that I agree with per se. I think it's just a problem of, I just
wish, I just feel like 'women' should include me. And so I don't feel like I'm
nonconforming." When I asked her why she felt she couldn't just list her
gender identity as 'woman,' she said, "Beyond getting snarky messages like,
'Why does yours say woman?' . . . Yeah, so that's a bummer. . . . It's like the
categories they care about mean nothing to me." As she explained, she was
open to sex and relationships with people with a range of gender identities,
yet found herself questioned and rejected as misrepresenting herself by
heterosexual men who expected a feminine-presenting woman.

But appearance norms certainly were enforced by LGBQ people as
well. Kylie explained the challenges of getting the queer aesthetic right: "I
feel like it's very, very segmented in that way and so it's weird because if we
present too yuppie to like someone in social justice, they judge you. If you
present too—I just constantly feel like I'm kind of giving off some sort of

vibe that doesn't—I don't know." Sean said, "The lesson you learn in the gay world is that appearance is everything. And I'm sort of consciously averse to that. Which is one reason I've distanced myself from the community. I don't go to the Castro[18] very often and all that." Yet even Sean admitted to being influenced by these appearance norms: "But at the same time, I naturally am attracted to these idyllic visions, which is annoying to know that about yourself." Evan also said he often rejected men for very small imperfections: "Mostly I don't want to see guys again. I'm an awful person when it comes to this. There'll be this one thing and I'm like, 'Ugh. He was too hairy there.' Or 'I don't like his tooth.' Picky bitch, that's me." Thus, while LGBQ people sought partners outside of heteronormative constraints, they also frequently confronted, or enforced, alternative norms that were similarly constraining and often heavily gendered.

REIMAGINING SEX

Rather than regulate their sex lives with guidelines, most LGBQ people focused on having sex when the time felt right, or simply because they wanted to have sex. This could be in the context of a burgeoning relationship or a casual encounter. Compared to heterosexual men and women, less focus was placed on what the sex "meant." Certainly there was less judgment of and concern about sex outside the context of a committed relationship. Lauren said, "I don't have an attachment effect in the way that I have heard other people do, in terms of it being something sacred that you only do with someone you're in a relationship with or you would only do that with someone you see potential with. I like to have sex. If I'm comfortable, if I feel safe enough, I feel fine doing that." Adah preferred to have sex in committed relationships but still expressed their perspective that it's okay to have sex in any context: "Sometimes things just feel like magic and fun and right." Instead of following particular rules on when it's appropriate to have sex, they said, "I think it's different every time—when it feels right." Karina, a 37-year-old queer cis woman, said, "It just happens. I don't predict that I will be aroused in twenty minutes." Sam had a similar perspective. When I asked them under what circumstances they'd be willing to have sex with someone they'd just met, they said, "Any circumstances."

Only a few people were conservative in their approach to sex. Emma said, "Sex has always felt like kind of a big deal to me, and despite what my mom says, it feels really intimate and kind of vulnerable to show that side of yourself to somebody, and to be that up-close and personal with a stranger's body has never felt right for me." While her mother had encouraged her to explore her sexual desires in whatever manner she saw fit, Emma preferred to have sex in committed relationships.

There was a wide range in how assertive people were willing to be when seeking or initiating sex; some were very aggressive and upfront and others waited for the other person to make the first move. Tina said, "We were mutually into it. So I felt like she would initiate some of the time, I would initiate some of the time. I never felt like I was being needy or desperate, you know, and initiating as often as I was." But she was reluctant to initiate the first sexual encounter, saying, "There have been many dates where if the other person hadn't made the first move, nothing would have happened physically." Patricio said they pursued sex "negotiation style. Hey, like you hit me up via cruising, like let's have this negotiation. . . . Is this a possibility? Should we not?" Evan was very direct and discussed all the online apps he used to find partners for sex: "Nude Dudes. Manhunt. Grindr." He described his profile: "Top seeking NSA [no strings attached] fun. Hot, smooth, young, white bottoms. Profiles are pretty short. . . . I do do profiles a little bit longer. . . . Naked videos and pictures of me. Me fucking. Me jacking off. And then that attracts a lot of guys." He expects the same from a potential partner: "Be forward with me. I'm really forward. You want to fuck? Let's fuck." Still, Evan said he would be less direct with a potential dating partner than with a sexual partner. He explained, "If you're actually properly dating, I don't bring up sexual positions [when arranging the date]. If I'm meeting somebody to go out on a date and we are fucking, *then* I'll bring up sexual positions needed or wanted. Things I like to do. Common interests." In this, he expressed a sentiment similar to heterosexual men and women—that if you're interested in a relationship, you shouldn't be as explicitly sexual right away.

While heterosexual people of course also engage in casual sex, there was less stigma among LGBQ people, as for the most part they refrained from judging their partners for their past sexual behaviors. In contrast to heterosexuals, there was very little discussion over the number of previous partners. Karina didn't care to hear about former partners, saying, "No, it's pretty easy for me to detach myself from trying to imagine what they did, because this person's right here." Riley said, "I mean, we've all had a history before we got here, right? I've done things and she's done things, but we're here now." In fact, rather than limit the number of former partners, people preferred those who had sexual experience, knew what they wanted, and knew what they were doing. Tina said, "In fact, I find it kind of exciting when people have a lot of sexual experience. I think maybe I can learn something new from them. Or that they'll be like really good in bed." Ella made a similar point: "I prefer they're experienced. They have more sexual experience. I mean I had one experience with a woman who was inexperienced and that was boring, it sucked, and she wasn't really willing to reciprocate. Not that that would be all inexperienced women, but I prefer that they've had sex with women, good sex with women, know that they want to be with women." Samuel, a 37-year-old gay cis man, also made the connection between openly identifying as LGBQ and good, exciting sex:

> If someone is recently out or never had sex with a gay man before, I would not want to break someone in. . . . I live in the Castro. I indulge in a lot of fetish behavior, and I have seen a lot of stuff that many gay men haven't, and I'm not even that far gay. Like there are some men who are way campier gay than I am. So if someone is not comfortable with their own sexuality or feels too conservative, that's a turn-off.

Still, in a few instances this directness and openness to sex, and casual sex in particular, made people feel uncomfortable. Those who didn't engage in casual sex felt somewhat alienated from gay life, as they felt outside the norm and in some cases struggled to find partners. For example, Jack said,

> Like when I moved to San Francisco, there's an Olympic fucking community here that I'm just so divorced from. I have to take a Klonopin[19] like hearing about some of this shit. It's like I'm such a buttoned-up person. When I talk to gay people here, it's like they know the ingredients that are in their lube, which condoms feel the best. It's like they just really understand all the angles of it. And they can go for hours.

He went on, "Like I can't date in the Castro. Like that's a very ossified gay community here. It's very starched in a mind-set that's like sexually liberal, very, very forwardly progressive. . . . I think it's very shallow. . . . I can't deal with people who are just all about sex. And I find that a lot here." Marco, a 30-year-old gay cis man, had a similar perspective, discussing how he felt when he was still dating: "I was really feeling myself in critique of the gay community. I found myself really hesitant to want to hook up with guys who I felt were all about consuming as many sexual partners as they could." Marco explained that he didn't have a problem with casual sex per se but didn't like the way it was approached by many gay men as sport. Indeed, this critique was only brought up by gay cis men.

Connected to the lack of judgment about sex, particular emphasis was placed on being experimental and imaginative during sex.[20] Over and over again, people told me that this was what made their sex lives good with partners. Tina said, "She's very spontaneous and I was excited about how experimental a lot of the sex we had was. But it was also very tender too." Sam discussed two different partners and what made the sex so good with each of them. One partner was very adventurous. As Sam said, "We went to like the student center, and to answer your question, I don't remember who made the first move, but it was on a pool table. It was like on the second floor, but you could look down to the first floor—yeah, but she fucked me on the pool table. That's when I was like, you're so awesome." Of another partner, they explained, "She was like oh, do you want to go to this sex party, it's an all-women sex party? I was like, what? She was all into these things. . . . This one was at someone's house and there were toys and there was some kink involved." Manuela, a 36-year-old queer genderqueer person, said, "A turn-on definitely is to be really creative or exploring kink."

By contrast, sex was deemed not good or less than ideal when it was not experimental. For example, Jocelyn said what she liked least about a former relationship was the sex: "She wasn't—or she didn't have much libido when we were together and she wasn't that into trying new stuff. Not very adventurous. 'Cause she had her own issues with being closed off about sex and so, yeah." Sam said, "Sex life was good, I just—it sounds horrible, but I had had better sex. Like it wasn't terrible, it wasn't bad, it was mediocre, but it was missing that—yeah, like punch if you will. . . . I felt like she was very vanilla." Indeed, at least an openness to trying new things was seen as important. Emma said, "Like I think I'm open enough that I would say if

this is really, really important to you in terms of sex, like I'll see how comfortable I am, let's see what we can work out together. But yeah, there's no
behavior I can think of that would be absolutely we're done." Riley, too,
connected variety in sex to communication and the need for partners to
work out what they wanted during sex: "We have so many options, too,
so there's always communication about like, well, what do you want to do?
Which is awesome." Tina saw herself as distinct from her heterosexual
friends, in particular noting how their norms and behaviors around sex
were very different: "I think I've been more promiscuous than them and
probably more into weird sex than they are." Again, queer sex was positioned as more experimental and queer people as less judgmental.

In spite of the desire to break out of rigid standards of behavior, there
was quite a bit of pigeonholing around sexual practices. Some embraced
this, while others felt frustrated by the boundaries constructed by others.
Evan was okay with it, describing himself as a "top" and declaring San
Francisco "a city of bottoms."[21] As he explained, "One of my phrases is
'young and smooth' or 'smooth and tight.' It's got to be tight. Or, like it's got
to be smooth. I'm all about a smooth hole and my friends just know me as
this pervy top—I like smooth assholes." In fact, in spite of Evan's claim
about San Francisco, most of the gay men I interviewed saw themselves as
versatile and wished those men who wanted to exclusively top would be
more open to alternating topping and bottoming. Jen saw exclusive "topping" as a power play that she wanted no part of, saying of a woman, "So I
went over to her house and we hung out all day and then we decided to
have sex and then I'm naked and then she's like, 'Okay, I'm gonna fuck you,
but you're not gonna fuck me back.' That was a deal breaker. So basically
that kind of power dynamic where you get to do me, but I don't get to do
you back does not work." Nicholas expressed the same sentiment when
discussing an ex-boyfriend: "I broke it off. And I broke it off because of the
sex. The difference of him being 80 percent top and 20 percent bottom,
and I didn't feel comfortable asking him to do something that he wasn't.
He wasn't really a bottom; I don't want to force somebody." Instead, he
preferred a more reciprocal sexual relationship.

Sean and Kylie resented that their appearances seemed to dictate how
others understood them as potential sexual partners. Sean, who found
himself fetishized as a bear, said that when men simply wanted to have sex

with him rather than start a relationship, they wrote "Woof!" "That sort of dumbfounded me when it happened the first time. It just means I like the way you look. Or you seem like a big burly man that I like, I guess is what it means." As he said, he, like Jack, tended to avoid the Castro as a result, especially because he was more interested in a committed relationship. Kylie, a queer cis woman, was frustrated that she was frequently treated as gender nonconforming and thus not seen as a potential partner for het-erosexual men. "I mean I absolutely love scrawny little straight men who I can totally bend over." However, the heterosexual men seeking partners online didn't view her as sufficiently feminine and refused to be open to her as a potential partner.

Jocelyn, a trans woman,[22] explained that there was a period where she couldn't get any dates online because the only people who were contacting her were those she called "tranny chasers." As she explained,

> So with porn, there's this sort of image that's put up there where trans women are dominant and they're going to be the dominant one in the rela-tionship. So guys want you to fuck them, they want you to like come all over them, like that's the specific type of guy that comes looking for that. But it's this image that's in porn; it's not really very realistic. There's a few trans women who are like that, but like when you take a testosterone blocker, it changes everything. First of all, you're sterile, you can hardly get an erec-tion, like just for me everything changed. And so I physically couldn't do all these things. And most of my friends couldn't do them either, my trans friends.

As she said, the cis men contacting her identified as straight, which didn't feel right to her. She felt fetishized through porn images, sought out by straight men who simply wanted one thing from her, and she struggled to find more enjoyable and mutual sex and partnerships. As a result, she had very few sexual partners for a while.

"DON'T SAY WE ARE ONE; WE'RE TWO PEOPLE"

The overarching ambivalence to marriage discussed in chapter 2 did not, for the most part, translate to an ambivalence to long-term commitment or the desire for a life partner. It was simply that LGBQ people wanted to construct their partnerships on their own terms rather than through the expectations of normative relationships. Evan was one of the few who was avoiding long-term commitment for the time being: "I don't do that. My whole mantra right now is whatever's meant to be is meant to be. I don't need to force—for some reason, I need to force sex—but, I don't need to force a relationship. I don't have to force dating. I'm a catch. Whatever falls at my feet . . . and if it works, it works." He explicitly compared his approach to that of heterosexual women: "My girlfriends are so desperate seeming and it's not cute because they seem desperate. And they seem to want a relationship so bad, and I'm like, 'Ugh. Just go along in life and see what happens.'"

Part of the resistance to marriage was reflected in how LGBQ people made sense of companionship. In particular, they worried about losing their independence and personal space, given the expectations that come along with settling down together. Kylie said of a former partner, "I finally got my own apartment and then it just kind of became the assumed thing I guess that she was gonna move in. I think she more assumed and I was just kinda like, sure, yeah, sure. So I would say it was a foolish lack of speaking. It's not that I didn't want her to move in; I just didn't really reflect on it or on the ramifications of it." When I asked how living together affected the relationship, Kylie said, "Negatively. It's just I think I really do need personal space. I am an introvert. I do need to recharge that way and I just never had that space because she was always home." As she explained, "Like I have some friends who are like disappearing up each other's vaginas and I'm like, it's just so bad. Like moving in together, like only operating as a 'we' and like not having individual activities."

Tina had a similar experience in an early relationship: "I guess it was my first long-term relationship with a woman and that did bring with it—We could be mutually needy, you know, the U-Haul thing was definitely an effect that happened where it was like she felt like I was moving too fast and then I felt like she was moving too fast." As a result, she worried when her current partner brought up moving in together. However, given her previous experience, she knew she needed to make clear her expectations:

I was a little scared when he first brought it up. I'm pretty introverted and haven't lived with roommates for a while and really, really need my alone time. He's more extroverted than I am so I worry about that. So what helped me feel ready was talking about these issues with him actually. Just talking it out and saying, like, "Look, I need to have a separate room from you," you know, I need all these crazy things that would seem crazy to another person probably. I don't necessarily need a separate bedroom, but a separate bed.

Jen said the same thing: "I want a two bedroom. I want my own bedroom, I need alone time, and I need my own space or I start to freak out." Interestingly, this sentiment seemed evenly distributed across the sample, with no one of a certain gender or sexual orientation stating it more than another.

Given the focus on creating non-normative relationships, many of the participants didn't want to get married. Kylie said, "So marriage—kind of against the institution, kind of against the prioritization of the legalization of getting married over the safety of others. Like I just think the heteronormalization of everything is just kind of bad. . . . I just don't want to fall into that structure of like married, kid and house, dog something." Evan concurred, saying that his main feeling toward mainstream relationship messages was "disgust. Disgust that you have to be in a committed monogamous relationship, or you have to buy somebody a disgusting diamond ring and marry off and have kids. It's awful. I think it's sick." Jen was more ambivalent: "Some days I'm like how great would it be to plan a future with someone and have that team and stability. And then sometimes I'm like no one shall own me. Like I'm as free as the wind. Don't say we are one; we're two people."

In spite of these sentiments, almost everyone wanted a long-term commitment in at least some form and many were happy to have the right to marry, even if they didn't necessarily want to do so themselves. Many connected marriage to legal rights but also to the desire to demonstrate to the world their commitment to and love for another. Ella said, "I'm so glad we have gay marriage. I'm not one of those people who's like, 'Oh, keep queer queer.' Like I'm really glad that gay marriage exists. I think we deserve it. The tax and the hospital benefits and all those things." Yet she also said she would construct marriage on her own terms: "I would get married if I had a life partner. But I think it would be like Dan Savage monogamous-ish kind of thing where like there could be breaks from monogamy, we could have threesomes." Indeed, many hoped to incorporate some form of non-monogamy into their relationships.

But Manuela struggled with what they wanted from a relationship and the messages they received about being queer: "It's like, why am I queer? You know, like I'm supposed to be going against the grain. I guess maybe these ideas about long-term relationships or monogamy or love, it's just like actually that doesn't exist for queers." Yet at the same time, when I asked them if they wanted to get married someday, they answered, "Yes and no. The yes part of me has this fantasy, like would love to have that long-term commitment with one person." But given that they identified as queer, they leaned not toward marriage but to having a different type of ritual to celebrate their commitment. They explained that they wanted something similar to a certain commitment ceremony they had heard of: "A bunch of witches went to this ceremony, called a webbing." As they explained, this ceremony involved the visualization of the participants' interconnectedness with community. This resonated with Manuela as it reflected how they wanted to construct a partnership—not as two individuals isolating themselves but rather as members of a community, living as part of that community.

Contrary to heterosexual courtship scripts, which dictate that the man should "surprise" the woman with a marriage proposal and wedding ring, only a few of the participants desired a one-sided marriage proposal. Ella explained, "I've been dreaming about that since I was little. The proposal has to be a big grand gesture preferably with lots of planning and maybe the involvement of others. I want to be proposed to." When I asked her why this was important to her, she said, "'Cause I see it in the movies and it's like Disney Princess Ariel and it would be fun. I'm really like a social theatrical person and I like a good story." But most respondents explicitly discussed a reimagination of the proposal script. Elizabeth, a 27-year-old bisexual cis woman, said of the marriage proposal, "I imagine that it would probably be something that we talk about and decide on." Emma said, "I think if we did it, I like the idea of me asking her and her asking me, so like two proposals." Riley said of his fiancée:

> She's like, "This is really silly that I have a ring and you don't." And I was like, "I thought I was going to have to wait for that." 'Cause I really wanted one, but I was prepared to wait because I'm masculine or whatever, you know?

And she was like, "That's stupid; we're queers and we write our own script."
. . . And then a couple weeks later the ring came and she proposed back . . .
I like that it was important to her to propose back.

As in Riley's narrative, there was generally a sense that queer relationships could transcend gender and that gender expression and action did
not have to match. Manuela said, "Masculine-of-center people are
expected to be the ones to make decisions or take up more space or to be
assertive. But I've noticed that in the queer community, people just do
what they do, regardless of how they appear." Jamie had a similar reaction
when she got engaged to her partner through a series of conversations: "A
lot of people assume that because [my partner] is more masculine presenting that she popped the question and it was a big surprise and there
was this big to-do. And it wasn't like that at all. . . . Even though I'm very
feminine and she's very masculine, we really don't want to get caught up
in gender roles."

Yet Jamie also indicated that while she and her partner felt free to challenge scripts that did not feel right to them, they also felt free to embrace
rituals they did like. They both wanted rings because they felt rings sym-
bolized the seriousness of their relationship, both to each other and to
those around them. She said, "It's assumed that because we're queer, we're
gonna be very non-normative and nontraditional. . . . And it felt like this
is a rite of passage for all people so why shouldn't we have a right to have
engagement rings like anybody else." Noah, a 28-year-old bisexual cis
man, also focused on the symbolism of getting engaged and how it signified commitment: "I think a lot of the gays in the city are very cynical; they
thought it was just another fling and didn't know it was serious. So I think
people have more respect for our relationship now." Thus, while many of
the respondents focused on "normative resistance,"[23] some also saw elements of conformity as acceptable practice when enacted with intention.
Indeed, there was also a sense among participants, as voiced by Jamie,
that queer individuals should not be excluded from important life mile-
stones and practices simply because they were queer. Brian made a similar
point when discussing his engagement to his partner:

You know, I don't think either of us ever thought that we would get married.
I was reading a lot of Butler and I was sort of like, I don't know, like resent-

ing the act of like needing the state's permission to sanction blah-blah-blah. But that being said, I think we knew we wanted to be life partners and all that. We actually got engaged before the DOMA [Defense of Marriage Act] thing happened and so it felt a little transgressive still and I knew from my parents that it would mean a lot to my family to support us and to have a ceremony. And I think both [my partner] and I like ritual in the sense of like there are certain occasions where like there is something really nice about marking that with everyone in your life.

These comments show a deliberate engagement with scripts by the participants rather than a full-scale, knee-jerk rejection. In practice, people are picking and choosing what works for them rather than following expectations complacently.

Finally, LGBQ people sought to demonstrate their commitment to equality through the symbolism of their naming practices. Tina said she would not change her name if she married: "I think it's part of my resistance to marriage being like the woman giving herself up to the man in this very traditional way. And I think for a lot of people that's a meaningful gift, like giving up your name for someone else. But for me I would prefer not to sort of fall into the gender roles that way." Emma said, "We would both keep our last names. Both of us feel that like this is who we are. And there's also that weird power imbalance of being the one to take the other person's name." Brian and his partner created a whole new last name together and used their respective last names as their middle names. This allowed them to demonstrate their relationship through their last name without prioritizing the name of one partner over the other, or assuming that one partner needed to sacrifice their identity to create a family identity.

NOT IMMUNE

Although most of the LGBQ people discussed trying to limit or avoid gendered behaviors in their romantic relationships, a few respondents desired gendered scripts. Ella was one of the few:

This one butch woman who was like early fifties, I loved it. She opened the car door for me every time. She always paid for our dates. She'd bring me flowers. It was so sweet and I love that chivalry . . . God, 'cause it felt like this old-fashioned fifties-style romance. I'm not immune to it, even though I'm feminist and I'm a lesbian, I'm not immune to the man takes care of the woman script.

Amid the shift in her generation to nongendered dating scripts, Ella was the only person in the sample who admitted being raised with an image of courtship that she still desired; further, she felt she could only enact these scripts with older lesbian partners. This was in contrast to the majority of the sample, who instead discussed how foreign these scripts felt. Growing up, many of the respondents worried that they would never find a partner because gendered scripts sounded so unappealing. Rather than emphasizing their desire for chivalry and elaborate marriage proposals, they discussed being alone for the rest of their lives.

While Ella was unapologetic about her desire for gendered scripts, she acknowledged that some might see a disconnect between this and her identity. More frequently, given the pressures to contest normative relationship patterns, respondents emphasized gender as play, possibly to undermine the potential critique they anticipated receiving for gendered behaviors. Andie said, "I sort of like that playful aspect of the gender dynamic . . . I like the idea that I'll give you my jacket if you're cold because I'm so tough and cold doesn't matter to me, but I'll take care of you. But again, it's always in a little bit of a tongue-in-cheek way, but I still really like it." This narrative allowed Andie to have fun with the elements of gender she enjoyed while still maintaining a critical distance from compulsory adherence. This was important both for her understanding of herself as a queer person and to avoid the negative reactions from her queer community.

Some respondents also enjoyed playing with explicit gender role reversal. Jen, for example, talked extensively about butch-femme dynamics and how she appreciated them in some regards as long as she could turn them on their head in other ways. Jen identified as femme, and she discussed how a former partner, who identified as butch, had found her attractive specifically because she was unexpected and unpredictable:

> I would pay and she [liked that]. Just because I saw how unexpected it would be because I think she was also kinda hanging out with femmes who always expected her to pay, open the door, like fall into those typical gender

roles. I had a steady job also and I think she was just getting out of college then. So I had more money than her. So I would pay. But I also enjoyed taking care of her and I enjoyed the gender reversal.

Here the pleasure was from going against normative expectations rather than conforming to them.

Interestingly, cis women dating other cis women were the demographic most likely to engage in gendered dating practices, perhaps because courtship scripts resonate with women more than men, or possibly due to the historical legacy of strict butch/femme dynamics in lesbian communities.[24] In addition, a few of the cis women who dated both men and women reported feeling more comfortable enacting normative gender behaviors with women than with men. When I asked Melanie what she might wear on a first date, she said, "I would definitely dress more down for a man and more up for a woman. I don't want to be leading with my looks with men and I don't want to be trying to be sexy for men. I really like the energy of dressing up for women and I just don't like it for men." Those who said this tied it back to a resistance to heterosexual dating practices, aware of the heavy pressure they experienced to conform and looking for ways to actively reject these pressures. In particular, they didn't want to signal a desire for an unwanted gendered relationship script, giving male partners the wrong idea about the desired dynamics. These same dynamics in same-sex relationships just didn't raise the same concerns. But many of the respondents also acknowledged that they lived in a unique location that provided them with a space to challenge these norms. As Melanie said, "I feel like I live in this weird bubble of super, super, super progressive people like politically, sexually, gender, dating." Living in the progressive, urban Bay Area allowed respondents to feel more confident of finding like-minded individuals with whom they could successfully remake relationship scripts.

Still, others struggled with the expectations that come with male/ female or masculine/feminine relationships. While Melanie said that she would rather dress up for a woman than a man, others indicated the opposite, citing the pressure to conform to normative beauty standards. As Tina said,

I do think I put on more makeup for dates with men. I mean I've always felt more physically attractive with women. Oh, the other part is I'm like very

anxious about my butt being big. That just means that I have body image
issues basically. But I only bring that up because I don't feel those as acutely
when I'm with women. And so for that reason in general I just feel a little bit
more confident with women so I don't wear as much makeup. I wear clothes
that make me feel attractive, but I don't necessarily overthink it as much
with women as with men.

Tina also admitted to following men's lead more than women's when
dating, explaining, "All the lessons about patriarchy, all the horrible patriarchal lessons my mom taught me, I really swallowed hook, line, and
sinker. I think it really is this fear of seeming needy, though, or seeming
desperate. I think it's a very real factor that some guys do have it in their
head that same formula where it ought to be the guy [to initiate dates.]"
Lauren had this perspective confirmed during a relationship with a heterosexual cis man, describing how he chastised her for being too assertive
in the relationship: "He was like, 'I think you think I'm going to float away
if you don't come to me all the time. I'm not. Let me initiate.' Basically he
felt like I had stopped letting him initiate [hanging out and sex]. Then,
after that, I felt like I was walking on eggshells trying not to overstep, trying not to initiate too much. I just felt really weird."

This challenge to undo heteronormative practices was especially acute
in the relationships bisexual or queer cis women had with heterosexual cis
men. Tina discussed this challenge in her current relationship:

> Although he's been very flexible and resilient and like remarkably willing to
> change and sort of roll with the punches of my weird—not weird but like
> mildly unconventional approach to dating I guess, he still comes from a
> much more traditional background than I do in terms of that stuff. So
> I think, yeah, he's definitely got like the heterosexual paradigm in mind and
> every so often I kind of have to remind him that he's not in a straight relation-
> ship I guess. And I guess I take credit for also being the first woman he's been
> with who even calls those things into question, you know? So, yeah. It's been
> an interesting challenge and being with someone who didn't have like the
> same liberal arts "gender is a construct" sort of thing that I've had and to like
> get to explain those things to him and hear what he thinks about them. Still
> he's not quite eye-to-eye with me about the gender thing, but yeah, yeah.

Although I interviewed only one queer cis man who was dating a heterosexual cis woman, he too faced a similar challenge. When I asked Amit

what queerness looked like in the context of an ostensibly heterosexual relationship, he explained,

> I mean it's just, it's very heteronormative, it's just we fall into a trope state. . . . I mean definitely when we're together it's actually been really challenging because she wants someone that's a much more masculine guy than I am, you know, that tough guy, that's what turns her on. It's like her exes have been kind of like big kind of macho guys whereas I'm not. And I am more like, hey, let's snuggle and I, like I'm very gentle and soft. Not tough guy. Tough in other ways. So that's been hard. And I think it's been hard for both of us also to look at like our relationship as something physical as opposed to being friends, you know, like and trying to think of each other in a sexual way and get into that.

Amit said that he and his partner were going to therapy to find a way to make the relationship work in spite of their different perspectives on how gender should play out in their relationship.

But the more common reaction to the emergence of gender inequality in romantic relationships was an intentional effort to change. It wasn't as though gender didn't play a role in relationships, but rather that people tried to notice when it perpetuated inequalities and then challenge it. As Patricio remarked, "I notice it comes out in some of my relationships so I question it. Like patriarchy or like the person on top pays or whatever, you know? I'm like, is this a reenactment of heterosexual norms?" Amit found his current partner's insistence on a more traditional masculinity especially difficult as he had been working to challenge his "masculinity, patriarchy, and male privilege." As he explained, "So about my masculinity, challenging my notions of what it means to be genderqueer, what it means to be dating a genderqueer or trans person and to be in an intimate relationship with them. How my masculinity shows up in intimate spaces and sex and in romance." Amit continued,

> For example, like when [a former partner and I] first started sleeping together and having sex we would take turns topping each other. And as the relationship progressed I was the top more often than not. And there were fewer times that they would penetrate me or like there's fewer times that we used a strap-on. And we didn't often talk about it. But as we were deconstructing our relationship in the breakup process, all these things came up and we started talking about it more.

Since that relationship, Amit had spent a great deal of time journaling and reflecting on the ways he felt he enacted male privilege in his romantic relationships, in an effort to change those dynamics. As we shall see in the next chapter, a critical and reflective approach to intimate relationships matters. By engaging with relationship practices with greater intention and awareness of the potential inequalities that can result, LGBQ people had more-equal courtships. This is not to say that they didn't recreate inequalities, as is clear from their narratives; but it is to say that they viewed relationship dynamics as an ongoing project to be consistently addressed.

NEW NORMS, NEW NARRATIVES

The language of queer dating suggests that liberation is about individualistic self-determination and going beyond norms. While respondents discussed a lack of rules, community-level queer norms encouraging the rejection of socially sanctioned practices have supplanted heterosexual norms. LGBQ people faced pressures to create egalitarian relationships, have adventurous sex, split the check, contemplate nonmonogamy, and voice suspicion toward marriage. These pressures constrain the range of available, acceptable relationship practices, and in many ways respondents found these new norms just as imperative as those they were attempting to transcend. Yet in embracing these counter-normative practices, they "queered courtship," finding ways to make their courtships more egalitarian and in opposition to the expected romance practices. Those who did choose to engage in gendered practices were forced to reframe these preferences in ways that would insulate them from critique and accusations of homonormativity.[25] This is similar to the self-identified feminist heterosexual women and men who wanted so badly to understand themselves as egalitarian and progressive in spite of their many traditional gendered behaviors. Given the variation in gender, sexual, and racial and ethnic identity in the sample, the lack of variation in narratives indicates how widespread these new norms are becoming for queer young adults, at least in progressive social environments.

6 The More Things Change . . .

Courtship behaviors matter in their own right because they reflect beliefs about appropriate interactions between genders. As chapters 3 and 4 showed, in spite of a strong stated preference for egalitarian relationships, the majority of heterosexual women and men continue to engage in rituals that highlight their perceived differences, indicating strong support still for essentialist beliefs about gender. In contrast, the majority of LGBQ people endorse greater equality between partners in their dating and courtship practices and frequently tie this to their more fluid understandings of gender. How much does all this matter in the long run? Are these merely meaningless rituals perpetuated by personal preference, as many of the heterosexual people asserted, or do they translate into greater inequalities as argued by many of the LGBQ people working hard to resist these behaviors?

In this chapter, I examine the relationship between the narratives employed during courtship and how labor and care work are conceived in long-term relationships. Significantly, the narratives drawn on to justify dating practices are similar to those used in respondents' committed relationships. As I show, heterosexual men and women believe they have different interests, different skills, and different availability for their personal lives. These assumptions of "difference" limit their ability to question and challenge these preferences and arrangements, and they perpetuate gender inequality in their relationships in the process. On the other hand, LGBQ people, drawing on narratives of equality and interrogating enactments of inequality, emphasize egalitarian and flexible care work and labor in committed relationships. The way people date may set the stage for the dynamics in their long-term relationships.

THE UPSTAIRS/DOWNSTAIRS MYTH REVISITED

During heterosexual courtship, the overt expression of romantic interest is delegated almost exclusively to men. Women are expected to simply react to men's gestures. As their romantic relationships progress, however, women also communicate interest and love in gender-appropriate ways. In particular, women are expected to do more of the "labors of love."[1] This labor is often routinized household labor and emotional work, both of which are romanticized and portrayed as care.[2] The burden of sustaining relationships transfers to women in the process, as they are called on to perform affective labors that include nurturing their partners and their relationships, as well as recognizing their partners' desires and needs over their own.[3] Men and women perform different types of relationship work, and in the process, "gender is reproduced" in the context of romantic relationships.[4] These relationship practices disadvantage women and privilege men in heterosexual relationships, preventing the formation of egalitarian peer relationships. But how do self-identified empowered heterosexual women justify these practices?

Labors of Love

It has been 30 years since sociologist Arlie Hochschild identified the ideological work that heterosexual women do in order to reconcile their desire for egalitarian relationships with their lived realities.[5] Indeed, her discussion of the upstairs/downstairs myth (the woman manages all the rooms where people live, while the man takes care of the basement) clearly revealed how women were able to make unequal arrangements appear fairer than they were. Today, in spite of years of rapid social change, heterosexual women continue to narrate arrangements as more equal than they actually are. When I asked heterosexual women how they made decisions about household labor, half simply said that each person did what they preferred, similar to how they narrated gendered courtship as mere preference as well. For example, one person might prefer cooking while another might hate cooking but not mind cleaning. Many said that they didn't even have to formally discuss the issue as it all worked itself out fairly. Caroline, 31, said,

> It has sort of evolved organically. We're both kind of anal, but about different things and we both have sort of slightly different obsessions. So I really like to not have dirty dishes out and to have clean dishes all the time. I do a lot of the dishes. Meanwhile he does a lot of fixing stuff around the house. Like we needed motion sensor lights, so he's been researching that and bought them and installed them, and I didn't want to have anything to do with that. Like buying speakers. He's been doing that. He likes to research and buy shit, which is fine with me because I don't want to spend my time doing that.

Many women appealed to the argument that men prefer to do outside work, fix things around the house, or deal with the electronics for the family. What they failed to examine, however, was the relative time and value of each task; almost invariably women took on the more frequent, time-consuming, everyday tasks. Caroline had broken up with a man while in graduate school after she realized they had different visions for their lives. He wanted a traditional marriage with a stay-at-home wife, while she wanted an egalitarian marriage and had no interest in staying at home with kids. But like many of the women, Caroline failed to look beyond her own childcare obligations and career opportunities to other aspects of relationships inequality, such as the type of household labor each was expected to perform. As a result, she was willing to divide the work with her current husband as the arrangement "evolved organically" on the basis of interests rather than as preordained by gender. That preferences might be the result of gender socialization was not considered.

Ashleigh, 29, had the most traditional relationship of any of the heterosexual women in that she was the only one who had quit her job to stay at home with her children. She was also one of the more traditional when it came to the enforcement of gender difference during courtship. Yet even she wasn't willing to take on the majority of the burden of household labor when it was framed by gender. As she explained, she laid out the ground rules with her husband: "I wrote down everything that the house needed and everything inside and outside. And he kind of thought it was going to go, man does outside, woman does inside. I was like, no, because outside is easier than inside. So here is how it's going to work. And he agreed to that." As it turned out, a gendered division of labor was only acceptable if it appeared to be the result of preferences rather than the result of an explicit discussion of what is expected of men and women by virtue of their being men and women. Indeed, Ashleigh described how authority was assigned in the relationship on the basis of talents and interests: "I allow him to make the financial planning decisions for our future. A lot of times, if it's a strength for him, then I'll kind of default to him. Or if it's a passion for him. If it's a passion for me, he'll let me kind of take over. Like decorating I love to do, and he realized that early on in our relationship and has allowed me to sort of make all those decisions."

Still, there was a strongly held belief that women are just more attentive to household issues and will thus end up doing a greater share of the household labor. In spite of her gender-neutral argument for the division of labor, Caroline acknowledged this: "Because I care more about the quality of our relationship. Because I care more, I'm less tolerant of stuff that I find to be not exactly the way I want it. And I don't know if it's a woman thing or what, but I was very sensitive to creating precedent." Here the assumption was that women are more willing to do work for the well-being of the couple. Interestingly, Caroline also noted she was worried about "creating precedent," which to her meant not allowing certain negative behaviors (such as socks left on the floor) to slide. As a result, she took on a greater burden of the household labor, but also took on the role of the taskmaster for the couple.

In addition, there was a sense that men couldn't be trusted to take care of household tasks due to their inattentiveness. Aashi, 29, said, "I can see myself being the one that handles the day-to-day expenses just because I'm better at opening mail, mailing stuff out." She explained that she did more of the housework and gave laundry as an example: "My boyfriend has a tendency to mess up his clothes, shrink things, so I end up doing laundry." Katie, 32, noted too that women are more attentive to household work than men, distinguishing between what she considered ideal and what she considered probable as a result of their respective traits:

> Ideally, if you notice that there's something wrong, let's do it together. Or could you take care of that? I know in an ideal world that that doesn't ever happen, because girls notice a lot more than guys do, by and large, not all the time. And so . . . I would want the guy to help me out. I mean, I know that just by the nature of me being quick to notice a lot of things, I'm going to end up taking the burden of doing the chores a little bit more. Not necessarily because it's my job *as the woman* to take care of all the household things, but just because I'll end up noticing them more. And wanting to do something about it.

While Katie acknowledged that women and men have different standards for household cleanliness, she failed to connect this to a different willingness to take care of chores. Rather than translate to a discussion between partners on an agreed-upon level of cleanliness, it became the woman's job to maintain the standard *she* wanted. In essence, the attitude was that if you don't like it, you deal with it, no matter if both of you benefit from your work. In Katie's mind, it wasn't her role as a woman to do the majority of the household labor, which would have felt regressive to her, but merely the result of a different level of perceptiveness to this particular issue. This distinction was subtle but significant to women, as it meant the difference between feeling pigeonholed by gender expectations versus the inevitable result of natural differences between men and women. It didn't matter if the end result was the same; why men and women have different standards of cleanliness and why women notice messes more was never called into question. When I asked Katie if it bothered her that the household labor might not be divided 50–50, she said,

> Now that I'm older, it probably won't bother me as much, but when I was younger it would bother me a heck of a lot. I remember getting really mad that my dad wouldn't do the dishes after dinner. And my mom would do everything. It's like, "Mom, you had a long day too. Why is Dad doing nothing?" I remember getting really mad. And then my mom said, "You know, you should just take care of the things that you notice. And do things out of love for somebody else. Even if it means something that you might not want to do."

As with housework, very few of the women had concrete ideas about how to handle childcare and assumed it would "evolve organically." Because only five had children, this wasn't an issue most had had to directly confront yet. Instead, like with housework, it appeared they expected everything to fall neatly into place when the time came. This was even the case among those who were already married. Amelia, 33, said that although she and her partner planned to have children in the future, they hadn't discussed how they would handle childcare. Many, like Heather, 27, said that they couldn't fully anticipate what they would want for the future at the present moment: "I don't know for sure. I'm assuming I'll go back to work, but I'm not a parent. I don't know how I'll feel in general. I'll probably figure it out. I probably won't even know that when I'm pregnant." This left an opening for them to maintain identities as working women, while also making space for them to fall back on gendered caregiving patterns when the time came and "maternal instincts" kicked in.

As shown in chapter 2, though, most said they didn't want to stay at home and, reflecting their class privilege, instead anticipated that they would pay someone to take care of their children or rely on retired and geographically mobile grandparents rather than have their partner step in. Common responses were, "His mom, I guess," or, "Daycare." Aashi explained, "I would hope I would have some type of nanny that would help me and that's what I would probably need." As she explained, a stay-at-home dad "would make me really uncomfortable." Others made essentialist points about men's need to be in the workplace. Emily, 31, said, "I think it has to do with a man's ego. Like it's our human evolution. They have been the ones to go out there and hunt for food." Ashleigh claimed she was open to her husband staying home with their kids, although she ended up being the one to do so. Still, she said, "I don't think he would like it. He's a guy. I don't know; I think guys need to be working." Even Amanda, 31, who expressed great fear at being financially dependent, preferred to stay home: "I would not want my husband to stay at home at some point. I want him to be a provider and work. I guess in my head because that's what a man does."

The few women who already had children were doing the majority of the childcare, potentially pointing to the future for those who did not. Breanna, 36, said,

In general, the given responsibility, if it's related to the children, it's me. The expectation is, in general, I should do it. For example, one of our fights is around this. If I want to do something, the assumption is, who is going to watch my kids? I have to make arrangements—either ask him to do it, have someone do it, or arrange for them to be somewhere. But him—at the spur of the moment—can just take off and be gone.

Brooke, 36, also indicated that she had the ultimate responsibility for her kid: "He'll take [our son] on bike rides with him. But in the middle of the night, I'm the one getting up. And whenever [our son] is sick, I'm the one that's freaking out at 2:00 in the morning." She added that she feeds her son and bathes him, doing the main caregiving tasks, while her partner sporadically does the fun stuff. She even said, "Like for me to be out like this [at the interview], I had to make sure there was dinner stuff there for him." Anna, 40, was in the process of getting a divorce, saying of her husband, "He was not understanding that I needed to do other things with my life and he just wanted me to be at home and I couldn't do it. Yes, we had a little girl, but there were other things that I wanted to do with my life and I needed his support."

Still, as with housework, there was resistance to labeling these as gendered expectations for women in particular. As Olivia, 26, explained, "I want to stay home for a couple of years, but if anyone was like, I expect a woman to stay home and raise the kids, that's a deal breaker." Rather, like Ashleigh, this arrangement was more palatable when arrived at in a supposedly gender-neutral manner: "We made the agreement that whoever makes less money stays home with the kids." Luckily, that "just happened" to be her, given that "he was raised by a stay-at-home mom, so that's what he wanted for his kids. And that's kind of what I always wanted to do too."

Mommying Their Men

Many of the women argued that caring was done differently by men and women and that women's way of caring for men (and their families) was often reflected in their willingness to pick up the slack at home. Men's unwillingness to do housework or caregiving wasn't seen as an indication of their lack of care, as they merely showed care in other ways. Mia, 39, explained how she and her long-term boyfriend showed care for each other:

> He's very considerate of me, and he's attentive. Do I need anything to drink? Do I want anything else? That kind of thing. . . . Very good manners. Always opens my car door, and closes it once I get in. . . . I like all that stuff actually. Because I think it illustrates care and thoughtfulness. . . . Because [those gestures] do make me feel special on some level. . . . And it makes me feel—protected is a little too strong—looked out for? Cared for? It demonstrates care.

When I asked her how she cared for him, she said, "I cook for him a lot. I do a lot of cleaning up. And I demonstrate care by asking him about all of his problems and listening to all his problems . . . which can be really annoying. . . . I always keep an eye on what needs to be updated and I try to care for him in that way. Sometimes it feels a little maternal, which feels a little bit creepy. And I guess that line between maternal and wifely can be slim." Keira, 36, made a similar argument when discussing how she and her husband care for each other differently:

> I do all of the cooking in the house, but once again, I enjoy it. He makes our house better. I know that sounds weird. One thing that [my ex-husband] never did was, if the doors were squeaky, he never fixed them. I admit it's very traditional by gender, but [my husband] will naturally go with a can of oil and lubricate all the hinges. He rigged up his old iPod into the kitchen so I had music when I was cooking. I would bring in my little iPod and try to hook it up and extend the cord. He's like, "You're just dirtying your iPod." He sacrificed his old one, downloaded all the music I liked onto it, and bought speakers and a dock and rigged it up for me. Those are the sort of things he does for me and for the household. He doesn't really do laundry. He had such a bachelor existence for so long. If he had laundry, he would just take it to a dry cleaners where they'd wash all his clothes and bundle them up. That's what he was used to. He'll take the garbage out. He'll change the litter in the litter box. He doesn't want me to hurt myself. So if I have to change a shower curtain, he's like, "I'll do that." There are times when he'll say, "Why don't you do this and I'll vacuum?" He doesn't volunteer a lot, but there are times when he knows I'm frazzled with my professional work. I tend to work on the weekends, too. He'll know and be like, "Let me do the vacuuming and you focus on your work," which is nice. When he knows I'm really tired, he'll offer to do the dishes. Generally I don't mind doing the dishes. I do more of the housework, but it's also because I'm a little particular about how things are done.

Keira was one of the women in the study who was staunchly against traditional gender roles, including the symbolic aspects, but who went along with them anyway to please her partners. When she described care work in her relationship, it appeared in many ways to be what she had resisted. She worked significantly more hours than her husband and earned 70 percent of their income, and she still did the majority of the housework. But she wasn't trapped at home, taking care of kids and dependent on her husband, and that was different enough from her mother's life so as not to raise red flags for her. The household labor was clearly her job, and because her husband offered to help here and there when he knew she needed it, and because she enjoyed certain aspects of housework, she was content to take on more than her fair share. And she was willing to define it as fair because she viewed herself as more particular and enjoyed cooking, while he had spent all of his adult life in a "bachelor existence" during which she assumed he didn't need to be attentive to housework. By defining men's care work as intermittent, symbolic gestures, women were able to reconcile men's unwillingness to participate equally in the second shift with their own desire for an egalitarian relationship, all while still feeling loved.

As they argued, caring could be done differently (and should be, due to gender) but still result in an equitable relationship. As Ashleigh claimed, men and women need different things from their relationships. She and her husband read books together to better understand each other and what each needed, based solely on their genders:

> The one we're reading right now is how I can understand him better and what his needs are and his strengths and how I can build him up. And, like, add to our relationship. . . . It says men need respect . . . and women need to be loved and feel loved. . . . [My husband] will always feel like I love him if I'm respecting him. Even if he's not acting in a way that deserves respect all of the time. . . . You want to build him up. You need to know that sex is important to them, that it's not just . . . it's not what it is to a woman; it's part of something that helps them feel that they're living as who they're supposed to be or something.

He, in turn, was expected to tell her that she's beautiful: "Every woman kind of has this feeling—well, not every woman, but most women—that they just want to feel beautiful." Thus, just as during courtship, standard cultural narratives based on pop wisdom were appealed to as justification for the differences that appeared in their relationships.

Keeping the Peace

Many of the women also felt that they were more dominant in their relationships precisely *because* they did the majority of the relationship work and work around the house.[6] Keira said that she was the more dominant partner in her relationship with her husband:

> I probably am in terms of making decisions. I say that his middle name is inertia. I'm like, "Hey, this paperwork won't fill itself out." I basically take care of bills. That usually means just setting things up online. I'm also the one who has to remind him to get his paperwork together when it's time to do taxes. In terms of decisions not concerning finances, it's always a negotiation. If I want to go out to dinner and he doesn't, I'll say, "How do you feel if I just go out with friends?" He's perfectly okay. I've learned not to make that into an argument. If I want to go out and he doesn't, I don't need to make him go out.

She also said that her husband didn't enjoy going to the farmers market like she did, so he would pick her up there when she was done rather than go with her. This too was interpreted as a sign of caring. Yet at the same time, the underlying assumption was that men won't, and don't need to, change or accommodate women's interests, while women are more adaptable. Mia, too, acknowledged that it was hard for her partner to adjust to the needs of others, although she was able to connect this unwillingness to compromise to relationship inequalities:

> He gets his way in a lot of ways because he's practically incapable of adjusting to anything. But I still feel like I have power in the relationship in the sense that if something's really not cool, I can put my foot down and get what I want. I can get what I want, but it takes a lot of energy—I have to throw a fit. I have to want it, but, if it's important to me, I can get what I want. About certain things . . . there are certain things that I don't have any power over . . . like problems in our relationship that he won't even consider changing.

Even when women tried to address the inequality that appeared in their relationships, most felt rebuffed and attributed it to their partners' personalities. Brooke said of her husband, "He's just like that. Sets his mind to something and just doesn't budge." She said that she does "90 percent of the household stuff." When I asked her if she wanted her husband to do more, she said, "He doesn't listen. . . . He'll take his pants off in the living room and I tell him, 'Don't take your fucking pants off in the living room,' and he still does." Still, she acknowledged that he was indeed capable of doing more housework, as the division of labor had been much more equal when they first moved in together: "When you're in the first stages of googoo la-la land romance, cooking dinner and vacuuming and doing the laundry together is romantic. Well, he did more laundry then, I'll tell you that." Jenna, 26, had concluded that the unequal household load wasn't worth the battle: "It's definitely a battle that's not worth it to me. I don't mind cleaning that much and I will bring it up if I'm really bothered by it or stressed out. I will say, 'You have to help me.'" She also justified her partner's lack of help, saying that he made a lot more money than she did so it was only fair for her to contribute more at home, in spite of the fact that she too worked full-time.

Samantha, 31, was one of the few women who made a connection between dating behaviors and the dynamics she discovered she hated in her marriage. As she explained,

> Even from the beginning . . . it just wasn't as overt. He is just very dominant. He is very aggressive. He was very aggressive in his pursuit of me, and then everything was his suggestion all along the line. Like, me move in. He proposed. That kind of thing. So I'd say he was very aggressive. . . . That was the pattern with him, is he would essentially wear me down. Wear down my resistance to the point where we would fight about something, but over time you just get tired of fighting and then you passively would just be like, whatever, I'm tired of fighting over it.

While hers was an extreme example, his dominance was disguised as mere ritual during courtship but became more apparent after they got married. At that point, he began monitoring everything she spent, started huge fights over her desire to keep her maiden name, stopped doing housework, and eventually canceled her phone, which she discovered while attempting to make a call for help after barricading herself in their bedroom when a fight turned physical. Samantha told me that before she marries again, she will make sure to have a conversation with her partner, explicitly discussing how each thinks a marriage should function: "Because it's very indicative of where your relationship will go, if you have different perceptions of what a relationship should be like in terms of your relation to the other person." As she explained, while she and her now ex-husband were dating, because she accommodated him, he thought they were of the same mind about the relationship. He had said he liked certain traits of hers, so she thought they would be valued in the marriage. As she later told him, "'You said when you married me that you loved these things about me—I'm independent, I'm intelligent, I voice my opinions, that kind of things.' But it sounded like he wanted me to subvert all of that once we were married to become what he wanted. Which is a contradiction of, I like these things about you, but once we're married, you don't?" They decided to divorce after he called her on the phone: "He was like, 'You know what? You're not the great Catholic wife I thought you were,' essentially. 'And we're obviously not going to see eye-to-eye.' I was like, 'That's all right.' We said all that we're going to say. It's done. And then three days later was our one-year anniversary."

Samantha said that moving forward she will look for someone who values her interests, as for her that now signals caring. Unlike Keira, who was content to be allowed to pursue her own interests, Samantha wanted someone to care enough about her to pursue them with her as it showed a willingness to value her perspective in the relationship:

> Like, for example, if I want to go to the theater, but he wants to go see a tennis match—I'm just using that as an example because I think it's boring—he doesn't really like going to the theater, but he'll do it occasionally to make me happy, or I'll do the thing for him to make him happy. But there is that balance. There wasn't that balance [with her ex-husband]. I told him this months before I left. If he did not place a value on something or think it's important, he would disregard it.

There was a sense then among heterosexual women that they were the ones who were able and willing to do the work required for the relationship to succeed, although they didn't have the language to describe it in these terms.

While women resisted the idea that the dynamics in their relationships were the default result of gender, they appealed to conventional notions of

gender difference to discuss them. Men were considered unable or unwilling to do housework properly, but this was viewed as normal due to preferences and skills rather than as unfair. Men were also seen as more naturally suited to labor outside the house and were thus let off the hook for
taking on a significant share of childcare. In order to feel okay about their
relationships, women searched for other ways that men cared for them or
contributed to the household. In doing so, they used the same process to
defend inequality in their long-term relationships as they did to justify
their preference for gendered courtship.

FAIRNESS AS EQUALITY

Just as heterosexual women narrated inequality in their relationships as
the result of preferences and skills, so too did heterosexual men. When I
asked Dave, 34, who was more dominant in his marriage, he said,

> There are issues that we care about, where we will stake out a definite posi-
> tion. Like, she cares more about the décor of the house. I don't particularly
> care. I might stake out a position on some things. So therefore she gets the
> dominant say. I care more about . . . I'm better at finances than she is. So by
> that logic, I think that I should have a dominant say. And I will have a domi-
> nant say—I will argue stronger for that. With kids, I'm going to defer to her.
> Because she knows.

As a result, heterosexual men were able to build inequality into their relationships by perpetuating a separate but equal philosophy.

Gendered Expertise

Men allow women greater authority in areas that are perceived as feminine and therefore undervalued.[7] But as with women, men were able to
use this division to discuss their relationship as egalitarian rather than
question the relative value of decision-making authority in each area and
the assumptions around women's expertise. Like Dave, Ryan, 28, said that
he was in charge of securing his and his girlfriend's financial future: "She
doesn't know a whole lot about it so she kind of trusts me to make sure we

have retirement and everything taken care of. Then she'll just do what she needs to do." Ethan, 38, said of his marriage, "It's pretty equal. It's something I miss, dominating." When I asked who got their way more or who made more decisions, he said, "It depends on the area. The food stuff, she tends to make more decisions. Maintenance here and there like if there's something you could do, or put in, things like upgrade, she's not that interested in doing that. If we need a water heater, I'll go figure out what kind to get. I'll deal with that. The taxes. And it's not really like it's traditional male/female roles, it's just, that's my background."

Interestingly, many of the men who avowed their feminist credentials still used gender to explain dominance in their relationships. Jake, 34, justified this by claiming that each partner had something to contribute: "I was the dominant one, but I wanted her. But we both knew that I was the one calling the shots. . . . I was deciding when we were breaking up or getting back together. It was like I was man, she was woman, but I totally needed and respected everything she was providing." A number of other men said that *women* enforced men's dominance in the relationship. Gavin, 31, felt that his dominance in the relationship was expected, which made it acceptable to him. It became the result of her personal preference rather than an attempt by him to control the relationship, and thus didn't violate his notions of equality. Brad, 32, explained,

> We pretty much do what I want. I pretty much make most of the decisions about, it feels like, almost everything, which is really trying for me. That's not the relationship I want for myself. I don't want to feel like I'm this caretaker. I haven't really felt that I am, but I feel like in my relationship, I have to be. I think that's part of what she wants. Yeah, from sex to money to decisions about little things, whether it's her daughter's schooling.

Gregory, 33, was one of the few men who said that his wife was the more dominant party: "By virtue of being female, she tends to be a little more long-term thinking. She's more of a long-term planner so she decides what she wants to do and then explains it to me and I'm okay." Still, he used gender as an explanation for her ability to plan. This was one way that men could let themselves off the hook for not contributing to the maintenance of the relationship. Certainly, the majority of the men who stated their wife or girlfriend was more dominant attributed this to her control of the household. Taking care of the house, and the authority that comes with it, was interpreted as women having more power in the relationship.[8]

A number of men recognized the relative value of this expertise and allowed women to get their way in certain low-stake realms as a means of getting their *own* way in areas they considered more important. Logan, 29, considered himself dominant in his relationship with his fiancée because he got his way much more often:

> [My fiancée's] solution to a lot of situations is to just not care about whatever it is. So instead of standing her ground on something or firmly believing in something, she'll just decide that position is not important to her. Not worth arguing. So I feel like I end up imposing a lot of things that I care about. We have a lot of stupid arguments about the shoes I will or will not wear because they're uncomfortable shoes—and she wants me to wear shoes that look good. So, she'll choose to fight about that, and then not fight about something that I feel is very important . . . whatever that might be.

As Logan recognized, battling over choice of clothing was less significant in the long run of a relationship than finances, over which he had a greater say. By giving in on clothing preferences, however, there was a sense that he was not solely in control. Men could then focus on getting their way in areas they valued or considered to be men's expertise.

Fair Enough

In addition, two-thirds of the men in committed, cohabiting relationships or marriages resisted an equal division of household labor, even though they either failed to see it as unequal or came up with excuses why it wasn't. Andrew, 35, said he knew that the division of labor would be egalitarian in his household from watching his wife's parents: "It was pretty clear to me that [my wife] was raised sort of in an egalitarian house where general rules were not adhered to. Even though her dad did most of the outdoor work and her mom did most of the indoor work, it wasn't because they were male or female; it was because he didn't like indoor work and she didn't like outdoor work." Again, just as women did, men failed to analyze how preferences and skills might be cultivated as a result of gender socialization.[9] Brad claimed very strongly that he was intensely unhappy with the traditional relationship he was in, arguing that he wanted an egalitarian partnership. Still, he failed to take responsibility for the unequal division of labor in his household, claiming it was due to his girlfriend's desire for tradition and his own particular circumstances that made it difficult for him to contribute:

> Once I moved in, I'm not a great cook, but I can do a couple things. I would do one or two meals a week and she would do the others. She doesn't have a dishwasher, so we both do dishes every night. I also hate doing dishes. . . . . She'll do the dishes and I do the drying. [She] also does all the laundry. That's not something we ever communicated. She also does my laundry. I'm a grown man. I've done my laundry. I've lived on my own. It's something she does. . . . She does all the cleaning, too.

According to Brad, severe asthma and allergies gave him a "great excuse" not to divide the housework evenly, although this could not be applied to cooking, laundry, and dishes. But he also attributed her behavior to her gender: "She's also a woman. She *loves* a clean house. I *like* a clean house, but I'm willing to let things go much longer than she is." Gavin fell back on a similar justification. In spite of a hired house cleaner to deal with housework, he and his girlfriend still had to negotiate the dishes and the laundry. Gavin said,

> She really, really hates having dirty dishes in the kitchen for whatever reason. It really bothers her. So she wants the dishes done right after dinner. . . . After dinner I want to just relax and watch TV, and I'll clean the dishes tomorrow. That's something I had to do as a kid [that I now reject] because I always hated doing that. Before dinner, maybe, like I'll just do whatever. But she needs to have them done right away. What ends up happening is she does them, I let her do them, and then she kinda resents that after a while. So there's that kind of thing. And she'll do the laundry, it's sort of a nice thing to do, but eventually I'll just kind of let her do it. . . . So she'll just want to start doing the laundry all the time and get resentful. Or I'll say like, "Hey, I really need T-shirts. I thought you said you were gonna do the laundry." 'Cause she'll say she's gonna do it but then can't. And she'll say, "Well, you can do it." I get that kind of [reaction]. But again, with the house cleaners it's really down to dishes and laundry. And frankly, we can work those out.

Rather than address his girlfriend's desires as valid, he attributed her demands to a personality quirk and his desire to avoid these chores as mere preference. In fact, he explicitly stated that their division of labor wasn't about gender: "I always looked up to strong women so it was never a hard leap for me to see women [as more than] people who just cooked and cleaned. . . . I don't like cooking, but it's not really a gender thing. Like [my girlfriend] loves to cook, she cooks all the time and it's sort of domestic, but it's like you don't have to, but I like it when you do and I'm not gonna do it." This narrative, in which his girlfriend's cooking was defined as a hobby, allowed him to justify his unequal share of household duties, while preserving his understanding of himself as a "feminist." While women may indeed have absorbed a higher standard for cleanliness due to cultural expectations, men failed to challenge the mentality that this was then women's problem. Certainly, accommodating these desires was not seen as an obligation on their part due to their love of the person and their duty to share the household work. Instead, men's desire to do less housework trumped women's desire for cleanliness.

Just like during courtship, some of the men even used what they did do around the house as a justification for what they didn't do, implying that they could only be expected to do so much. Aaron, 40, described a fight he had with his ex-wife over the chores he prioritized. After she saw him ironing his shirt before work, she told him to make sure that he put the ironing board away as she was tired of it being left out. He went to work without putting it away. Getting off work early due to rain, he came home, and instead of putting the ironing board away, he proceeded to do yard work:

> I go out and I'm literally cleaning the yard for four hours in the pouring rain. I'm coated from head to toe with mud. I'm pulling like brush and leaves and everything out of the yard to get it cleaned up. . . . She comes home at the end of the day and, you know, she comes home as I'm driving away with a dump truck full of crap out of the yard to go get rid of. And when I come home, she's fuming because the ironing board is still out. . . . So no acknowledgement that I have accomplished anything positive that day, just punishment for the thing I didn't do.

Aaron felt unappreciated for his contributions to the household and was especially angered when his willingness to do certain chores didn't get him out of doing others, such as cleaning up after himself. In his mind, because he had taken on a more arduous chore, he didn't need to respect or accommodate his wife's wish to not have to continue putting the ironing board away for him. Just as during courtship, one concession justified the lack of another.

Like Gavin, half of the men referenced housekeepers as the ideal solution to conflicts over the division of labor. This approach served the same purpose: it allowed men to shirk an opportunity to reject a gendered division of labor, while allowing them to view themselves as egalitarian. They failed to see their use of hired help as a continuation of gender inequality—now with a class and racial element—and even with this help, they were unwilling to divide the remainder of the housework fairly.

Finally, they relied on notions of fairness rather than equality to divide up household chores. This allowed men with greater incomes or hours at their jobs to divide the household labor unequally. A quarter of the men said that the partner with more free time should be the one to do more of the housework, a gender-neutral arrangement on its face. Given the nature of many of their professional careers, however, this inevitably meant that their partners would be picking up the slack around the house. The same reasoning went for income. In a humorous turning of the tables, however, a few men discussed how this approach was then used against them by women. Mark, 32, said,

> She cooks all the time, but for herself. And she makes her lunch for [work]. But the kitchen gets messy. I spend a lot of time cleaning dishes. I do our common laundry—like sheets and towels, and that kind of stuff. I feel like it is my house; so there is a feeling that I own it and. . . . She said that she didn't want a house because it was a bigger space and this was my thing. So it was more my commitment. Anything that has to do with fixing the house I have to be responsible for. I think a lot of it is translated to me doing a lot of the cleaning. Also, another thing is that she works [a lot]. So she doesn't have any time to do it, so I fill in a lot there. . . . She'll be helpful and I'll probably direct some of the chores. Take out the trash, that kind of stuff.

Ben, 33, discussed his frustration at how his wife used her greater earning power to hire someone and thus "buy her way out of" her share of the duties after they discussed how to fairly divide up the household labor:

There was this conversation about what things we hated doing and what things we didn't mind doing, so I'm like I don't mind cooking, I don't mind doing dishes, I hate vacuuming. . . . A very amusing argument around the fact that she agreed to take on a certain subset of household activities and then promptly hired a cleaning lady, so I'm like, "You abdicated all responsibilities," and she's like, "Well, but I'm paying for it." I'm like, "It's the same pile of money, you're just not doing your chores." The cleaning lady is the right decision, but we did have a little fight around that, around basically the fact that she agreed to do something and then didn't do it.

Heterosexual men drew on similar narratives when discussing childcare. As with women, very few were parents at the time of their interview. As a result, few had concrete ideas about what they wanted to do when they had kids, and their guesses were wide-ranging. Some thought they would pay for care; others thought they would divide the care equally or swap back and forth; a few wanted grandparents to pick up the slack; and others hoped their partners would take time out of the workplace. In particular, there was a widely held belief that a woman staying at home with kids would only cause problems in the marriage. Daniel, 26, said, "I think if we were to go down that road with kids, I would highly advise that she not stay at home. Because I know how career driven she is." But he also didn't want to stay at home, saying, "I mean, if there was a time where it was like for six months or something, but certainly I would absolutely, could not do a stay-at-home dad for multiple years."

Indeed, four of the five men who had kids were either divorced or on the brink of divorce, partly over issues related to the division of labor. Mateo, 33, discussed how his ex-wife staying home increased her emotional dependence on him at the same time that it increased her resentment: "Like I thought it was a good thing, her staying home with the baby, but it made that side worse." In the future, he says he wants "someone who has friends, a profession." Two men discussed how their wives were angered that they didn't have enough money to maintain a middle-class lifestyle on one income, lashing out at them as a result. Alexander, 38, said,

Once again the credit cards started getting high. And she says to me, "Well, I have a lifestyle to maintain. And you're not earning." And she wasn't working; she didn't work for six months after [our son was born.] And then with [our daughter] she was able to do the same, but only went back to work three days a week. But in the meantime, I was never making enough money in her eyes. And that's accumulated. So I mean it's a vicious argument. . . . You know, "You're the biggest mistake I made." You're lazy, you're this, you're that.

Michael, 38, felt the same resentment toward his now ex-wife:

I actually felt pretty abused in that relationship because I supported her for a long time financially because we were having kids, we decided she was going to stay home, and it was like there were certain expectations that I had to go to work, had to keep my job. . . . But it's like I'd have the kids all week-end because she'd go out shopping, she'd disappear all weekend and she had a "maintenance" budget that was $250 a month.

Thus, it appeared a number of the men were picking up on Brad's point, that both partners need to work "or resentment builds." At the same time, while women felt the right to unilaterally decide to stay home with kids, men did not feel they could dispute this decision.

Still, a handful of men either wanted wives who stayed at home for a bit, or said their wives wanted to stay at home. Alexander, who recounted all the resentment in a marriage currently hanging on by a thread, still said later, "I like women who can be women. So I guess a little traditional," while discussing his ideal marriage. Henry, 28, said, "I think the role of mother and father for us will be very traditional. The mother would be very domestic, would be interested in keeping the home, providing care for the children, whereas the father would maybe be the primary bread-winner. The father would take the young boys out to Little League practice or play catch with them."

Aaron explained the benefits of having a wife who stayed home as both an advantage for himself and a gift to his wife:

I love it. Because completely self-centered motive, number one. Hey, look what I can do. So there's a personal pride part of it, for sure. But at the same time, I look at all the stuff my wife is able to do. My wife likes to go and hang out with her friends and go to the gym with her friends. My wife was able to be with my daughter. My daughter never saw the inside of a daycare. Never once. And when she went to kindergarten my wife is able to volunteer in the classroom as much as she wants. So she spends a whole day a week in the classroom volunteering. She gets to go on every fieldtrip my daughter goes on, which my daughter loves. There's never been a conflict as far as, oh there's a parent-teacher conference, I've got to get the afternoon off work. Or calling in sick to work if one of the kids is sick.

Indeed, given the economic privileges of many of the men, many were able to envision options such as living on one income or paying people to take care of their children. As Armaan, 28, put it when asked about childcare, "Pay someone else to do it. That's the great thing about having money is that it allows you to do stuff like dry cleaning, bullshit like that. Someone else can do it and you can spend your time doing the stuff you really want to do." As a result, it appeared that most of the men were not prepared to pick up a significant share of the childcare. Rather, they either planned to outsource the labor or fall back on their wives, justifying this decision with their incomes and expectations for breadwinning. As Robert, 30, said of his wife, who out-earned him, "I think it bothers her. She'd like me to make more money, to be able to support the family more." Only two men seemed very committed to staying at home for any significant period of time. And only Ben had actually scaled back his career ambitions temporarily to stay at home with his infant daughter three days a week while his wife worked full-time. This was especially significant given that he had high earnings potential with an MS, an MBA, and a career in start-ups.

Roses as Romance

While heterosexual women discussed caring as evolving throughout the course of the relationship, with housework coming to symbolize care and love, heterosexual men continued to show care through intermittent gestures that were conventionally gendered. Henry said of his relationship with his fiancée, "In a lot of ways, we have a very traditional, old-fashioned relationship. I am the man so . . . I'm supposed to provide a romantic environment. . . . I'm supposed to make her feel attractive about herself. I'm supposed to get her interested in sexual activity, that kind of thing." William, 32, recognized that symbolic gestures could be used as a substitute for a more substantial engagement in the relationship: "So every little thing, every little detail meant so much to her, and I liked that, because it was an easy thing for me to do. I felt like if she could define happiness in her relationship by those simple things, it was easy for me to supply that, whereas it was difficult for me to supply any sort of real emotional foundation building." Certainly, the main focus by men was on showing care by buying gifts and flowers and "wining and dining" women. Jake went into great detail discussing how he made his live-in girlfriend feel special in this manner:

> I would go to the shops and I would power-shop for her and put stuff on hold and go back and say, "Go take a break from work, I'll watch the store. Go here, here, and here, ask them for the stuff I picked out and I'll buy"—it was our money—"We'll buy you the stuff you like." And so I just started buying her stuff. I knew what she felt comfortable in and liked. I'd buy her stuff that was a little racier than what she would buy and she loved it, she like felt like a little princess, and when we went out the response from the general public was overwhelming. "You guys are beautiful or she's beautiful!" She was on my arm and she just felt like a million bucks 'cause we had, with grubby clothes, an amazing relationship. And then when we got all dolled up, like she was wearing a nice outfit and her hair was brushed, she felt amazing. So we'd go march out and everybody just loved us. . . . Like any chance you got, you wanted to pamper your partner. But ultimately that was kind of the most romantic thing. That was our thing. Every couple months when she needed something to wear, we'd go somewhere. Like for her birthday, for example, I made a reservation at a really nice restaurant. Her dad found out what restaurant, called, and bought us a nice bottle of wine off the menu. On the way, she didn't have a nice pair of shoes to wear to the nice restaurant so she was wearing flip-flops and a nice dress, so we'd stopped off at Nordstrom's and bought her a really cute pair of shoes, a really expensive, cute pair of shoes to wear to dinner and it was just her most special day. Like she just had a blast, she felt like she was being spoiled and it was totally for her.

In his monologue, Jake managed to touch on almost every cultural stereotype about what women need to feel cared for and loved, mostly revolving around financial sacrifice and helping them feel beautiful. In this manner, he didn't sound much different from Ashleigh's discussion of what women need from their romantic relationships. As a result, as many of the men described it, these romantic excursions took the place of any larger sacrifices they might have otherwise made, such as sharing the housework and respecting their partners' needs on a daily basis. Still, one man, Adam, 33, seemed to recognize how these practices led to an imbalance in relationships, although he erased his partner's greater contribution to care in the process:

> I was a poor student. Sometimes I knew I couldn't afford roses and I would always give her like one rose per week on a Friday. And then her biggest romantic thing that she does for me would be cooking me dinner. It's almost an everyday thing. So for her it's more like living instead of doing something abnormal or out of her way. Now that I'm older and I look back at it, it's like she's really treating me more like a younger brother or someone who's under her.

Adam interpreted this to mean that his partner's caregiving was maternal and infantilized him, yet he also seemed to think that he did more for his partner since his romantic gesture wasn't an everyday occurrence, but rather an out-of-the-way practice. He failed to differentiate between the time and financial investment in buying a rose every Friday and cooking dinner every night.

ALTERNATIVE PATTERNS OF ROMANCE AND CARE

Caring activities are crucial to the maintenance of romantic relationships as people "do" love through both everyday acts and symbolic gestures used to signal one's attention to a partner's emotional and material needs.[10] As we've seen, these acts and gestures are gendered, as certain behaviors are expected of men and others of women in heterosexual relationships.[11] LGBQ people must find alternative ways to communicate romance, love, and care to their partners, given their commitment to challenging conventional heterosexual behaviors in their dating and romantic relationships.

For Each Other

Frequently, LGBQ people simply reimagined normative practices as egalitarian. In heterosexual relationships, for example, chivalry is a way for men to show care for their partners. LGBQ people, however, expressed distaste for this approach and argued that romantic behaviors and caregiving should be mutually performed. Adah, a 34-year-old queer genderqueer and gender-fluid person, said of chivalry, "That doesn't sound fun to me, but what does sound fun is certain aspects of that—like people showing care and consideration in those little ways, like opening the door for *each other*. . . . Like not that one person needs to do it for another, but when both people are doing those little considerate things for each other." Kylie, a 29-year-old queer cis woman, indicated that heterosexual conventions were a way for people to avoid the real intimacy work required in relationships, something certainly reflected in William's statement when he argued that romantic gestures were an easy way to make his partner happy in the absence of real emotional engagement. Kylie said, "You just come up with some cheesy romantic gesture and it's okay." As she argued, partners should be approached as individuals with specific needs, instead of simply viewed and reacted to through the lens of gender stereotypes. Karina, a 37-year-old queer cis woman, provided a great example of this when she explained how her former partner had showed love to her. "Cool presents. . . . She found a tin box. It looked like a mailing box and she filled it with a bunch of pictures she made. She drew pictures of genitals, vaginas with vegetables. That was so cute." There were many of these individualized gestures that people found endearing. Jen, a 31-year-old queer cis woman, discussed a partner who "tagged my neighbor's fence with my name. . . . It was so sweet and so unexpected." Another time, her partner found her bike parked at the BART station, "and it had been raining and I found she had put a plastic bag over my seat."

For many, the focus was on mutual gestures, and respondents frequently discussed the romantic practices that they and their partners did for each other. As Santiago, a 34-year-old queer trans person, stated, "We're big-surprise oriented. I surprised him and flew his brother out here for his birthday. We picked him up from the airport and surprised him with this blindfold, rented this beach house, and invited all his friends. He surprised me and took me to Hawaii for my birthday. We're pretty into grand gestures." Beck, a 33-year-old queer trans man, said, "We make cards for each other. . . . And I like to cook for him and he likes to cook for me." Tina said, "We have a running poetry contest together where we'll each take a different form of poetry each month and write to the other person in that." The poetry example turned out to be big, as many people brought it up. Karina mentioned a similar way of doing romance: "Take a piece of paper and then close it. Write a poem like that. A person writes a line [and then the other person writes the next line]." Thus, the emphasis was on romantic practices they valued as a couple and which they *both* used to show care. Many of the examples given were private rituals that partners used to communicate love in personal ways, specific to the relationship. Only a few people engaged in gendered care. Ella, a 26-year-old gay cis woman, was one of the few people who really liked gender roles during courtship, and this translated into her understanding of care work. As she said, "I like feeling like a pretty princess and the one who's taken care of." She also demonstrated her care through nurturing in very feminine-typed ways: "Oh, massages, cook for them, shower them with kisses and hugs. Being sweet, just like if they're sick, taking care of them. Bringing them tea."

A Balanced Approach

Interestingly, unlike in heterosexual relationships, household labor wasn't conceptualized as caregiving but rather as home maintenance in which both partners were expected to participate. Beck, who was home on disability, said, "Even though [my partner] is the one with the job, he knows that it's his responsibility to work on housework too. Which is something that we had discussed, but we both already knew that, so it was nice that there was no arguing about it." Brian, a 30-year-old cis man, and his partner took a different stance, but still one which they felt was equal: whoever was working less did more housework, but that shifted seasonally, given their respective jobs. "I don't think anyone feels like they're put in a particular role." Diana, a 27-year-old bisexual cis woman, explained, "I don't like organized chores. The whole concept of, it's this week so it's my turn to do this and you'll do this and this. It doesn't really work from what I've seen. I'm very much team oriented. Your job could be dishes, but be part of the whole. The whole is to keep the house clean." When I asked her what she would do if a partner didn't do their share with this approach, she explained that she wouldn't feel obligated to pick up the slack for someone: "I'd probably stop covering for them. Like their laundry wouldn't get done. I'd have clean laundry. I would probably take dishes and get a one-person set and keep them clean. You can't touch it. I will eat off of it, clean it, and bring it into the sink. I'm not going to do everything. I'm also not going to fight about it and then someone digs their heels in." Diana didn't find it "productive to micromanage another adult" and was against the idea of asking for help when overwhelmed or creating a "honey-do" list as many of the heterosexual women did when a partner refused to share the labor.

Instead, relationships in which the balance of housework started to feel off and began to emulate a gendered division of labor were treated with great suspicion. Adah said, "I wasn't really doing anything besides just being there and cleaning and cooking and hanging out with the dogs. I was like, oh, what is this housewife shit? Like I don't want to do this. . . . She'd be out chopping wood and I'd be like, okay, I guess I'm making corn-bread. How did I wind up in this straight relationship?" Adah noted that it was this shift to gendered dynamics that led them to leave the relation-ship: "I liked most the care and comfort that we provided for each other early on. But then ultimately she started making decisions from a self-centered place." As they explained, "I love to cook and things like that, but I couldn't tell if it was something that was actually happening or just something that was triggering and reminding me of the kind of relation-ship I didn't want to have." While Adah might have been happy to contrib-ute to the household by cooking, they wanted similar gestures back. Instead, cooking became a gendered task and a red flag that the relation-ship was taking on an unequal dynamic in which they weren't interested.

Given the importance placed on balance and equality, only a few LGBQ people wanted a more traditional division of labor where one partner stayed home with children while the other focused on paid labor. Many resolved this potential tension between goals and the reality of caregiving by simply opting out of parenting altogether, either emphasizing the importance of work or indicating that they didn't feel capable of taking responsibility for another human. As Sam, a 30-year-old queer genderqueer person, said, "When I think about future plans, I think I would want to have chickens." Only a third of the 40 LGBQ respondents were sure they wanted children, and none had them at the time of their interview. But those who did want kids in the future struggled with how to best proceed. Unfortunately, given the lack of structural supports for childrearing in the United States, this was one area that was more difficult to reimagine as egalitarian in novel ways. As a result, for most the default was to assume that they would pay someone to take care of their kids. This response was especially common among gay cis men and often took on a gendered element, such as when Jack, a 25-year-old gay cis man, said, "The lady that we would hire to clean would also double as that [child caregiver]. She'd have to be very good about that. I very firmly believe that there needs to be a maternal influence." Lesbian and queer couples were more likely to discuss switching off primary caregiving roles either by child or by a child's life stage.

But there was also much more discussion among LGBQ people that these practices required resources that they potentially might never have. Beck didn't see himself raising children with his partner, owing to their lack of resources combined with a lack of drive to do so: "We're like, oh, that would be kinda nice if we had all these other factors like the money and the space and lots of family and if healthcare in the country were better and there was like parental leave and all this; like yeah, it could be nice. But neither of us grew up being like, I want to be a parent." Adah explained,

> I would love to have a kid or maybe more than one kid and one of the things that's been hard for me is feeling like I'm never going to be financially stable enough. Definitely not on my own and maybe not even with a partner. Like as queer people, as mostly people of color who I've dated, most of us as transgender, nonconforming people, even when you have a job that feels secure, it's always in some kind of context where you're just not getting the same stability and perks as privileged people who are like straight and white or married.

As they went on to say, "I don't value money, like I don't need a lot of money in life to be a successful person, but if I'm going to have a kid, I would love to feel pretty sure that they're always going to have a roof over their head and enough food and healthcare and things like that."

As a workaround, a few people discussed searching for creative ways to engage in childrearing while not taking on the primary care of a child. They emphasized a more communal approach to childcare. Jessie, a 28-year-old queer genderqueer person, said, "Probably none [children] of my own when I think about it because that to me feels like a really weird selfish take on resources in the world. But I would not mind raising other people's children. I don't think I would adopt a child. I think it would be communal, like if someone had children I would be okay with raising that child." Manuela, a 36-year-old queer genderqueer person, agreed: "Definitely community. I remember when I was living in Santa Fe I was friends with so many single moms and they would all just take care of each other, you know. And I feel like that's just an example of what a lot of other cultures do too and it's not really emphasized so much in this culture."

Brian was also in the process of deliberately rethinking what family can be, asking, "How do we take kinship structures and ideas about futurity and reproduction and what happens if we break from just looking at the heteronormative family or the patriarchal family?" As he added,

> I actually talked yesterday to a close friend of mine who she and her partner are interested in having kids. They need a donor and like we've talked in the past about me being a donor and being kind of involved, but not being a primary parent. And I think there's something about that sort of nontraditional formation that's really interesting to me. I think love and communication are sort of the key things for making a kid feel safe more, for me, than the structures. Just 'cause those structures are sort of alienating to me in general.

Marco, a 30-year-old queer cis man, had a similar idea but ran into resistance from his partner: "I've kind of presented this idea about coparenting with another set of parents, but he has more traditional views." As a result, he fell back on paid care, saying, "I guess I had some feelings about it in that I wanted us both to work. I guess I'm holding some sort of expectation about there being childcare." While LGBQ narratives around parenting were still theoretical given that no one had children at this point, they suggest a more intentional engagement with the variety of forms childcare can take, as well as the barriers to achieving egalitarian arrangements without significant resources and policy supports. While heterosexual women and men articulated more individualistic solutions to this conundrum and never mentioned possible policy changes, a handful of LGBQ people were thinking more communally about what it means to be a parent in this society.

Space, Flexibility, and Changing Needs

Focusing on flexibility and renegotiation, many LGBQ people also emphasized how care work changed throughout the relationship. At different points, one might need to give more than receive, but respondents indicated that this should even out over time. Santiago said, "The first year was definitely about him. [My partner] came out as trans to me, came out as a survivor of sorts. There was a lot of crying; there was a lot of processing trauma." Yet later in the relationship, Santiago discussed how their own needs took priority and their partner was there for them during a hard time: "He'd just do everything for me. I wouldn't ask and he didn't hold it against me; he would just do things because he knew I needed them." LGBQ people frequently emphasized providing partners with space to be who they needed to be as an individual. Marco appreciated how he and his partner provided each other space to explore their own interests and independent selves without being shamed by the other.

Instead of reenacting scripts, the focus was on constant communication, evaluation, and renegotiation. Nothing was considered set in stone but instead was always up for discussion. Checking in with one's partner consistently was paramount and a way to allow space for each other's changing needs. Patricio, a 25-year-old queer nonbinary person, discussed renegotiating the terms of a relationship with a partner, something they felt a previous partner had not done for them:

At that time [my partner] had said she didn't want to have sex with me anymore. I was like, oh, okay, well, I still want to be with you and if you don't want to have sex with me, that's perfectly fine. That was the issue with [my ex-partner]. I told her I didn't want to have sex with her, but I still wanted to be with her. And she was like, well if you don't want to have sex with me, then what's the point of being in a relationship. So I was making sure with [my partner], I was like, look, if you don't want to have sex with me right now, that's okay. . . . But don't ever feel like you have to have sex with me to have this type of relationship.

Jessie made a similar point, stating, "My very important relationships with people tend to be a flowing, adapting, flexible, always changing kind of thing. Or how people feel at the moment. And I feel like that is much more honest." When I asked Riley, a 29-year-old lesbian trans man, how often he and his fiancée discussed what they wanted out of the relationship, he said, "I think all the time. We negotiate." He explained that his fiancée had wanted their relationship to be nonmonogamous. As he said,

"I've had a lot of exposure to the idea . . . but I wasn't sure it was something I actually wanted to do. So when she brought it up, it was a stretch for me . . . I was like, well, let's give it a shot. But it hurt the relationship. . . . And so we closed it. And we constantly reevaluate and we're always talking about it." Participants viewed this flexibility as a form of care work, in that it gave partners the understanding that their needs were important and that they had space and support to grow and change as a person. But people also aimed to make this process balanced, as each partner discussed working to accommodate the changing needs of the other.

At the time of the interview, Riley and his fiancée were again in the process of reevaluating their relationship. Riley had just started testosterone: "For her she's struggling a little bit because she's always been a lesbian and she's not sure, you know. Like she's worried about attraction and if like one day she wakes up to a man mug, she might not be totally into it. And also there's like the piece that she's femme and a lot of her visibility is in being seen with a butch. So like there is that piece that can make it hard for her too." Femmes may be called on to perform a certain femininity in order to reinforce trans masculinity, but in the process lose their own queer identity.[12] While Riley wanted to be seen for who he was, he also made sure to see his fiancée for who she was, demonstrating that this affective affirmation of each other's genders was not one-sided. This was an important form of care work in that as respondents or their partners struggled with or navigated their gender or sexual identity, they found they had emotional support in the form of their partner witnessing their changing needs and providing important recognition.[13]

DIFFERING CONCEPTS OF EQUALITY

While heterosexual women and men assert that they want egalitarian relationships, they tend to cling to the idea of gendered preferences and skills. For instance, women are seen as better suited to household labor simply because they are more attentive to it. The idea that women are simply fulfilling an expectation isn't considered. As heterosexual women form long-term relationships, cooking, cleaning, and caring for the household become the chief ways that they demonstrate care. Heterosexual men, on the other hand, continue to engage in generic visions of romance culled straight from the movies, just as they did during courtship. Romance and caring isn't doing half the load at home but, rather, flowers, jewelry, dinner, and a movie every few weeks. Each approach reflects the beliefs in gender difference established at a young age and reinforced during courtship.

While "romance" is one way that men can make up for unequal relationships, the other is through the gendered assignment of expertise, allowing both partners to feel as though they just happen to be dominant in different ways. The relative value of these areas of expertise goes unquestioned, however, as men generally take control over finances while women are in charge of decorating the house and dressing their partner. By assigning women dominance and expertise in household chores, men feel more comfortable abdicating responsibility and leaving women with the ultimate control of housework, but also obligation to do it. In other ways, however, men felt that women *expected* them to be dominant, given the relationship patterns that were established when they began dating. In addition, as women take on the household labor that they may feel is expected of them, men are able to argue that women "just do it." Men also emphasize what they do perform around the house in order to justify what they don't, similar to their justifications for inequality during courtship. Without a compelling reason for men to change, which is difficult to muster given that housework tends not to be viewed as fun and women find battles over it not to be worth the trouble, men are often content to just ride out the arrangement. Certainly, women expressed greater difficulty getting men to value their needs than the reverse.

Although heterosexual men and women were already building gender inequality into their committed relationships in numerous ways, one of the major barriers to egalitarian relationships is childrearing. Because of the lack of supports for childrearing in this country, many couples who previously managed relatively balanced relationships fall back on a gendered division of labor when they have kids.[14] Very few of the people in the study had children, yet it was clear that the same patterns held true for this group. Although they might have had the best of intentions, structural barriers to evenly dividing parenting and paid labor, combined with gender-essentialist narratives about who was best at what tasks in the home, resulted in unequal parenting practices. Those without children appeared to be on the same path, although given their economic resources, many anticipated outsourcing this labor so that both partners could at least remain in the workplace. Almost no one had thought beyond work schedules to consider how the ongoing care of a child would be managed. Given the respondents' narratives about the relative strengths of men and women, there is reason to believe that they will fall back on parenting practices that place the bulk of the responsibility on women.

LGBQ people's practices, by contrast, demonstrate the potential for greater relationship equality. When heterosexual partners fail to deconstruct gendered practices, they inscribe inequality into their relationships even as they express the desire to be egalitarian. LGBQ people, by making the conscious choice to reject normative practices, create a mindful space that allows them to seek new ways to demonstrate romance and care to their partners. Because many queer relationships do not, and in some cases cannot, rely on well-established practices and ideologies, norms are often questioned, evaluated, and then rejected, with the goal of making space for the creation of egalitarian practices instead. In the process, many couples incorporated the elements they felt were important to a successful relationship, emphasizing constant communication, evaluation, and negotiation. The aim was greater individuality and equality, and they actively worked to balance their own needs with the needs of their partners in ways that didn't rely on unequal scripts. While they did not always succeed, they found greater balance in their relationships than did heterosexual men and women.

WHERE THE RUBBER MEETS THE ROAD

While these findings indicate important benefits to rethinking taken-for-granted relationship practices, they should not be overstated. In many of the queer relationships, it was unclear what would happen over time, in particular as partners either had children or fell into relationship patterns. After all, many of the people interviewed were in relatively new relationships or were currently single. Just as with heterosexual couples, behaviors may not live up to expectations in the long run. It's easier to consistently rethink expectations at the beginning of a relationship than later on, as people fall into routines. Still, the greater equality present in those relationships that *were* long term does provide some hope.

That said, the structural barriers to equal parenting are also present for LGBQ people. None yet had children, but a third hoped to. While the majority wanted an equal division of paid labor and caregiving, their hope for balance and flexibility in these realms may be hard to achieve. After all, if one person is a higher earner, it starts to make less sense for that person to cut back at work. And the same pattern will probably hold for any kids beyond the first, pushing one person to focus more on home and the other more on paid labor. While I emphasize the need for cultural change, we also need change in the form of family-friendly policies if we want to see more egalitarian relationships. Finally, the LGBQ people I interviewed should not be understood as representative of that population as a whole, as they included a higher percentage of quite radical queers. This means that any challenges to norms they represent will have limited visibility and impact beyond their own community. But they do demonstrate the potential present when people consciously and consistently reflect on how to make relationships more equal rather than simply falling back on well-worn expectations.

7 Dated Dating and the Stalled Gender Revolution

As we have seen throughout the course of this book, the popular idea that young adults no longer date or seek committed relationships has been vastly overstated. Yes, the old dating script has certainly come into question and people are often left wondering about the best path to take as they attempt to secure long-term romantic partners. But while these scripts may be in transition, they are certainly not obsolete. Traditional courtship rituals coexist in an uneasy tension with new norms surrounding gender relations. The majority of college-educated young adults want to work, many in careers that require substantial investments throughout the life course. This has led to shifts in how people seek out romantic partners, as previously gendered relationship practices are now in conflict with class-based mobility scripts that call for two highly educated, highly ambitious professional partners to meet and marry as equals. As shown in chapter 2, achievement scripts for college-educated men and women, especially those seeking professional careers, are very similar. Women and men receive clear instructions for how to proceed through young adulthood in order to get where they want to go, and women, even more so than men, are under intense pressure to launch lucrative careers. Young adults are expected to set aside their personal lives to some extent, and romantic relationships in particular, in order to focus on establishing themselves in careers in a timely, lock-step manner—what sociologists Laura Hamilton and Elizabeth Armstrong refer to as the "self-development imperative."[1] Part of this is figuring out who they are as individuals and creating a sense of themselves as autonomous people who don't "need" others. Only then will they be sufficiently established to settle down into a serious relationship.

One of the key factors in consolidating class privilege is partnering with an equally accomplished mate. College-educated young adults want partners who are just as ambitious professionally as they are. But this is not only about securing economic stability; they also believe that by dating "equals," they are more likely to create the mutually satisfying relationships they crave, in which they are valued for their own individual accomplishments *and* can engage with each other in a challenging and stimulating manner. This model explicitly rejects the conventional expectation that male breadwinners seek out female homemakers, that a woman's economic standing reflect her husband's, and that "feminine charm" be the currency women use to attract husbands.[2] Instead, just as academic achievement and credentials are seen as the key to professional success, they are now too seen as the key to relationship success.[3] Young adults then seek to meet each other as equals and most now express a desire for egalitarian relationships. These narratives downplay gender difference and indicate that heterosexual men and women are looking for relationships in which gender does not determine the behaviors of each partner.

Yet from the very outset of the relationship, the persistence of gendered courtship undermines these goals. As we saw in chapters 3 and 4 (and in contrast to the popular hook-up narrative), heterosexual women and men continue to engage in traditional ritualized patterns in which the man asks and pays for early dates, determines the pace of the relationship, and proposes marriage. The culmination of courtship remains a relatively traditional ceremony in which a father walks his daughter down the aisle and "gives" her away to her partner, after which the couple further symbolizes the transfer of property by filling out paperwork for the woman to take her husband's last name. This trajectory was accepted *and embraced* by the majority of the heterosexual men and women with whom I spoke. While aspects were called into question here and there, most respondents liked and wanted these conventions, or at least took them at face value, thereby not challenging them. The handful who disliked them found them hard to avoid given their widespread appeal. Usually, they just went along with them anyway.

But given the desire to create egalitarian partnerships, why do these highly gendered courtship conventions persist? I found that in spite of wanting egalitarian relationships and seeing themselves as professional equals, men and women continue to believe that they are innately different. Courtship conventions are therefore used to reflect these supposed differences while also allowing men and women to establish the intentions of the other person. Dating can be confusing and fraught with emotions. But dating norms provide a script that men and women can comfortably follow to ensure they are relating to each other in the expected ways, thereby lessening the tensions that go along with getting to know someone new. The possibility of a misstep that may take you off the other person's radar decreases. Classification in terms of gender is engaged in partly for cognitive simplification, but it is based on essentialist beliefs, and it has consequences.[4] Men are assumed to like certain behaviors by virtue of their being men, while women are assumed to like certain behaviors by virtue of their being women. These assumptions limit the range of human preference and force us to get to know one another in a partially predetermined manner.

The cultural narratives about what women and men want from their romantic relationships surround us. They are on television and in the movies, explained in songs, and presented as advice in magazines and books. Women are told, *He's Just Not That Into You,* and given *How to Get a Man without Getting Played.*[5] Men get to explore *What Women Want in a Man* and *Why Women Love Jerks.*[6] The embedded assumptions are that most men are commitment-shy dogs out for sex and women need to be able to distinguish between them and the men willing to commit to marriage. Men, on the other hand, must learn to walk a fine line between being chivalrous and coming off as overeager, and to appear as dominant but not domineering. After all, the fun for men is in the chase, while women enjoy the validation that comes with being pursued and desired. Of course, men don't need as much advice since women are naturally dying to commit—scroll through a few pages of dating-advice books for men on Amazon and you inexplicably find yourself sorting through piles of dating-advice books for women on how to get men to commit. These narratives are consumed as general knowledge about what it means to be a man or a woman.

In fact, the majority of heterosexual women do want to get married. Yet they are constantly bombarded with messages that men either do not or are extremely reluctant to commit in this manner. Courtship rituals serve as a way to ferret out those with the same relationship goals. Allowing the man to ask and pay for dates, confirm the relationship, and propose serves this purpose. If he is allowed to set the pace of the relationship, there can be no worries of coercion. He is willingly committing. Meanwhile, women focus on making themselves attractive to men. This means making sure that they do not come off as overly aggressive or interested, traits that supposedly signal their desperation for commitment and are an automatic turn-off for men. Heterosexual men, for their part, feel that they must prove themselves to be reliable mates who can financially take care of their wives, while at the same time distinguishing themselves from the domineering, disrespectful masses. After all, they are looking to date and marry highly accomplished, self-sufficient, independent women. Thus, they must find ways to be confident without being overly aggressive, showing that they can take charge without controlling.

At the same time, courtship conventions aren't seen as threatening to men's and women's feminist identities. They are downplayed as mere preference, something they like and do for fun but that has no lasting consequences in their relationships. As long as women can maintain their careers and financial independence, the gendered relationship rituals don't undermine their personal narratives of empowerment, which focus almost exclusively on their professional lives. As sociologist Paula England argues, the push for gender egalitarianism has been limited to aspects of life that connect to upward mobility, such as educational and workplace opportunities, "but otherwise gender blinders guide the paths of both men and women."[7] For their part, men can engage in sexist behaviors that are coded as kind rather than as hostile. They view courtship conventions as just doing nice things and caring for their partners rather than a reflection of any deeper beliefs about gender. After all, they certainly want their partners to work, and they support women's professional goals. They aren't the man on the street yelling slurs at women, or insisting their wives stay home to take care of the kids. Interestingly, both men and women manage to hold these contradictory messages simultaneously. On the one hand, courtship conventions supposedly reflect the different needs and desires of men and women and are considered necessary. On the other, they are meaningless rituals that don't reflect beliefs about unequal genders. This disconnect serves the purpose of allowing men and women to take comfort in two important, but often conflicting identities: they get to maintain deeply held gender identities *and* consider themselves progressive, independent, and professionally oriented.

Certainly, I don't want to understate the progress that has been made. Many of the women were extremely aggressive in setting the pace of their relationships, although they often tried to conceal their nonconforming behaviors. Others rejected these relationship goals altogether, rejecting gendered courtship in the process. Many of the men resisted the expectation that they shoulder the financial burden of dating and enjoyed relationships with women who were happy to make their desires known and actively help navigate the direction the relationship would take. They certainly weren't resisting commitment, and many were determined to make a life with a permanent partner.

Others wanted to resist but found it hard to do so, given how ubiquitous the expectations for these gendered behaviors are. I still remember the reaction I received when I referred to myself as engaged without receiving a formal marriage proposal from my then partner. One man told me I wasn't really engaged. In spite of the many conversations my fiancé and I had about getting married, it would only count *after* he initiated a proposal in a traditional fashion. Another man told me the marriage was sure to fail because women shouldn't "push" marriage; rather, they should wait until the man initiated to ensure that he was actually ready and willing. I wasn't to even voice my opinion on the matter! I remember feeling confused, enraged, and embarrassed, all at the same time. I chafed at the gender stereotypes being pushed on me, but I also couldn't shake the feeling that perhaps I was doing something wrong, that my partner didn't really love me, and we wouldn't work out as a result.

It turns out we didn't. But I like to think it had nothing to do with the way we got engaged. Still, the message stuck with me, as I'm sure it sticks with many others. The only thing that would legitimize my relationships was doing things the "right" way. And so while many of the people I interviewed readily embraced traditional dating practices, others felt compelled to follow in spite of their own misgivings. Maybe their partner would want traditional practices and ditch them if they weren't followed. Maybe their friends and family would serve as a chorus, urging on conformity. If their own nagging voice in the back of their head didn't put on the brakes, someone else's would.

The nagging voices are different for LGBQ people. LGBQ people start out hearing that the only acceptable relationship choice is heterosexual, or that the way to a happy and stable life is remarkably similar to the path taken by heterosexual men and women. Build a career; settle down into a monogamous marriage; raise children. Some LGBQ people embrace this. They may engage in minor challenges to the expected relationship pathways and behaviors provided to heterosexuals, but for the most part they enjoy living a similar existence.

But for others, the nagging voices are those coming from the queer community, urging them to reject this one-size-fits-all version of romantic life and embrace radical ways of creating and sustaining intimate relationships. This group of LGBQ people has the additional challenge of navigating the courtship rituals that they often grew up valuing and expecting, but which no longer reflect their priorities. As they embraced their LGBQ identities, they found themselves instead drawing on queer cultural narratives and seeking alternative ways to build romantic meaning in their relationships. As a result, as we saw in chapter 5, LGBQ people were more likely to resist courtship norms and dated in significantly more egalitarian ways than did heterosexual couples. Payment for dates wasn't the sole responsibility of one partner, nor was it expected to be, and money wasn't used to determine how someone felt about the relationship. Nor was it the job of just one person to ask for a date. Having wide sexual experience wasn't stigmatized, although "vanilla" sex seemed like a potential deal breaker.

LGBQ people instead focused on communication, negotiation, flexibility, and building balanced relationships that made space for each individual's often-changing needs. This approach had a real effect on the types of relationships they built. They were not immune to gendered expectations and often enforced conventionally gendered behaviors in themselves and their partners. They also confronted new norms coming out of queer culture and dictating "how to be" in a relationship. But rather than take these as given, they frequently questioned them, challenging the inequalities that persistently pop up in all intimate relationships as a cornerstone of their relationship and care work.

Whereas sociologist Arlie Hochschild found a conflict between slower-changing men and faster-changing women, heterosexual college-educated men and women are now in general agreement over how they want their relationships to function.[8] Women are a bit more likely to support traditional courtship and men are a bit more likely to expect women to do more of the housework and childcare, yet the majority of women and men state a desire for traditional courtship and egalitarian long-term relationships. The conflict, then, is now an internal one between their commitment to equality and their commitment to gender difference, two extremely prominent narratives in our society. At present, heterosexuals lack alternative scripts for dating and courtship to counter the culturally hegemonic, gendered one. While there is now an egalitarian ideology for marriage, providing men and women with a way to discuss and formulate ideals that contrast with the male breadwinner / female homemaker model, there is no similar egalitarian ideology for courtship. This makes alternative pathways hard to conceive. Women and men are thus left unsure how to balance an independence that rejects gender complementarity with committed relationships, where desire and romance are traditionally rooted in the enactment of gender difference. And in contrast to gendered marriage, gendered courtship is easy to view as harmless and enjoyable, without stopping to consider possible negative outcomes.

In contrast, LGBQ people *do* have alternative scripts, but these have not been taken up by the majority of heterosexuals. These scripts give LGBQ people space to question the taken-for-granted assumptions about romantic relationships and how they should function and proceed. As gender scholars argue, it can be hard to create change when imagination is limited,[9] and traditional scripts limit the imaginations of heterosexual people as to the range of possibilities.

On June 26, 2015, I was on an airplane coming home after finishing my interviews with LGBQ people, when the Supreme Court handed down its decision on *Obergefell v. Hodges*. Same-sex marriage would be the law of the land; now all states would be required to perform and recognize the marriages of same-sex couples and provide the attendant rights. It has only been a few years since the ruling, and it remains to be seen how this decision will influence queer communities. But as sociologist Abigail Ocobock argues, after marriage equality, critiques against assimilation and normalization will be harder to sustain and legal marriage is likely to "have a profound impact on the character of LGBQ culture and communities." In particular, she asserts that people need the space to imagine alternatives and *Obergefell* undermines this: "Dominant (heterosexual) cultural scripts about marriage—as symbolizing personal choice, love, and achievement—emphasize the private, individualized nature of marriage and make it harder to see (or at least stay focused on) how it also operates as a constraining social institution."[10]

I hope that moving forward, LGBQ communities won't lose the imagination they possess to challenge normative understandings of romantic life. Rather than see LGBQ people assimilate to heterosexual norms, heterosexual men and women need to learn from the creative queer reimaginings of personal life. While the assumption has been that certain pathways are ideal for stable relationship formation and the concern is how to make these pathways available to everyone, perhaps there is certain value to be found in having to rethink how relationships can and should look.[11] Given that courtship and marriage are traditionalizing practices that reify gender-essentialist narratives, how might alternative expectations and pathways create space for more egalitarian practices? Future research should continue to examine how a lower investment in courtship practices in groups excluded from the supposed ideal makes space for rethinking the relationship between gender and family.

BREAKING THE ROMANCE TRANCE

We may merely be in a period of transition, with gender equality in romantic relationships all but inevitable as we move toward greater structural equality. As I stated in chapter 1, scholars have argued that the intransigence of gendered courtship norms is less significant to the goal of gender equality than is the strong preference for egalitarian relationships and professional

opportunities.[12] Certainly there has been a sense that as the material inequalities between men and women fade, so too will the status inequalities.[13]
After all, the theory of cultural lag posits that changes in beliefs often lag
behind structural changes but eventually catch up.[14] But this ignores an
important element, the possibility of a feedback loop—that as long as people
continue to insist that men and women are fundamentally different in what
they desire from their romantic relationships and how they should behave
within them, difference narratives will be consistently reinforced and then
applied to other aspects of men's and women's lives. There is evidence for this
in the finding that many LGBQ people couldn't use gender-essentialist narratives in the same way as heterosexuals and used their critical lens to more
successfully challenge inequality in their relationships.

As chapter 6 showed, the heterosexual men and women in this study
wanted egalitarian relationships and had the educational credentials and
material resources to meet each other as equals in their households. Yet they
did not. While almost none were forming the male breadwinner/female
homemaker families that we associate with the traditional marriage, the
division of household labor, care work, and decision-making authority
remained highly gendered. These aren't 1950s relationships by any means,
as both partners are expected to work and men to at least chip in with
housework and childcare. But those who'd had highly traditional courtship
patterns also had more traditionally gendered long-term relationships.
During courtship, men showed their care for women through symbolic
rituals based in gender difference that emphasized their commitment to the
relationship. As the relationship transitioned to marriage, women showed
care and commitment by changing their last names and taking on a greater
share of the household labor.

The cultural narratives about the assumed fundamental differences
between men and women evoked during courtship were used to explain
the unequal arrangements in long-term relationships. In fact, not only
were they used to justify inequality, but they became the reason why inequality should not be *understood as such*. If these differences merely
reflect the essential traits of men and women, then they can't be seen as
the result of culturally enforced inequality. Not only did these narratives
then prevent reflection as to how preferences, skills, and traits may be
socially constructed, but they hindered attempts to challenge unequal

arrangements. Indeed, many of the women struggled with their partners' unwillingness to help with an equal share of the housework, eventually chalking up men's intransigence to their innate stubbornness and inability to compromise. By contrast, LGBQ people downplayed mainstream gender narratives and instead emphasized egalitarian and flexible care work highly attuned to individual needs in relationships. Challenging old norms and drawing on new ones didn't mean they never struggled with problematic relationship practices, but it did give them a different set of tools with which to work, and their relationships were more equal as a result.

We have seen great changes in the American family over the last fifty years, yet the gender revolution has stalled and one of the main reasons is our inability to dismantle the gendered family.[15] Until we begin to fully challenge the assumptions about men's and women's innate traits that are used to justify these particular arrangements, we will continue to experience substantial inequality in our intimate relationships. Courtship conventions validate and celebrate these assumed differences between men and women as necessary, but also as fun, romantic, and harmless. Yet gender difference is associated with value, and women remain disadvantaged in their long-term relationships as a result of our determined emphasis on gendering men and women.[16] These beliefs will end up affecting these relationships, even in the ways couples seek to avoid. As they start to have children and confront the unyielding workplace, there is little doubt that they will draw on gender to formulate "Plan B."[17]

Contesting traditional courtship norms will help undermine the go-to understandings and expectations that young adults fall back on. Yet other changes needs to occur as well. Family-friendly work practices and social policies, such as flexible workplaces, a limited work week, extended paid parental leave, and free or affordable universal childcare, enable partners to enact egalitarian behaviors.[18] While I've emphasized the cultural changes that need to occur, these need to be supported and even encouraged through policy change. For example, as research on paternity leave shows, when fathers are forced to take extended parental leave through use-it-or-lose-it policies, they become more involved fathers rather than simply taking on the helper role.[19]

Shifting our roles in society shifts what we believe people are capable of, undermining essentialist narratives about the differences between genders.[20] While I contest the argument that people are as egalitarian as they say they are, I do agree that attitudinal shifts can come from policy shifts, thus interrupting the feedback loop. Change is difficult, and I hope that young adults and policy makers continue the hard work of dismantling gender inequality in this country, creating a variety of pathways that allow for a range of relationship experiences.

Summary of Interview
Respondents

Table 1   List of Respondents

Name*	Age	Gender	Sexuality	Race/Ethnicity
Aaron	40	cis man	heterosexual	white
Aashi	29	cis woman	heterosexual	Asian
Abby	33	cis woman	heterosexual	white
Adah	34	genderqueer/fluid	queer	MENA
Adam	33	cis man	heterosexual	Asian
Alek	38	cis man	gay	white
Alexander	38	cis man	heterosexual	Asian
Alice	34	cis woman	heterosexual	Asian
Alison	27	cis woman	heterosexual	white/Latina
Alyssa	28	cis woman	heterosexual	Asian
Amanda	31	cis woman	heterosexual	white
Amelia	33	cis woman	heterosexual	Asian
Amit	27	cis man	queer	Asian
Amy	26	cis woman	heterosexual	white
Andie	27	genderqueer	gay	white
Andrew	35	cis man	heterosexual	white
Anming	29	cis man	gay	Asian

(continued)

Table 1   (Continued)

Name*	Age	Gender	Sexuality	Race/Ethnicity
Anna	40	cis woman	heterosexual	white
Ariana	30	cis woman	heterosexual	MENA
Arjun	25	cis man	heterosexual	Asian
Armaan	28	cis man	heterosexual	MENA
Ashleigh	29	cis woman	heterosexual	white
Beck	33	trans man	queer	white
Ben	33	cis man	heterosexual	white
Brad	32	cis man	heterosexual	white
Breanna	36	cis woman	heterosexual	Asian/white
Brian	30	cis man	queer	white
Brooke	36	cis woman	heterosexual	white
Caitlin	30	cis woman	gay	white
Caroline	31	cis woman	heterosexual	white
Charlie	32	trans man	queer	white
Chloe	26	cis woman	lesbian	white
Christopher	34	cis man	heterosexual	white
Claire	26	cis woman	heterosexual	white
Daniel	26	cis man	heterosexual	white
Dave	34	cis man	heterosexual	white
Diana	27	cis woman	bisexual	black
Elizabeth	27	cis woman	bisexual	white
Ella	26	cis woman	gay	white
Emily	31	cis woman	heterosexual	Asian
Emma	27	cis woman	gay	white
Ethan	38	cis man	heterosexual	white
Evan	27	cis man	gay	white
Evelyn	30	cis woman	heterosexual	Asian
Gavin	31	cis man	heterosexual	white
Gregory	33	cis man	heterosexual	Latino
Hailey	31	cis woman	bisexual	white
Heather	27	cis woman	heterosexual	white
Henry	28	cis man	heterosexual	white
Isabella	29	cis woman	heterosexual	white
Ishan	29	cis man	heterosexual	Asian
Jack	25	cis man	gay	white
Jake	34	cis man	heterosexual	white
Jane	31	cis woman	heterosexual	white

Jamie	30	cis woman	queer	Latina
Jen	31	cis woman	queer	black/white
Jenna	26	cis woman	heterosexual	white
Jennifer	27	cis woman	heterosexual	white
Jeremy	30	cis man	heterosexual	white/Latino
Jessie	28	genderqueer	queer	Asian
Jocelyn	36	trans woman	bisexual	white
Karina	37	cis woman	queer	white
Katie	32	cis woman	heterosexual	Asian
Keira	36	cis woman	heterosexual	Asian
Ken	33	cis man	gay	black/American Indian
Kylie	29	cis woman	queer	Asian
Lauren	29	cis woman	queer	white
Leslie	25	cis woman	lesbian	white
Logan	29	cis man	heterosexual	white
Luke	26	cis man	heterosexual	white
Manuela	36	genderqueer	queer	white/Latinx
Marco	30	cis man	queer	white
Mark	32	cis man	heterosexual	white
Mateo	33	cis man	heterosexual	Latino
Matthew	29	cis man	heterosexual	white
Melanie	29	cis woman	queer	black/Asian
Mia	39	cis woman	heterosexual	white
Michael	38	cis man	heterosexual	white
Michelle	31	cis woman	heterosexual	black
Nicholas	36	cis man	gay	white
Nicole	28	cis woman	heterosexual	white
Noah	28	cis man	bisexual	Asian
Olivia	26	cis woman	heterosexual	white
Patricio	25	nonbinary	queer	Latinx
Paul	34	cis man	heterosexual	white
Peter	29	cis man	heterosexual	Asian
Rachel	27	cis woman	heterosexual	white
Rebecca	40	cis woman	heterosexual	Asian
Riley	29	trans man	lesbian	white
Robert	30	cis man	heterosexual	Asian
Ryan	28	cis man	heterosexual	Asian
Sam	30	genderqueer	queer	Latinx
Samantha	31	cis woman	heterosexual	white
Samuel	37	cis man	gay	white

(continued)

Table 1   (Continued)

Name*	Age	Gender	Sexuality	Race/Ethnicity
Santiago	34	trans	queer	Asian
Sarah	31	cis woman	heterosexual	white
Sean	26	cis man	gay	white
Shreya	29	cis woman	gay	Asian
Sienna	30	cis woman	heterosexual	white
Sofia	26	cis woman	heterosexual	Latina
Steven	30	cis man	heterosexual	Asian
Tina	27	cis woman	bisexual	white
Tommy	27	cis man	heterosexual	white
William	32	cis man	heterosexual	white
Yang	36	cis man	gay	Asian

*All names are pseudonyms.

Table 2   Demographic Characteristics

Variable	Measure	N	Percentage
Gender	Cis woman	50	47
	Cis man	44	42
	Genderqueer/nonbinary	6	6
	Trans	5	5
Sexual orientation	Heterosexual	65	62
	Queer	16	15
	Gay	15	14
	Bisexual	6	6
	Lesbian	3	3
Race/ethnicity	White	62	59
	Asian	25	24
	Bi-/multiracial	7	6
	Latino/a/x	6	6
	MENA	3	3
	Black	2	2
Class background	Middle to upper	70	67
	Poor to working	35	33
Educational attainment	Bachelor's	73	70
	Master's	18	17
	Professional degree	11	10
	Doctorate	3	3
Personal income	>$200,000	3	3
	$150,000–199,000	2	2
	$100,000–149,000	12	12
	$80,000–99,000	6	6
	$60,000–79,000	18	17
	$40,000–59,000	18	17
	$20,000–39,000	14	13
	>$20,000	14	13
	Decline to state	18	17
Relationship status	Single	40	38
	In a relationship	13	12
	Cohabiting	24	23
	Married	20	19
	Previously married	5	5
	Remarried	3	3

(continued)

Table 2   (Continued)

Variable	Measure	N	Percentage
Parental status	Children	10	10
	No children	95	90
Age	Mean age: 30.8		
	Standard deviation: 3.9		

Interview Guide

COURTSHIP BEHAVIOR STUDY

BASIC INFORMATION

I.D. Number _____

I'd like to start by getting some basic information about you.

B.1. Your first name is _____, is that right?
B.2. How old are you?
B.3. What is your relationship status?
B.4. How do you identify in terms of gender and sexual orientation? What are your pronouns of reference?
B.5. How do you identify in terms of race and/or ethnicity?

Now I'd like to ask you some questions about your current situation.

B.6. What is your current living situation?
B.7. What is your educational background? (PROBE: What did you study/are you studying in school? Did you do well in school? Do you have any interest in continuing your education?)
B.8. What is your current employment situation?

FAMILY BACKGROUND

I'd now like to ask you some questions about your family while growing up as well as your relationship with your mother and father now.

F.1. Where did you grow up?

F.2. Who did you live with while growing up? Did your living situation change at all while you were growing up? If yes, how?

F.3. Do you have any siblings? If yes, what are their ages? What is their current relationship and work situation?

F.4. Describe your mother's job(s). Did she stay at home?

F.5. Describe your father's job(s).

F.6. What would you say your socioeconomic status was while growing up? (PROBE: Low income, working class, middle class, upper middle class, upper class?)

F.7. Describe your parents' relationship(s). Were they happy, unhappy, or somewhere in between? How did that change over time?

F.8. Describe your relationship with your mother while growing up. (PROBE: Would you say you were close/distant/somewhere in between?)

F.9. How has it changed? What brought about this change?

F.10. Describe your relationship with your father while growing up. (PROBE: Would you say you were close/distant/somewhere in between?)

F.11. How has it changed? What brought about this change?

Now I'd like to ask you some questions about your parents' expectations for you.

F.12. Thinking back as far as you can remember, did your mother or father express any expectations or hopes regarding your future? (PROBE: Did your parents agree with each other or did they express different ideas?)

F.13. What expectations did (they/he/she) have regarding education? Work? (PROBE: Was the importance of education stressed? Was a certain career stressed?)

F.14. What expectations did (they/he/she) have regarding relationships and marriage? (PROBE: Did they stress getting married a lot / some / not at all? Did they stress a particular type of partner or lifestyle? Did they discuss a good age to get married? Did they emphasize dating around versus committed relationships before marriage? Did they stress establishing a career before marriage or did they stress marriage as the most important accomplishment?)

F.15. Did/do your parents offer you any dating/relationship advice? If yes, what kind of advice do they offer you?

F.16. Finally, is there anything I missed about your family that you think is important for me to know?

COURTSHIP HISTORY

I'd like to ask you some questions about your dating and relationship experiences.

First, I'd like to get an overview of your relationship history.

C.1. Growing up, what were your expectations regarding dating, love, marriage? How old did you want to be when you got married?

C.2. How old were you the first time you had a relationship or became romantically involved?

C.3. Starting with your first romantic or sexual involvement, can you give me an overview of your dating and relationship history? I'd like to hear about periods where you were single or dating casually as well as about relationships you had.

GO THROUGH THE RELATIONSHIP HISTORY IN CHRONOLOGICAL ORDER USING QUESTIONS MARKED *R* FOR PERIODS OF COMMITTED RELATIONSHIPS, QUESTIONS MARKED *D* FOR PERIODS OF CASUAL DATING, AND QUESTIONS MARKED *S* FOR PERIODS OF NO DATING.

FOR EACH COMMITTED RELATIONSHIP ASK THE FOLLOWING QUESTIONS. IF MORE THAN FIVE, ASK ABOUT THE FIVE MOST SERIOUS RELATIONSHIPS:

I'd now like to ask you some more detailed questions about the committed relationships that you discussed.

R.1. You have had ____ committed relationships, correct?

R.2. When and how did the relationship start? (PROBE: How did you meet? What kinds of things did you talk about? Did one of you pursue the other? How did you present yourself to your potential mate? How did you contact one another after the initial meeting?)

IF MET ON INTERNET, ASK THE FOLLOWING QUESTIONS:

R.2.a. On what site did you meet? Why did you choose that site?

R.2.b. What did your profile say? (PROBE: Why did you choose to present yourself in that way? What type of person were you trying to meet with this profile? How often did you update your profile and what prompted you to do so?)

R.2.c. Who contacted whom?

R.2.d. How did you know you were interested in the person? What did you look for in their profile? What did you like about your online interactions?

R.2.e. What kind of online exchanges did you have with the person? (PROBE: What did you discuss? What kinds of things did you reveal about yourself? What did they reveal about themselves? Did you exchange pictures? How did you choose your picture?)

R.2.f. How long did you have online exchanges before contacting each other outside of the internet? Who initiated this contact? (PROBE: What type of contact did you have? Did you immediately meet each other or did you talk on the phone first?)

R.2.g. How did you decide when to meet? Who initiated the meeting?

R.2.h. Do you take any safety precautions?

R.2.i. Why did you decide to use the internet to meet people? (PROBE: Do you prefer the internet to other types of meetings? Do you feel you meet different types of people on the internet than when you go out?)

R.3.   What was going on in your life at the time?

R.4.   What made you romantically interested in this person? (PROBE: Did they have a particular appearance that you liked? Personality? Other traits?)

R.5.   Tell me about the early stages of your relationship when you had just begun dating. (PROBE: Describe your first date. Who asked whom? How did you meet up? Where did you go? Who paid? How did the relationship progress from there?)

R.6.   What types of meetings did you have? (PROBE: Where did you go? Who initiated these dates? Who paid? How did you decide who paid?)

R.7.   How often did you see each other?

R.8.   Were you dating more than one person at the same time? Was your partner?

R.9.   Did you take any safety precautions?

R.10. Did you put any special care into your appearance?

R.11. In what ways did you signal romantic interest to your partner?

R.12. Did you become sexually active before or after committing to this person? (PROBE: If before, what made you decide to do so? If after, why did you decide to wait?)

R.13. Who initiated sexual activity?

R.14. How did you know you wanted a committed relationship? (PROBE: Did you look for something specific from a partner before you decided to commit? What did you look for? Did anything specific happen in your life at the time that made you want to commit at that point?)

R.15. How long did you know this person before you knew you wanted a committed relationship?

R.16. How did you and your partner decide to have a committed relationship? (PROBE: Did you have a conversation about it or did it just happen? If you had a conversation, who initiated it? What was discussed in this conversation? Did you discuss what you wanted from the relationship?)

R.17. How did your behavior change in a committed relationship versus noncommitted? (PROBE: Did you change your appearance in any way? How did the activities you engaged in change? Who paid for your activities? How did you decide who paid? How did your sexual behavior change? How did your conversations change?)

R.18. What activities did you expect to do with your partner after committing? (PROBE: For example, did you meet the families, attend events as a couple, go on trips, spend the holidays together? How were these activities decided on? Who tended to initiate the conversations? Who paid?)

R.19. When and how often did you discuss what you wanted out of the relationship? Who tended to initiate these conversations?

R.20. Did you feel that one of you had more power in the relationship? Why or why not?

R.21. Did you consider yourself to be in love with this person? Why or why not?

R.22. How did you decide whether to increase the level of commitment, such as move in together and/or get engaged? Who initiated these conversations? (PROBE: If you never considered living with this partner or getting engaged, why not? If you've never considered living with any partner or getting engaged, why not? Do you hope to one day?)

R.23. If you lived together, where did you live?

R.24. If you lived together, how did your living arrangement affect your relationship? (PROBE: How did you decide how to divide the household labor? Were there any conflicts over this? Did living together change your sexual activity in any way?)

R.25. What did you like most about the relationship? What did you like least?

R.26. What were/are the biggest conflicts in the relationship?

R.27. How long did the relationship last? If ended, how did you decide to end the relationship? What factors did you take into consideration? Was the breakup one-sided or mutual?

R.28. Did the relationship change you in any way? (PROBE: Did it affect what you want out of a future relationship?)

R.29. Are there any interesting experiences that you want to tell me about? Is there anything else that I missed that you think is important?

FOR EACH PERIOD OF CASUAL DATING, ASK THE FOLLOWING QUESTIONS:

D.1. What was going on in your life at the time?

D.2. Were you interested in a committed relationship at this time or were you only interested in casual dating? Why or why not?

D.3. In what ways did you meet potential mates? (PROBE: Did you go out with friends? Go to parties? Bars and nightclubs? Participate in extracurriculars? Did you go on the internet?)

D.4. Can you give me a brief description of the casual relationships you had during this period?

    D.4.a. How did you meet? (If met on the internet, ask questions R.2. a–i).

    D.4.b. How did you arrange to see each other again?

    D.4.c. What types of meetings did you have? (PROBE: How did you meet up? Where did you go? Who initiated these dates? Who paid? How did you decide who paid?)

    D.4.d. How often did you see each other?

    D.4.e. Were you dating more than one person at the same time? Was your partner?

    D.4.f. Did you take any safety precautions?

    D.4.g. Did you put any special care into your appearance?

    D.4.h. In what ways did you signal romantic interest to your partner?

    D.4.i. Were you sexually active during this period?

    D.4.j. Why did this relationship end? Did one of you end the relationship?

FOR EACH PERIOD WHEN NO DATING TOOK PLACE, ASK THE FOLLOWING QUESTIONS:

S.1. What was going on in your life at the time?

S.2. Were you open to the idea of meeting a potential partner at that time? If no, why not?

S.3. Were you actively trying to meet a potential partner at that time? If no, why not?

S.4. If yes, in what ways did you try to meet potential mates? (PROBE: Did you go out with friends? Go to parties? Bars and nightclubs? Participate in extracurriculars? Did you go on the internet?)

IF YES TO USE OF INTERNET, ASK QUESTIONS S.4. a–h. IF NO, SKIP TO QUESTION S.5.

S.4.a. Why did you decide to use the internet to meet people? (PROBE: Do you prefer the internet to other types of meetings? Do you feel you meet different types of people on the internet than when you go out?)

S.4.b. What kinds of sites do you use to meet people? (PROBE: Why did you choose these sites?)

S.4.c. What does your profile say? (PROBE: Why did you choose to present yourself in that way? What type of person are you trying to meet with this profile? How often do you update your profile and what prompts you to do so?)

S.4.d. How do you decide if you are interested in another person online? What do you look for in their profile?

S.4.e. How do you make contact with that person or show your interest? Do you tend to make the contact or do other people tend to contact you? Why?

S.4.f. Do you tend to pursue/interact with more than one person at a time?

S.4.g. What kinds of exchanges do you have online with potential mates? (PROBE: What do you discuss? What kinds of things do you reveal about yourself? What do they reveal about themselves? Do you exchange pictures? How do you choose your picture?)

S.4.h. Did you pursue a face-to-face interaction with anyone you met online? If no, why not? If yes, what happened?

S.5. When you went places where you might encounter potential mates, what kind of effort did you put into your appearance? (PROBE: Did you have a beauty routine? What type of clothing did you wear?)

S.6. Were you sexually active during this period? If yes, how did you meet sexual partners? Why were you uninterested in pursuing a relationship with these partners?

S.7. Why do you feel that you weren't able to meet anyone who interested you during this period?

ENGAGEMENT

I'd now like to discuss engagement with you.

IF NEVER ENGAGED OR MARRIED, SKIP TO QUESTION E.7.

FOR EACH ENGAGEMENT, ASK THE FOLLOWING QUESTIONS:

E.1. Do you consider yourself to be in or entering into a marriage, a civil union, or a domestic partnership? (PROBE: Why? How did you decide on your particular status? Do you consider the distinction to be important to you?)

E.2. How did you and your partner go about deciding to make a lifelong commitment? (PROBE: Did one of you propose? Did you have a conversation? Did one of you initiate the conversation?)

E.3. Was there a ring? How important was the ring to you? Was it a surprise or did you pick it out together? Who paid for it?

E.4. How did you decide you wanted to be married/committed to this person? (PROBE: What was going on in your life at the time? What are the characteristics that you value in a spouse/partner?)

E.5. Did getting engaged/partnered affect your relationship in any way?

E.6. Did the engagement result in marriage / civil union / domestic partnership? If not, why did you break up?

IF ENGAGED OR MARRIED, SKIP TO QUESTION E.11.

E.7. Do you want to get married (or partnered / enter into civil union)? Why or why not?

E.8. How would you feel about never getting married or entering into an expected lifelong commitment?

E.9. What are you looking for in a spouse/partner? (PROBE: What do you look for in terms of personality? Appearance? Career? Money?)

E.10. In what ways do you think you will approach the marriage market differently than dating? (PROBE: Will you behave differently around potential partners? Will you look for a particular kind of partner?)

E.11. What do you consider to be an ideal proposal/engagement?

COURTSHIP PREFERENCES

Now I'd like to ask you about your courtship preferences and ideals.

IF RESPONDANT IS ENGAGED/MARRIED/IN A LONG-TERM COMMITMENT, ASK QUESTIONS IN PAST TENSE.

P.1. What do you look for in a potential mate? (PROBE: Do you tend to look for a certain type of person? What do you look for in terms of personality? Appearance? Career? Money? How has this changed over time?)

P.2. Do you prefer to date casually or do you tend to be mainly involved in committed, long-term relationships?

P.3. Do you tend to be the one to approach or do you tend to be approached? (PROBE: Are you more comfortable being approached or approaching? How do you feel when the situation in reversed? Are there any circumstances under which you would do the reverse?)

P.4. How do you like potential mates to approach you? What approaches do you find to be a turn-off? (PROBE: Do you prefer an aggressive approach or one that is more subtle?)

P.5. How do you signal to someone that you are interested in them? (PROBE: What kind of body language do you engage in? What kinds of things do you say to them? Are you direct or do you prefer to give hints? How do you signal that you are not interested?)

P.6. What types of things do you talk about when you first meet a potential mate? What do you avoid discussing?

P.7. Would you ever go home with someone / take someone home the same day/night that you meet them? (PROBE: Why or why not? Under what circumstances?)

P.8. What is your ideal first date? (PROBE: What would you do? What kind of person would you want to be with? Do you pick the date up, get picked up, or meet somewhere?)

P.9. How do you prepare for a first date? (PROBE: What type of clothing do you wear? What is your beauty routine? Do you do any other types of preparation such as coming up with conversation topics, investigate topics of interest to the other person, come up with an exit strategy?)

P.10. What are some of the things that you like/dislike on a first date? (PROBE: Are there certain topics that you like/dislike discussing? What kinds of behaviors do you like/dislike? How physical should your date be? How aggressive should your date be? Do you like people to play hard to get? What type of appearance do you expect from your date?)

P.11. Is there a certain way that you like to present yourself on first dates? For example, do you like to present yourself as carefree or do you like to be upfront about wanting marriage?

P.12. Do you have any rules for first dates? What are they? (PROBE: Are there certain things that you won't reveal about yourself? Do you have rules for sexual behavior?)

P.13. Who usually pays? Do you have any guidelines for who pays? (PROBE: Does this tend to be an uncomfortable situation or are there obvious "rules"? Does there tend to be a discussion? How does this vary by the activity of the date?)

P.14. Are you willing to be sexually active on a first date? How do you decide? (PROBE: If yes, where do you go? Do you tend/prefer to go to your place or their place?)

P.15. How do dates usually end? (PROBE: Does someone take the other home? Do you make follow-up plans?)

P.16. Do you take any safety precautions?

P.17. How do you know if the other person is interested / not interested in you? Are there any signals?

P.18. How do you demonstrate interest in the other person?

P.19. Who usually initiates the first contact after a date? How is that contact usually made? How soon after the first date is it appropriate to make contact? (PROBE: What do you do if your date contacts you, but you are not interested in having a follow-up date?)

P.20. Are there other ways that you enter into relationships besides through dating? Do you prefer dating or other approaches?

P.21. Do you tend to date more than one person at a time? How about your partners?

P.22. What are some of the factors that would make you continue seeing someone? What are the factors that would make you end it? (PROBE: Personality, appearance, behavior? What are your deal-breakers? Do you have any "tests" for a partner?)

P.23. When you are dating someone, do you have any rules? What are they? (PROBE: What do you talk about, what do you avoid? What behaviors do you consider important/unimportant?)

P.24. How do you manage your appearance? Does it tend to change over time?

P.25. How do you like your partner to look? Do you have any expectations regarding how they take care of their appearance and what clothes they wear? How important is appearance to you? What are physical turn-ons and -offs?

P.26. How/when do you decide to be sexually active? Who tends to initiate sexual contact? What kind of approach do you consider to be a turn-on versus turn-off?

P.27. Do you have any rules for your own sexual behavior?

P.28. Do you have any expectations regarding the past sexual behavior of your partner? What types of past behavior would you consider a turn-off? What would you consider to be a deal-breaker?

P.29. Who should pay for activities? (PROBE: Does it vary by type of activity? Do you discuss this issue?)

P.30. How do you (expect to) organize household finances with your partner while cohabiting? Married? What do you consider to be the ideal arrangement?

P.31. How do you (expect to) organize household chores with your partner while cohabiting? Married? What do you consider to be the ideal arrangement?

P.32. Where do you turn for advice on dating and relationships? (PROBE: Do you read any magazines or self-help books? Do you watch any television shows?)

P.33. Do you feel that your dating and relationship behavior is in line with that of your friends or do you feel that you are not in the norm? (PROBE: What do you consider to be the norm? How do you feel about your position inside/outside the norm? How would you feel about the reverse?)

P.34. Do you have any other guidelines for dating that I may have missed?

P.35. How have your attitudes towards and guidelines for dating changed as you've gotten older? Why?

P.36. Do you consider yourself a feminist? Why or why not?

CONCLUDING REMARKS

Well, that's all the questions I have. Is there anything you would like to ask or anything you would like to say that you haven't said?

If I need to contact you again, what is the best time and place to contact you? Do I have your correct phone number? Would you like to receive a report of my findings when the study is completed?

That's all. Thank you very much for your help.

. . . . .

INTERVIEWER OBSERVATIONS

Include description of respondent, residence, and family environment (if available), general description of family/life trajectory and current outlook, and notation of any outstanding events, notable circumstances, or especially interesting/important findings and observations. Make sure to note anything that seems important but would not be apparent by reading a verbal transcript.

Notes

CHAPTER ONE. THE PUZZLING PERSISTENCE
OF GENDERED DATING

1. Sciortino 2017.
2. England 2010: 149; Gerson 2010.
3. Bell 2013; Illouz 1997.
4. Lever, Frederick, and Hertz 2015; Rose and Frieze 1993, 1989.
5. Sayer 2016.
6. Ridgeway 2011; Stone 2007.
7. Stone 2007; Wong 2017.
8. Rehel 2014.
9. Tichenor 2005.
10. Green 2010; Pfeffer 2012.
11. Biblarz and Savci 2010; Green 2010; Pfeffer 2012.
12. Ocobock 2018; but see also Moore (2018) for discussion on the political significance of same-sex and queer marriage.
13. Biblarz and Savci 2010; Carrington 1999; Civettini 2016.
14. Williams 2013.
15. Williams 2013.
16. Fein and Schneider 1995; Rosin 2010.
17. Morris 2014.
18. Morris 2014.

19. Hess 2013.

20. Hess 2013.

21. Bogle 2008; but see also Clarke (2011) and Ford (2018) for how experiences differ for college-educated black women.

22. Edin and Kefalas 2005; Sassler and Miller 2017; Silva 2015.

23. Sassler and Miller 2017.

24. Dahl 2017; Kitchener 2018; Pardes 2014; Sciortino 2017.

25. Cate and Lloyd 1992.

26. Bailey 1988.

27. Bailey 1988: 19.

28. Bailey 1988.

29. Bailey 1988; Ridgeway 2011.

30. Bailey 1988; Cate and Lloyd 1992; Lever, Frederick, and Hertz 2015; Rose and Frieze 1993, 1989.

31. Illouz 1997.

32. Coontz 2005.

33. Collins 2000; Dill 1994; Espiritu 2008.

34. Coontz 2005.

35. Cherlin 2009.

36. England 2010; Gerson 2010.

37. Barnes 2016; Gerson 2010; Hamilton 2016; Lareau 2003; Risman 2018.

38. Barnes 2016; Hamilton 2016.

39. Damaske 2011; Wong 2017.

40. Cotter, Hermsen, and Vanneman 2004.

41. Hamilton and Armstrong 2009.

42. Cotter, Hermsen, and Vanneman 2004.

43. Finer 2007; Goldin and Katz 2002.

44. Dworkin and O'Sullivan 2005; Ortiz-Torres, Williams, and Ehrhardt 2003.

45. Cuddy, Fiske, and Glick 2007.

46. Casper and Bianchi 2002.

47. Landivar 2017; Stone 2007.

48. Damaske 2011.

49. Bureau of Labor Statistics 2018.

50. Parker and Stepler 2017.

51. Coontz 1997.

52. Gerson 2010.

53. Buss et al. 2001.

54. DiPrete and Buchmann 2006; Schwartz and Mare 2005; Sweeney 2002.

55. Gerson 2010.

56. Ocobock 2018.

57. Stacey 2011; Weston 1991.

58. West and Zimmerman 1989.

59. Risman 2018.

60. Pfeffer 2017.

61. Stacey 2011; Weston 1991.

62. Pfeffer 2012.

63. Giddens 1991: 58.

64. Cancian 1987; Coontz 2005; Giddens 1991.

65. Risman 2018.

66. I use the term "courtship" broadly to refer to the pathways people take as they move from postfamily independence to long-term commitment. This definition of courtship encompasses a wide range of behaviors, from hooking up to dating to cohabitation, but still focuses on how people pursue the selection of a committed mate rather than simply a sexual partner. In particular, I focus on the conventional dating practices associated with courtship and how they relate to young adults' intentions and abilities to secure a long-term partner. This definition can be fraught as some people may challenge the assumption of the supposed end goal. However, the majority of Americans continue to desire and form long-term romantic relationships. Those who don't can help reveal how challenges to normative practices can make space for reimagining possibilities.

67. Coontz 2013; Pedulla and Thebaud 2015.

68. Gerson 2010; Pedulla and Thebaud 2015; Stone 2007.

69. Pedulla and Thebaud 2015; Rehel 2014.

70. Gerson 2010; Stone 2007.

71. Cotter, Hermsen, and Vanneman 2004.

72. England 2010; Fate-Dixon 2017; Pepin and Cotter 2018.

73. England 2010.

74. England 2010.

75. England 2010.

76. Scarborough, Sin, and Risman 2019.

77. Pepin and Cotter 2018.

78. I use Cecilia Ridgeway's definition of gender. Gender is "a system of social practices within society that constitutes distinct, differentiated sex categories, sorts people into these categories, and organizes relations between people on the basis of the differences defined by their sex category" (2011: 9). See also Risman (2018) for a definition of gender as a social structure.

79. Ridgeway 2011: 35.

80. Eaton and Rose 2011.

81. Brooks and Bolzendahl 2004.

82. Carrington 1999; Hochschild 1989.

83. Gallagher and Smith 1999; Huber and Spitze 1981.

84. Hamilton, Geist, and Powell 2011; Ridgeway and Correll 2004: 511; Swim and Cohen 1997.

85. Cech 2013; England 2010.

86. Swim and Cohen 1997.

87. Ridgeway and Correll 2004: 511.

88. See appendix 2 for the interview guide.

89. I chose respondents from two college settings: a large, prestigious public university and a midsize, suburban state university with a high acceptance rate. I drew from two public universities in order to increase the diversity of the sample and target individuals from a variety of backgrounds and experiences.

90. In this wave, respondents received $50 for their participation in the interview, due to the availability of funding.

91. I use the term "LGBQ" rather than "LGBTQ" throughout, to emphasize that the comparison between the heterosexual and LGBQ groups is sexual identity rather than gender identity.

92. This is compared to 13 percent of the population as a whole, according to the US Census Bureau (2017).

93. This varies significantly from the general population and demonstrates the high level of privilege among the respondents. In 2015, when this research was concluded, 7 percent of American men and 10.4 percent of American women had a master's degree or higher (National Center for Education Statistics 2017).

94. Hamilton 2016; Hamilton and Armstrong 2009.

95. England 2011; Graf and Schwartz 2011.

96. Dellinger 2004; Pyke 1996.

97. Bridges 2014.

98. Pyke 1996: 532.

99. Hamilton and Armstrong 2009: 593.

100. Arnett 2004; Hamilton 2016; Hamilton and Armstrong 2009; Rosenfeld 2007.

101. But see Clarke (2011) and Ford (2018) for discussions of how college-educated black women don't reap these rewards of a college education.

102. Cherlin 2009; Sassler and Miller 2017.

103. This is similar to the racial demographics of the United States, which is 60.7 percent white alone, not Hispanic or Latino (US Census Bureau 2017).

104. Bailey 1988.

105. Illouz 1997.

106. Cherlin 2009.

107. Collins 2000; Edin and Kefalas 2005; Silva 2015.

108. England 2010; Hamilton 2016; Sassler and Miller 2017.

109. Given the small number of black and Latinx respondents, I was mostly unable to ascertain patterned differences between these groups and the more privileged white and Asian respondents. Overall, narratives sounded very similar. These groups were more highly represented among the LGBQ sample, however, so I include more discussion of racial and ethnic variation in chapter 5.

NOTES TO PAGES 16–25

110. See, for example: Clarke 2011; Edin and Kefalas 2005; and Edin and Nelson 2013; Ford 2018; Sassler and Miller 2017; Silva 2015.

111. Previous sociological research on gender undertaken in the San Francisco Bay Area (Gerson 1985; Hochschild 1989) has found men and women struggling with and negotiating traditional gender norms here as well, confirming that gender norms are entrenched everywhere. Yet at the same time, these tensions are affecting women in very different social locations as well. Even evangelical Christian women experience this push and pull between tradition and modernity (Burke 2016; Gallagher and Smith 1999). While people in the Bay Area might provide different narratives and pursue different strategies, all people must navigate these social changes.

CHAPTER TWO. THE QUEST FOR EGALITARIAN LOVE

1. All names are pseudonyms, and quotes have been edited for clarity, but not for content. Pronouns and identifiers used are those provided by the respondents.

2. The "MRS degree," where privileged women attended college in order to find economically successful husbands to support their homemaking, has been left behind as women pursue college as a pathway to their own professional achievements. See: Armstrong and Hamilton 2013; Hamilton 2014; Hamilton and Armstrong 2009.

3. At present, women earn more college degrees than men, increasingly choose masculine-typed fields of study, and have almost fully integrated MD, MBA, and JD programs. See: Damaske 2011; England 2010; England and Li 2006.

4. Given the opportunity costs of leaving the workplace and the social and economic supports necessary to maintain a professional career, highly educated women are now less likely than their less educated counterparts to be out of the workforce for childrearing for more than a limited amount of time over their life course. See: Damaske 2011; England 2010.

5. Bell 2013; Hamilton and Armstrong 2009; Sassler and Miller 2017.

6. Townsend 2002.

7. Hamilton 2016; Kane 2006.

8. Hamilton 2016.

9. As Hamilton (2016) shows, some parents see college as a mobility project in which a college degree is a way for daughters to ensure an economically stable or upwardly mobile future. Certain majors do a better job of ensuring economic stability than others, and success with certain majors can be contingent on the class background of parents. See also: Armstrong and Hamilton 2013.

10. Cherlin 2009.

11. That said, the majority of the women did not have children at the time of their interview.

12. Gerson 2010; Wong 2017.

13. This is similar to what Vasquez-Tokos (2017) finds in her study of Latino and white intermarriage. Certain Latinas preferred to marry out of their ethnic group in order to avoid what they assumed was a preference for male dominance among Latino men. Drawing on racial stereotypes, these women viewed white men as more committed than Latino men to gender equality.

14. Hamilton and Armstrong 2009.

15. Although college-educated black women are also encouraged to delay marriage and ensure financial independence, they have a harder time establishing relationships that move toward greater commitment (Clarke 2011; Ford 2018).

16. Armstrong and Hamilton 2013.

17. Ascher (2015) explains the "Failure to Launch Syndrome" as the inability of young adults to establish financial, emotional, and physical independence from their parents as they transition from adolescence to adulthood.

18. Pink-collar jobs refer to female-dominated professions, often paid caregiving work. Gerson (2010) found that women were more likely to cut back at work to support a partner when they found limited mobility in their own workplace.

19. Collins 2005. See Barnes (2016) for a discussion of how black professional women make different calculations when they decide how to balance paid labor and caregiving responsibilities. In particular, Barnes finds that black professional women are more likely to frame their decision to stay home as one made to counter negative stereotypes about black families rather than as an individualistic choice.

20. As Gerson (2010) found, if an egalitarian relationship seems unlikely, women are more likely to choose self-reliance than a traditional partnership that poses "the dangers of domesticity."

21. While this is a common sentiment among low-income women, who delay marriage to avoid a controlling partner, college-educated women saw their income as protecting them from that outcome and providing them with an out should they need one. See: Edin and Kefalas 2005.

22. Wong 2017.

23. See also: Gerson 2010.

24. Charles and Bradley 2009.

25. See: Cherlin 2009. Used to distinguish lower-income individuals from higher-income individuals, "responsible" personal choices become the way to establish a stable career and marriage, while instability in either is attributed to poor choices on the part of the individual.

26. Hochschild 1989.

27. This is consistent with current findings on mate selection. See: DiPrete and Buchmann 2006.

28. Townsend 2002.

29. Talbot and Quayle 2010.

30. As Bell (2013) shows, young women from poor and working-class backgrounds face a peer culture in which early pregnancy undermines educational and professional goals.

31. Riley is a trans man who identifies as a lesbian.

32. Klawitter 2015.

33. Edin and Nelson 2013.

34. Mollborn 2017.

35. Townsend 2002.

36. Cherlin 2009; Randles 2017.

37. Hamilton and Armstrong 2009.

38. Cherlin 2009.

39. Schalet (2011) shows how Americans support an "adversarial independence" in which young adults are expected to achieve independence before they are considered ready for serious romantic and sexual relationships.

CHAPTER THREE. NEW GOALS, OLD SCRIPTS

1. *The Rules* is a 1995 self-help book by Ellen Fein and Sherrie Schneider that provides dating advice for women who want to marry "the men of their dreams."

2. Miller 2015.

3. Miller 2015.

4. McCaughey 2007.

5. Ridgeway 2011.

6. Bogle 2008; Sassler and Miller 2011.

7. Rudman and Fairchild 2004.

8. This is consistent with Sassler and Miller (2017), who found that class-privileged women are more likely than service-class women to take an indirect approach to pursuing men, whereas those from less privileged backgrounds are more likely to wait for a man to make the first move.

9. Sassler and Miller (2017) also found that middle-class women often approached men, but then waited for men to initiate a formal date.

10. Bogle 2008; Hamilton and Armstrong 2009.

11. Geller 2001; McCaughey 2007.

12. This is similar to what Sassler and Miller (2011) found.

13. Hamilton and Armstrong 2009.

14. Ortiz-Torres, Williams, and Ehrhardt 2003; Seal and Ehrhardt 2003.

15. Bell 2013; Hamilton and Armstrong 2009.

16. This divide is even more fraught for women of color, who also have to contend with racial stereotypes about their promiscuity. See Collins 2005.

17. Geller 2001; Sassler and Miller 2011.

18. Sassler and Miller 2011: 482.

19. Sassler and Miller 2011.

20. This is potentially a result of the racial privileges the majority of the respondents enjoy. As Clarke (2011) shows, college-educated black women lack negotiating power in their dating relationships to secure greater commitment.

21. Hamilton, Geist, and Powell 2011.

22. Hamilton, Geist, and Powell 2011; Swim and Cohen 1997.

23. Becker and Wright 2011: 62.

24. Becker and Wright 2011; England 2010.

25. England 2010.

26. Stone 2007: 125.

27. McCall 2011.

28. Bell 2013.

29. Hamilton 2016.

30. Bell 2013; Gerson 2010.

31. Collins 2000.

CHAPTER FOUR. A FEW GOOD (HETEROSEXUAL) MEN

1. See Bridges (2014) for a discussion of how men simultaneously distance themselves from and participate in practices that perpetuate gender inequality.

2. Gerson 2010.

3. Eaton and Rose 2011.

4. The #MeToo movement is an online social movement that started in 2016 and was popularized in 2017 to demonstrate the prevalence of sexual harassment and assault.

5. Schrock and Schwalbe 2009.

6. The three-day rule is folk knowledge about dating, promoted in popular media; it states that a man should wait three days to call a woman after getting her phone number so as not to appear desperate, and to increase her level of interest.

7. Pascoe 2007; Schrock and Schwalbe 2009.

8. Sassler and Miller 2017; Shafer and Christensen 2018.

9. McCaughey 2007; Pascoe 2007; Schrock and Schwalbe 2009.

10. Dellinger 2004: 557.

11. Hamilton and Armstrong 2009.

12. Hamilton and Armstrong 2009.

13. McCaughey 2007.

14. Glick and Fiske 1996.

15. Glick and Fiske 1996.

16. Glick and Fiske 1996.

17. Gallagher and Smith 1999.

18. Gerson 2010.

19. McCaughey 2007; Pascoe 2007.

20. Hamilton and Armstrong 2009.

21. Bridges 2014; Pyke 1996.

22. Messerschmidt 2010.

CHAPTER FIVE. QUEERING COURTSHIP

1. Walters 2014.

2. By discussing LGBQ people as a group, I do not aim to erase the differences between lesbian, gay, bisexual, and queer histories and identities, but rather to focus on how queer narratives in particular shape resistance to heteronormative relationship practices.

3. Ward 2015: 202.

4. Pfeffer 2012: 578.

5. Green 2010.

6. Green 2010: 401.

7. Pfeffer 2014; Ward 2015.

8. Orne 2017: 220.

9. While Riley identified as a trans men, he still retained his sexual orientation as lesbian.

10. Orne 2017: 224.

11. Lamont 2014.

12. Benevolent sexism draws on stereotypes of women as in need of special care or protection.

13. Vasquez-Tokos (2017) discusses how some Latinas don't want to marry Latino men as they are seen as more rigid about gender norms. In my study, the majority of heterosexual women of color were Asian and many held the same perspective about Asian men.

14. Collins 2005.

15. QTPOC is an acronym for Queer Trans People of Color.

16. As Robinson (2015) demonstrates, gay men justify the exclusion of men of color from consideration as sexual partners by drawing on a discourse of "personal preference." Gay white men in particular also racially stereotype gay men of color.

17. In gay culture, the term "bear" refers to men who are hairy and have a large build.

18. The Castro is a well-known gay neighborhood in San Francisco.

19. Klonopin is a drug used to treat anxiety.

20. LGBQ people placed much more emphasis on good sex in their relationships and lives in general. This could have been because the sample was less likely than the heterosexual sample to be in long-term relationships, or they simply could have felt more comfortable talking about sex. In my interviews with heterosexual people, they appeared less comfortable discussing the topic. However, it could also be that a queer community norm is to value good sex.

21. Topping refers to the act of taking the penetrative position during sex, while bottoming refers to the act of being penetrated during sex. Someone who identifies as versatile is willing to take either position. Topping and bottoming can also refer to who takes the more dominant and more submissive roles during sex.

22. Jocelyn, a trans woman, shared that she could not afford a desired bottom surgery. As of the time of the interview, she had a penis.

23. Pfeffer 2012: 578.

24. See Faderman [1991] 2012.

25. Recent queer theory critiques homonormativity "as the neoliberal lesbian and gay rights movements' emphasis on assimilation to heteronormativity as a strategy" to normalize gay and lesbian relationships and access rights by emphasizing their similarity to heterosexuals (Schippers 2016: 8).

CHAPTER 6. THE MORE THINGS CHANGE . . .

1. Ward 2010: 239.

2. Erickson 2005.

3. Erickson 2005; Rao 2017.

4. Ward 2010: 239.

5. Hochschild 1989.

6. Hochschild 1989; Moore 2011.

7. Coltrane 1989.

8. Interestingly, Moore (2011) finds the same argument among black lesbian women who do the greater share of childcare in their partnerships.

9. Ridgeway 2011.

10. Carrington 1999; Illouz 1997.

11. Ward 2010.

12. Pfeffer 2017; Ward 2010.

13. Ward 2010.

14. Ridgeway 2011; Risman 1999.

CHAPTER SEVEN. DATED DATING AND THE STALLED GENDER REVOLUTION

1. Hamilton and Armstrong 2009: 593.
2. Hamilton 2016: 15.
3. Hamilton 2016.
4. Ridgeway 2011.
5. Behrendt and Tuccillo 2004; Bryans 2017.
6. Bryans 2013; King 2014.
7. England 2010: 150.
8. Hochschild 1989.
9. Risman 2018.
10. Ocobock 2018: 69–70.
11. The same lessons may hold true for other groups excluded from normative relationship practices. Low-income and black people face lower expectations for and rates of marriage and greater relationship instability in the form of breaking up and repartnering more frequently. While the policy solution has frequently been to promote marriage in these groups, there are dangers to this as well. See: Avishai, Health, and Randles 2015.
12. Graf and Schwartz 2011.
13. Jackson 1998.
14. Ridgeway 2011.
15. England 2010; Gerson 2010; Ridgeway 2011.
16. Ridgeway 2011.
17. Gerson 2010; Wong 2017.
18. Coontz 2013.
19. Rehel 2014.
20. Ridgeway 2011.

References

Armstrong, Elizabeth A., and Laura Hamilton. 2013. *Paying for the Party: How College Maintains Inequality*. Cambridge, MA: Harvard University Press.

Arnett, Jeffrey. 2004. *Emerging Adulthood: The Winding Road from the Late Teens through the Twenties*. New York: Oxford University Press.

Ascher, Michael. 2015. "Failure to Launch Syndrome: What You Need to Know to Help Your Dependent Adult Child." *Huffington Post,* March 2.

Avishai, Orit, Melanie Health, and Jennifer Randles. 2015. "The Marriage Movement." In *Families as They Really Are,* ed. Barbara Risman and Virginia Rutter, 2nd ed., 308–20. New York: Norton.

Bailey, Beth. 1988. *From Front Porch to Back Seat: Courtship in Twentieth-Century America*. Baltimore: Johns Hopkins University Press.

Barnes, Riche J. Daniel. 2016. *Raising the Race: Black Career Women Redefine Marriage, Motherhood, and Community*. New Brunswick, NJ: Rutgers University Press.

Becker, Julia, and Stephen Wright. 2011. "Yet Another Dark Side of Chivalry: Benevolent Sexism Undermines and Hostile Sexism Motivates Collective Action for Social Change." *Journal of Personal and Social Psychology* 101: 62–77.

Behrendt, Greg, and Liz Tuccillo. 2004. *He's Just Not That Into You: The No-Excuses Truth to Understanding Guys*. New York: Simon Spotlight Entertainment.

Bell, Leslie. 2013. *Hard to Get: Twenty-Something Women and the Paradox of Sexual Freedom*. Berkeley: University of California Press.

Biblarz, Timothy J., and Evren Savci. 2010. "Lesbian, Gay, Bisexual, and Transgender Families." *Journal of Marriage and Family* 72(3): 480–97.

Bogle, Kathleen. 2008. *Hooking-Up: Sex, Dating, and Relationships on Campus*. New York: New York University Press.

Bridges, Tristan. 2014. "A Very 'Gay' Straight: Hybrid Masculinities, Sexual Aesthetics, and the Changing Relationship between Masculinity and Homophobia." *Gender and Society* 28: 58–82.

Brooks, Clem, and Catherine Bolzendahl. 2004. "The Transformation of Gender Role Attitudes: Socialization, Social-Structural Change, or Ideological Learning?" *Social Science Research* 33: 106–33.

Bryans, Bruce. 2017. *How to Get a Man without Getting Played: 29 Dating Secrets to Catch Mr. Right, Set Your Standards, and Eliminate Time Wasters*. Scotts Valley, CA: CreateSpace Independent Publishing Platform.

———. 2013. *What Women Want in a Man: How to Become the Alpha Male Women Respect, Desire, and Want to Submit To*. Scotts Valley, CA: CreateSpace Independent Publishing Platform.

Bureau of Labor Statistics. 2018. News release. www.bls.gov/news.release/pdf/famee.pdf

Burke, Kelsy. 2016. *Christians under Covers: Evangelicals and Sexual Pleasure on the Internet*. Berkeley: University of California Press.

Buss, David, Todd Shackelford, Lee Kirkpatrick, and Randy Larsen. 2001. "A Half Century of Mate Preferences: The Cultural Evolution of Values." *Journal of Marriage and Family* 63: 491–503.

Cancian, Francesca. 1987. *Love in America: Gender and Self-Development*. Cambridge, UK: Cambridge University Press.

Carrington, Christopher. 1999. *No Place Like Home: Relationships and Family Life among Lesbians and Gay Men*. Chicago: University of Chicago Press.

Casper, Lynne M., and Suzanne M. Bianchi. 2002. *Continuity and Change in the American Family*. Newbury Park, CA: Sage.

Cate, Rodney, and Sally Lloyd. 1992. *Courtship*. Newbury Park, CA: Sage.

Cech, Erin. 2013. "The Self-Expressive Edge of Occupational Sex Segregation." *American Journal of Sociology* 119: 747–89.

Charles, Maria, and Karen Bradley. 2009. "Indulging Our Gendered Selves? Sex Segregation by Field of Study in 44 Countries. *American Journal of Sociology* 114: 924–76.

Cherlin, Andrew. 2009. *The Marriage-Go-Round: The State of Marriage and the Family in America Today*. New York: Vintage.

Civettini, Nicole. 2016. "Housework as Non-normative Gender Display among Lesbians and Gay Men." *Sex Roles: A Journal of Research* 74: 206–19.

Clarke, Averil Y. 2011. *Inequalities of Love: College-Educated Black Women and the Barriers to Romance and Family*. Durham, NC: Duke University Press.

Collins, Patricia Hill. 2005. *Black Sexual Politics: African Americans, Gender, and the New Racism*. New York: Routledge.

———. 2000. *Black Feminist Thought: Knowledge, Consciousness, and the Politics of Empowerment*. New York: Routledge.

Coltrane, Scott. 1989. "Household Labor and the Routine Production of Gender." *Social Problems* 36: 473–90.

Coontz, Stephanie. 2013. "Why Gender Equality Stalled." *New York Times*, February 16.

———. 2005. *Marriage, a History: How Love Conquered Marriage*. New York: Penguin.

———. 1997. *The Way We Really Are: Coming to Terms with America's Changing Families*. New York: Basic Books.

Cotter, David, Joan Hermsen, and Reeve Vanneman. 2004. *Gender Inequality at Work*. New York: Russell Sage Foundation.

Cuddy, Amy J., Susan T. Fiske, and Peter Glick. 2007. "The BIAS Map: Behaviors from Intergroup Affect and Stereotypes." *Journal of Personality and Social Psychology* 92: 631–48.

Dahl, Melissa. 2017. "Why You Still Want a Surprise Proposal Even If You Know You're Getting Married." *New York Magazine*, July 20.

Damaske, Sarah. 2011. *For the Family? How Class and Gender Shape Women's Work*. New York: Oxford University Press.

Dellinger, Kirsten. 2004. "Masculinities in 'Safe' and 'Embattled' Organizations: Accounting for Pornographic and Feminist Magazines." *Gender and Society* 18: 545–66.

Dill, Bonnie Thornton. 1994. *Across the Boundaries of Race and Class: An Exploration of Work and Family among Black Female Domestic Servants*. New York: Taylor & Francis.

DiPrete, Thomas, and Claudia Buchmann. 2006. "Gender-Specific Trends in the Value of Education and the Emerging Gender Gap in College Completion." *Demography* 43: 1–24.

Dworkin, Shari, and Lucia O'Sullivan. 2005. "Actual Versus Desired Initiation Patterns among a Sample of College Men: Tapping Disjunctures within Traditional Male Sexual Scripts." *Journal of Sex Research* 42: 150–58.

Eaton, Asia, and Suzanna Rose. 2011. "Has Dating Become More Egalitarian? A 35 Year Review Using Sex Roles." *Sex Roles* 64: 843–62.

Edin, Kathryn, and Maria Kefalas. 2005. *Promises I Can Keep: Why Poor Mothers Put Motherhood before Marriage*. Berkeley: University of California Press.

Edin, Kathryn, and Timothy J. Nelson. 2013. *Doing the Best I Can: Fatherhood in the Inner City*. Berkeley: University of California Press.

England, Paula. 2011. "Reassessing the Gender Revolution and Its Slowdown." *Gender and Society* 25: 113–23.

———. 2010. "The Gender Revolution: Uneven and Stalled." *Gender and Society* 24: 149–66.

England, Paula, and Su Li. 2006. "Desegregation Stalled: The Changing Gender Composition of College Majors, 1971–2002." *Gender and Society* 20: 657–77.

Erickson, Rebecca J. 2005. "Why Emotion Work Matters: Sex, Gender, and the Division of Household Labor." *Journal of Marriage and Family* 67(2): 337–51.

Espiritu, Yen Le. 2008. *Asian American Women and Men: Labor, Laws, and Love.* Lanham, MD: Rowman & Littlefield.

Faderman, Lillian. [1991] 2012. *Odd Girls and Twilight Lovers: A History of Lesbian Life in Twentieth-Century America.* New York: Columbia University Press.

Fate-Dixon, Nika. 2017. "Are Some Millennials Rethinking the Gender Revolution? Long-Range Trends in Views of Non-traditional Roles for Women." *Council on Contemporary Families,* March 30.

Fein, Ellen, and Sherrie Schneider. 1995. *The Rules: Time-Tested Secrets for Capturing the Heart of Mr. Right.* New York: Grand Central.

Finer, Lawrence B. 2007. "Trends in Premarital Sex in the United States, 1954–2003." *Public Health Reports* 122: 73–78.

Ford, LesLeigh. 2018. *That's the Way Love Goes: An Examination of the Romantic Experiences of Black Middle-Class Women.* Doctoral dissertation, Duke University.

Gallagher, Sally K., and Christian Smith. 1999. "Symbolic Traditionalism and Pragmatic Egalitarianism: Contemporary Evangelicals, Families, and Gender." *Gender and Society* 13: 211–33.

Geller, Jaclyn. 2001. *Here Comes the Bride: Women, Weddings, and the Marriage Mystique.* New York: Four Walls Eight Windows.

Gerson, Kathleen. 2010. *The Unfinished Revolution: How a New Generation Is Reshaping Family, Work, and Gender in America.* New York: Oxford University Press.

———. 1985. *Hard Choices: How Women Decide about Work, Career, and Motherhood.* Berkeley: University of California Press.

Giddens, Anthony. 1991. *Modernity and Self-Identity: Self and Society in the Late Modern Age.* Stanford, CA: Stanford University Press.

Glick, Peter, and Susan T. Fiske. 1996. "The Ambivalent Sexism Inventory: Differentiating Hostile and Benevolent Sexism." *Journal of Personality and Social Psychology* 70: 491–512.

Goldin, Claudia, and Lawrence Katz. 2002. "The Power of the Pill: Oral Contraceptives and Women's Career and Marriage Decisions." *Journal of Political Economy* 110(4): 730–70.

Graf, Nikki, and Christine Schwartz. 2011. "The Uneven Pace of Change in Heterosexual Romantic Relationships: Comment on England." *Gender and Society* 25: 101–7.

Green, Adam Isaiah. 2010. "Queer Unions: Same-Sex Spouses Marrying Tradition and Innovation." *Canadian Journal of Sociology* 35(3): 399–436.

Hamilton, Laura. 2016. *Parenting to a Degree: How Family Matters for College Women's Success.* Chicago: University of Chicago Press.

———. 2014. "The Revised MRS: Gender Complementarity at College." *Gender and Society* 28: 236–64.

Hamilton, Laura, and Elizabeth Armstrong. 2009. "Gendered Sexuality in Young Adulthood: Double Binds and Flawed Options." *Gender & Society* 23: 589–616.

Hamilton, Laura, Claudia Geist, and Brian Powell. 2011. "Marital Name Change as a Window into Gender Attitudes." *Gender & Society* 25: 145–75.

Hess, Amanda. 2013. "Technology Killed Courtship: Good Riddance." *Slate*, January 14 (online).

Hochschild, Arlie, with Anne Machung. 1989. *The Second Shift.* New York: Avon Books.

Huber, Joan, and Glenna Spitze. 1981. "Wives' Employment, Household Behaviors, and Sex-Role Attitudes." *Social Forces* 60: 150–69.

Illouz, Eva. 1997. *Consuming the Romantic Utopia: Love and the Cultural Contradictions of Capitalism.* Berkeley: University of California Press.

Jackson, Robert M. 1998. *Destined for Equality: The Inevitable Rise of Women's Status.* Cambridge, MA: Harvard University Press.

Kane, Emily. 2006. "'No Way My Boys Are Going to Be Like That!' Parents' Responses to Gender Nonconformity." *Gender & Society* 20: 149–76.

King, Patrick. 2014. *Why Women Love Jerks: Realizing the Best Version of Yourself to Effortlessly Attract Women.* Seattle: Amazon Digital Services.

Kitchener, Caroline. 2018. "Marriage Proposals Are Stupid." *The Atlantic*, March 23.

Klawitter, Marieka. 2015. "Meta-analysis of the Effects of Sexual Orientation on Earnings." *Industrial Relations* 54: 4–32.

Lamont, Ellen. 2014. "Negotiating Courtship: Reconciling Egalitarian Ideals with Traditional Gender Norms. *Gender & Society* 28: 189–211.

Landivar, Liana Christin. 2017. *Mothers at Work: Who Opts Out?* Boulder, CO: Lynne Rienner.

Lareau, Annette. 2003. *Unequal Childhoods: Class, Race, and Family Life.* Berkeley: University of California Press.

Lever, Janet, David A. Frederick, and Rosanna Hertz. 2015. "Who Pays for Dates? Following Versus Challenging Gender Norms." *Sage Open*.

McCall, Leslie. 2011. "Women and Men as Class and Race Actors: Comment on England." *Gender and Society* 25: 94–100.

McCaughey, Martha. 2007. *The Caveman Mystique: Pop-Darwinism and the Debates over Sex, Violence, and Science.* New York: Routledge.

Messerschmidt, James. 2010. *Hegemonic Masculinities and Camouflaged Politics.* Boulder, CO: Paradigm.

Miller, Kelsey. 2015. "The Dating Rules That Will Not Go Away." *Refinery29,* February 9 (online).

Mollborn, Stefanie. 2017. *Mixed Messages: Norms and Social Control around Teen Sex and Pregnancy.* New York: Oxford University Press.

Moore, Mignon R. 2018. "Reflections on Marriage Equality at a Vehicle for LGBTQ Political Transformation." In *Queer Families and Relationships after Marriage Equality,* ed. Michael Yarborough, Angela Jones, and Joseph N. DeFilippis. New York: Routledge.

———. 2011. *Invisible Families: Gay Identities, Relationships and Motherhood among Black Women.* Berkeley: University of California Press.

Morris, Alex. 2014. "Tales from the Millennials' Sexual Revolution." *Rolling Stone,* March 31 (online).

National Center for Education Statistics. 2017. "Digest of Education Statistics 2017." https://nces.ed.gov/programs/digest/index.asp

Ocobock, Abigail. 2018. "From Public Debate to Private Decision: The Normalization of Marriage among Critical LGBQ People." In *Queer Families and Relationships after Marriage Equality,* ed. Michael Yarborough, Angela Jones, and Joseph N. DeFilippis. New York: Routledge.

Orne, Jason. 2017. *Boystown.* Chicago: University of Chicago Press.

Ortiz-Torres, B., S. Williams, and A. Ehrhardt. 2003. "Urban Women's Gender Scripts: Implications for HIV." *Culture, Health and Sexuality* 5: 1–17.

Pardes, Arielle. 2014. "You're a Feminist . . . So Why Don't You Date Like One?" *Women's Health,* April 4.

Parker, Kim, and Renee Stepler. 2017 "Americans See Men as the Financial Providers, Even as Women's Contributions Grow." Pew Research Center. www.pewresearch.org/fact-tank/2017/09/20/americans-see-men-as-the-financial-providers-even-as-womens-contributions-grow/

Pascoe, C.J. 2007. *Dude, You're a Fag! Masculinity and Sexuality in High School.* Berkeley: University of California Press.

Pedulla, David S., and Sarah Thebaud. 2015. "Can We Finish the Revolution? Gender, Work-Family Ideals, and Institutional Constraint." *American Sociological Review* 80: 116–39.

Pepin, Joanna, and David A. Cotter. 2018. "Separating Spheres? Diverging Trends in Youth's Gender Attitudes about Work and Family." *Journal of Marriage and Family* 80: 7–24.

Pfeffer, Carla A. 2017. *Queering Families: The Postmodern Partnerships of Cisgender Women and Transgender Men.* New York: Oxford University Press.

———. 2014. "I Don't Like Passing as a Straight Woman": Queer Negotiations of Identity and Social Group Membership." *American Journal of Sociology* 120(1): 1–44.

———. 2012. "Normative Resistance and Inventive Pragmatism: Negotiating Structure and Agency in Transgender Families." *Gender & Society* 26(4): 574–602.

Pyke, Karen. 1996. "Class-Based Masculinities: The Interdependence of Gender, Class, and Interpersonal Power." *Gender & Society* 10: 527–49.

Randles, Jennifer. 2017. *Proposing Prosperity? Marriage Education Policy and Inequality in America.* New York: Columbia University Press.

Rao, Aliya Hamid. 2017. "Stand by Your Man: Wives' Emotion Work during Men's Unemployment." *Journal of Marriage and Family* 79: 636–56.

Rehel, Erin M. 2014. "When Dad Stays Home Too: Paternity Leave, Gender, and Parenting." *Gender & Society* 28: 110–32.

Ridgeway, Cecilia. 2011. *Framed by Gender: How Gender Inequality Persists in the Modern World.* New York: Oxford University Press.

Ridgeway, Cecilia, and Shelley Correll. 2004. "Unpacking the Gender System: A Theoretical Perspective on Cultural Beliefs and Social Relations." *Gender & Society* 18: 510–31.

Risman, Barbara. 2018. *Where the Millennials Will Take Us: A New Generation Wrestles with the Gender Structure.* New York: Oxford University Press.

———. 1999. *Gender Vertigo: American Families in Transition.* New Haven, CT: Yale University Press.

Robinson, Brandon Andrew. 2015. "'Personal Preference' as the New Racism: Gay Desire and Racial Cleansing in Cyberspace." *Sociology of Race and Ethnicity* 1: 317–30.

Rose, Suzanna, and Irene Hanson Frieze. 1993. "Young Singles' Contemporary Dating Scripts." *Sex Roles* 28: 499–509.

———. 1989. "Young Singles' Scripts for a First Date." *Gender and Society* 3: 258–68.

Rosenfeld, Michael. 2007. *The Age of Independence: Interracial Unions, Same Sex Unions and the Changing American Family.* Cambridge, MA: Harvard University Press.

Rosin, Hanna. 2010. "The End of Men." *The Atlantic,* July/August.

Rudman, Laurie, and Kimberly Fairchild. 2004. "Reactions to Counterstereotypic Behavior: The Role of Backlash in Cultural Stereotype Maintenance." *Journal of Personality and Social Psychology* 87: 157–76.

Sassler, Sharon, and Amanda Miller. 2017. *Cohabitation Nation: Gender, Class, and the Remaking of Relationships.* Berkeley: University of California Press.

———. 2011. "Waiting to Be Asked: Gender, Power, and Relationship Progression among Cohabiting Couples." *Journal of Family Issues* 32: 482–506.

Sayer, Liana C. 2016. "Trends in Women's and Men's Time Use, 1965–2012: Back to the Future?" In *Gender and Couple Relationships,* ed. Susan M. McHale, Valerie King, Jennifer VanHook, and Alan Booth, 43–78. New York: Springer.

Scarborough, William J., Ray Sin, and Barbara Risman. 2019. "Attitudes and the Stalled Gender Revolution: Egalitarianism, Traditionalism, and Ambivalence from 1977 through 2016." *Gender & Society* 33: 173–200.

Schalet, Amy. 2011. *Not under My Roof: Parents, Teens, and the Culture of Sex.* Chicago: University of Chicago Press.

Schippers, Mimi. 2016. *Beyond Monogamy: Polyamory and the Future of Polyqueer Sexualities.* New York: New York University Press.

Schrock, Douglas, and Michael Schwalbe. 2009. "Men, Masculinity, and Manhood Acts." *American Review of Sociology* 35: 277–95.

Schwartz, Christine, and Robert Mare. 2005. "Trends in Educational Assortative Marriage from 1940 to 2003." *Demography* 42: 621–46.

Sciortino, Karley. 2017. "Can I Be a Self-Sufficient, #Empowered Woman and Enjoy It When a Guy Picks Up the Check?" *Vogue,* November 15 (online).

Seal, David, and A. Ehrhardt. 2003. "Masculinity and Urban Men: Perceived Scripts for Courtship, Romantic, and Sexual Interactions with Women." *Culture, Health and Sexuality* (5): 295–319.

Shafer, Emily Fitzgibbons, and MacKenzie A. Christensen. 2018. "Flipping the (Surname) Script: Men's Nontraditional Surname Choice at Marriage." *Journal of Family Issues* 39: 3055–74.

Silva, Jennifer. 2015. *Coming Up Short: Working-Class Adulthood in an Age of Uncertainty.* New York: Oxford University Press.

Stacey, Judith. 2011. *Unhitched: Love, Marriage, and Family Values from West Hollywood to Western China.* New York: New York University Press.

Stone, Pamela. 2007. *Opting Out? Why Women Really Quit Careers and Head Home.* Berkeley: University of California Press.

Sweeney, Megan. 2002. "Two Decades of Family Change: The Shifting Economic Foundations of Marriage." *American Sociological Review* 67: 132–47.

Swim, Janet, and Laurie Cohen. 1997. "Overt, Covert, and Subtle Sexism: A Comparison between the Attitudes toward Women and Modern Sexism Scales." *Psychology of Women Quarterly* 21: 103–18.

Talbot, Kirsten, and Michael Quayle. 2010. "The Perils of Being a Nice Guy: Contextual Variation in Five Young Women's Constructions of Acceptable Hegemonic and Alternative Masculinities." *Men and Masculinities* 13: 255–78.

Tichenor, Veronica. 2005. *Earning More and Getting Less: Why Successful Wives Can't Buy Equality.* New Brunswick, NJ: Rutgers University Press.

Townsend, Nicholas. 2002. *The Package Deal: Marriage, Work, and Fatherhood in Men's Lives.* Philadelphia: Temple University Press.

US Census Bureau. 2017. "Quick Facts." www.census.gov/quickfacts/fact/table /US/PST045218

Vasquez-Tokos, Jessica. 2017. *Marriage Vows and Racial Choices.* New York: Russell Sage Foundation.

Walters, Suzanna Danuta. 2014. *The Tolerance Trap: How God, Genes, and Good Intentions Are Sabotaging Gay Equality.* New York: New York University Press.

Ward, Jane. 2015. *Not Gay: Sex between Straight White Men.* New York: New York University Press.

———. 2010. "Gender Labor: Transmen, Femmes, and Collective Work of Transgression." *Sexualities* 13: 236–54.

West, Candace, and Don H. Zimmerman. 1989. "Doing Gender." *Gender & Society* 1: 125–51.

Weston, Kath. 1991. "The Politics of Gay Families." In *Rethinking the Family: Some Feminist Questions,* ed. Barrie Thorne. Boston: Northeastern University Press.

Williams, Alex. 2013. "The End of Courtship?" *New York Times,* January 11 (online).

Wong, Jaclyn. 2017. "Competing Desires: How Young Adult Couples Negotiate Moving for Career Opportunities." *Gender & Society* 31: 171–96.

Index

aesthetics, queer, 122–25

aggression: in conflict with "good" man role, 81–83, 84–85; in conventional masculinity, 90, 91–92; in dating behaviors, in long-term relationship problems, 151–52; in LGBQ reimagining of sex, 126; in the sexual double standard, 96–97; of women, in pursuing relationship goals, 68, 177, 178

ambition, professional: in conceptualization of egalitarian relationships, 22–23, 26, 27–29, 30–31, 34–35, 38–40, 48–49, 52; in cultural narratives of masculinity, 6; as desirable quality in LGBQ partners, 118–19; in the gender revolution, 1–2, 7–8; in the self-development imperative, 174–75; women's, in conflict with traditional courtship, 77

American Dream narrative, 43

appearance, physical: attractiveness, 58–59, 89–90, 115–16, 119, 120, 177; in conceptualization of success and egalitarian love, 34–35; in inequality disguised as romance, 89–90, 99–102; in LGBQ courtship, 122–25, 137–38

assertiveness: in heterosexual dating scripts, 55, 58–59, 68, 78; in inequality disguised as romance, 79, 82–83; in LGBQ court-ship, 114–15, 126, 134, 138. *See also* initiative

attractiveness: changing interests in, 89–90; female, for heterosexual men, 99–102; in heterosexual dating scripts, 58–59, 177; in LGBQ courtship, 115–16, 119, 120

autonomy, women's, 49, 73, 75–76, 77–78, 90–91

barriers, structural: to equal parenting, 166–67, 171–72, 173; in women's achievement, 15

"bear culture," 124

beauty, 100–101, 120, 124–25, 137–38, 149–50, 162–63. *See also* appearance, physical

"benevolent sexism," 74–75, 103, 116–17, 177–78

breadwinning role: in American dating, 5, 6–7; in conceptualizations of success and egalitarian love, 18, 21, 29, 31, 37–40, 50–51; in division of household labor, 146–47, 159–61; gender revolution in decline of interest in, 8–9; in heterosexual women's dating scripts, 60; male breadwinner/female homemaker model, 5, 8, 12, 175, 180, 182; as masculine, 89–90, 102–3; paying for dates, as demonstration of, 85–86

butch-femme dynamics, 112–13, 135–37, 170

dominance: in conceptualizations of success and egalitarian love, 36–37; symbolic, in reconciling divergent ideals, 75–76; topping as, 210n21; use of gender in justifying, 153–54

double standard, sexual, 8, 63–64, 66, 93–97, 104–5

Dutch treating, 88–89, 115–18

earning power, 8–9, 29, 37–38, 52, 85–86, 118, 158–59

education, 13–14, 20–21, 34–35, 40–41, 42–43, 175, 205n4

egalitarianism: differing concepts of, 170–72; expectations of, 20–22; and gendered courtship, 11; in LGBQ courtship, 117–18; privilege in, 52; reconciling with traditional courtship, 74–77; structural equality in, 181–82; teamwork in, 31–40

egalitarian love, conceptualizations of: career success in, 20–21, 22–34; by heterosexual and LGBQ couples, 18; for LGBQ, 40–51; marriage as teamwork in, 31–40; privilege in, 52

emotional engagement in long-term relationships, 161–65

empowerment/disempowerment: feminist, and white privilege, 15; in heterosexual dating scripts, 54–55, 68, 70, 72, 77–78; middle-class male support for, 90–91; narratives of, in conflict with traditional courtship, 177–78; in paying for dates, 116–17; in upending gendered dating, 4–5

equality/inequality: in courtship downplayed, 75–78; courtship norms in persistence of, 181–83; domestic, 1–2, 3, 141–42, 143–44; financial resources in, 15; gender essentialism in, 2, 180; in LGBQ courtship, 3, 108–9, 118–19; in long-term relationships, 141–63, 170–72; material, 181–82; in the persistence of gendered courtship, 11; privilege in, 52; in professional contexts, 16; progressive identity in perpetuation of, 102–5; and romantic initiative, 81–83, 84–85; in shifting masculinities, 105–6; structural, 181–82; of study participants, 14

exclusivity, 2, 54, 61–64, 93

expertise, gendered, 19, 101–2, 141–42, 152–56, 170–71

families: in conceptualizations of success and egalitarian love, 20–21, 22–24, 25–26, 27–28, 33; in dating, 5; LGBQ couples

rethinking, 166–68; queer challenges to, in gender revolution, 9–10; in traditional marriage proposals, 71. *See also* parenting

Fein, Ellen: *The Rules*, 54–55

femininity, 34–35, 53, 70, 123–24, 165, 170

feminism: of Bay Area young professionals, 14, 15, 16; in conceptualizations of success and egalitarian love, 30; defined, in professional and dating culture, 1–2; "free choice," 12; and gendered courtship rituals, 12, 89, 177–78; and gendered dominance, 154; in heterosexual dating scripts, 19, 53–54, 55, 74–75, 76–77; in LGBQ courtship, 135–36; men's gendered courtship behavior framed as, 85–86, 102–3; reconciliation of, with traditional courtship, 74–75, 76–77; religion in animosity to, 91

finances/financial resources: in American dating, 4–7; differing expectations for men in, 39–40; financial independence, 30, 33–34, 36, 41, 48–49; financial responsibility, 39–40; financial stability, 23–25, 29, 30–31, 41, 86, 89–90; in LGBQ childrearing decisions, 167–68; in the persistence of gendered courtship, 10–11, 12; in strategies on gender inequality, 15

first dates: expectations of payment for, 59–61, 85–86, 116; in heterosexual dating scripts, 53, 54, 55, 58–61, 65–66; initiation of sex on, 86; in LGBQ courtship, 114, 116, 137

flexibility: in LGBQ care work, 19, 141–42, 168–70, 173; in LGBQ commitment, 46–51; in LGBQ dating practices, 18, 108–9; in LGBQ long-term relationships, 168–70, 179–80; in millennial and Gen X dating structures, 4

gender: defined, 203n78; presentation of, 9, 120–21, 123–24, 134; reversal of, 136–37

gender essentialism: in courtship rituals, 17–18, 176; in dated dating, 2, 176, 180, 181–84; in division of household labor and care work, 2, 19, 141–42, 143–45, 146, 152–53, 170–72, 182–84; in heterosexual dating scripts, 55–57, 75–77; in inequality disguised as romance, 91–92; in liberal tolerance narratives, 107–8; in the persistence of gendered dating, 6–7, 11–12; romance rooted in, 2; in the stalled gender revolution, 180, 181–84

gender revolution, 180, 181–84; strategy in, 83–85; surname changes as, 104; use of, to avoid household work, 161–63
Rules, The (Schneider & Fein), 54–55
rules for dating, 53, 93–97, 109–11

Schneider, Sherrie: *The Rules*, 54–55
scripts: cultural, 54–59; sexist, 111–14; social, 2–3, 11–12, 133–35, 174–75. *See also* heterosexual dating scripts
security, economic. *See* stability, financial
self-development imperative, 14–15, 18, 20–21, 30–31, 49, 52, 174–75
self-reliance, 7, 52
sex: destigmatization of, in LGBQ courtship, 125–27, 179; and emotional commitment, for "good" men, 91–93; emphasized in LGBQ relationships, 210n20; "good" men's rules for, 93–97; in heterosexual dating scripts, 62, 63–66; initiation of, 2, 64–66, 96–97; in LGBQ courtship, 125–30; sexual history, 8–9, 126–27
sexism: benevolent, 74–75, 103, 116–17, 177–78; hostile, 100–101, 103; for LGBQ people, 111–14; in the persistence of gendered courtship, 12
sexual double standard, 63–64, 66, 93–96, 105
sexuality: female, 54, 93–97; male, 91–92
skills, gendered, 19, 101–2, 141–42, 152–56, 170–71
social desirability bias, 12
socialization, gendered, 143–44, 155–57
space, personal, 131–32, 168–70
spheres: male, 75–76; private, 6–7, 30; public, 2, 5–7, 11, 19–20, 30, 74
stability, financial, 23–25, 29, 30–31, 41, 86, 89–90
stalled gender revolution, 1–2, 10–12, 174–84
stay-at-home parenting, 29–30, 38–39, 103–4, 143–44, 146–47, 159–61
stereotyping: in gendered divisions of labor, 161–63; in heterosexual dating scripts, 57; of men as sexually aggressive and predatory, 91–92, 105; racial, in intermarriage,

206n13; of strong men as aloof, 84; unchallenged in acceptance of traditional courtship, 78. *See also* gender essentialism
submission, 66–67, 75–76
success sequence, 31–34, 43–44, 52
surname changing, 54, 71–74, 103–4, 105–6, 135
symbolism: of men's care work, 149; romantic, in gendered division of labor, 161–62; of surname changes, 135

taboos, 55, 69–70
terminology, LGBQ, 112–13
three-day-rule, 208n6
trans people. *See* LGBQ people

upstairs/downstairs myth, 142–53

validation of relationships, 10, 46–47, 178–79
value: of gendered expertise, 171; of work, 153–54, 183

women, black, 206nn15,19
women, heterosexual: attachment of, to dating rituals, 4–5; competing desires of, 77–78; concepts of household equality by, 170–71; conceptualization of success and egalitarian love by, 18, 20–21, 22–31; in determining relationship status, 61–64; divergent ideals of, 74–77; emphasis on education and careers for, 22–31; expectation of, that men pay for dates, 59–61, 85–90; how-to guide to dating for, 54–59; marriage delayed by, 25–27; marriage proposals in scripts of, 66–71; men's dominance enforced by, 153–54; relational imperative of, 63–64; in relationships of with LGBQ men, 138–39; sexual initiative of, 64–66; as study participants, 14; as stylists for men, 101–2; on surname changing, 71–74; in unequal divisions of house and care work, 141–53
women, Latina, 206n13
work/life balance, 2s

Founded in 1893,
UNIVERSITY OF CALIFORNIA PRESS
publishes bold, progressive books and journals
on topics in the arts, humanities, social sciences,
and natural sciences—with a focus on social
justice issues—that inspire thought and action
among readers worldwide.

The UC PRESS FOUNDATION
raises funds to uphold the press's vital role
as an independent, nonprofit publisher, and
receives philanthropic support from a wide
range of individuals and institutions—and from
committed readers like you. To learn more, visit
ucpress.edu/supportus.